Simon Gray was born in 1936. His plays include *Butley, Otherwise Engaged, Quartermaine's Terms, Little Nell* and *The Old Masters*. He has also written many plays for television and radio, several novels and seven books of his memoirs, including *The Smoking Diaries, The Last Cigarette, Fat Chance* and *Enter a Fox*, published by Granta Books. He lives in Holland Park, London.

'A wonderful book, hilarious and poignant in turn, or even together, such as the beautiful and moving elegy for Alan Bates, a long-time friend and the actor most closely associated with Gray's work. Here the uncertainty is gone, the commentary razor-sharp with a delicate and revealing quality that takes the breath away. The book is a great exercise in openness, Gray seemingly at his most vulnerable as he relates stories of his youth, of his relationships with his wife, with Harold Pinter and with his pets, every one accompanied by his constant smoking' *Time Out*

'One of the funniest books I've read' Anna Ford, *Daily Express*

'Gray has a genius for fury . . . sit back and enjoy Gray's discourses on literary masturbatory habits . . . for all its shapelessness, *The Year of the Jouncer* is as carefully constructed as a clock . . . Roll on next year and the publication of *The Smouldering Diaries*' *New Statesman*

'Certain to be one of the funniest books of the year' *London Review of Books*

'Theatrical memoirs often produce sour and sticky candyfloss that is difficult to clean off. Simon Gray is remarkable for having written a second diary that, like his first, has a taste of honey . . . No one who didn't have that spring of wearied optimism inside could write like Gray, whose ear for dialogue gives his apparently-rambling recollections a crystal authenticity. His eye for absurdity is just as sharp and somehow he manages to place himself at the centre of the world he describes without casting the faintest shadow . . . His brushstrokes are masterly . . . No one will put down this book without marvelling at how so many apparently melancholy episodes can be turned by a kind of alchemy into such an invigorating cocktail. He makes you laugh on every page, and can draw you as a willing observer into the most bizarre scenes which might not have obvious appeal . . . You will be lucky to find a more delicious read this year' *Sunday Telegraph*

'Finding the right voice for truth-telling often means shedding, or fighting one's way out of, several key layers of wrong voice, but sometimes it can come like a wonderful blessing. However Gray reached it, reach it he did, and it's the unique and unforgettable voice heard in his diaries which makes reading them an experience so exhilarating . . . Long and vigorously may he continue to jounce' *Literary Review*

'Admirers of Gray's masterly *The Smoking Diaries* will be pleased to learn that its sequel is quite as funny and entertaining . . . Excellent and congenial company' *Mail on Sunday*

'More worth reading than most other memoirs that are likely to be published this year. For its jokes alone, you will want to buy half a dozen copies as presents' *Times Literary Supplement*

'Gray pondering, reflecting, remembering, grumping and brooding about Britain, people and life, in a malevolently funny autobiography . . . I'd love to spend a day in a pub with Gray, but just one day. His books I will spend weeks with' *Sunday Tribune* (Dublin)

'Gray's a very cunning craftsman. But also, thank goodness, a very funny one' *Scotsman*

'Addictive chronicles . . . Part memoir, part showbiz gossip, part meditation on the nature of aging, part tribute to the close friends he has lost, the books flit from Gray's childhood to a bewildered commentary on the absurdities and vagaries of modern life . . . Long may Simon Gray continue to jounce' *The Stage*

'*The Year of the Jouncer* once more finds The Silver Fox peering between the cracks of his life with wit, sardonic cussedness and a ramshackle verve that make this every bit as enjoyable as its predecessor . . . Think a chain-smoking Alan Bennett, but grumpier and bedevilled by stray cats and life's inconsistencies' *Metro*

'Gray is an absolute genius. The hazards of mounting his work in the West End; the viscissitudes of rehearsals; the ego of actors; the mercilessness of reviewers – the worse things get, the better the diaries become. Gray has developed a sophisticated comic act, a stream of consciousness and grumble that is as artful and rhythmical as improvised bluesy jazz . . . Gray's passage on his friend and colleague [Alan Bates] is tender and deeply humane – and the very best thing he has ever done' *Daily Express*

THE
SMOKING
DIARIES

The Year of the Jouncer

Simon Gray

Granta Books
London

Granta Publications, 12 Addison Avenue, London W11 4QR

First published in Great Britain by Granta Books 2006
First paperback edition published by Granta Books 2006
This edition published by Granta Books 2008

A CIP catalogue record for this book
is available from the British Library.

1 3 5 7 9 10 8 6 4 2

ISBN 978-1-84708-055-4

Typeset by M Rules
Printed and bound in Great Britain by
CPI Bookmarque, Croydon, CR0 4TD

For Ben and Lucy

PART ONE

A PRAYER ANSWERED

Here I am, sitting at my table, pigeons hopping about in the sun, little birds with yellow chests settling on the rim of my fruit punch, in front of me the sea in Caribbean blue and green, and from it the occasional purr and cough of small boats, the roar of a speedboat, brief and violent, and behind me the clatter of waiters laying tables while they talk to each other in incomprehensible Bajan – everything very much as you hope it will be when you're in London during Christmas, longing to be here.

So at least that's another Christmas gone, thank God. For me it has become the worst season, the season when people I love die, beginning with my mother, over thirty years ago, then a long gap, and then almost every other year, sometimes in consecutive years, for the last decade. Two years ago on Boxing Day it was Ian Hamilton, this year on the day after Boxing Day Alan Bates. No, that's wrong. Alan, who died three weeks ago, died in 2003, which is now last year, and Ian, who died two years and three weeks ago, died in 2001, which is now by the calendar three years ago. But on the day after Boxing Day and on Boxing Day respectively, in the Christmas season.

A SELF-PROHIBITION

My plan is to get down some thoughts and memories of Alan, but I don't think I can start today, not on the first day, with the pigeons hopping, and the little birds with yellow chests etc., one of which is now sharing my drink. Best let it happen when it happens, tomorrow perhaps, or later in the week, let it sneak up. Today the thing is just to be here, back here at the usual table, my yellow pad in front of me, free to go wherever – although I think I must make a pact with myself to lay off the subject of my age, and my physical deterioration, it's really time I outgrew all that, it's not becoming in a man nearing seventy, although I must confess that now I see those words actually on the page, 'nearing seventy', I find myself gaping at them. I can't think what it is that's nearing seventy, apart from my body, but the most significant parts of my body, the parts whose ageing have a significant bearing on my life expectancy – the liver (mistreated for nearly fifty years), the lungs (for over sixty years), the heart, the intestines, bladder and bowels – are all concealed from view, their condition reported on a couple of times a year in the form of figures printed out from blood tests. My doctor faxes them through to me and I study them with attentive ignorance, looking for asterisks. If he puts an asterisk by a number it means that the number is either too high or too low. These days the number to do with the prostate is too high, but I'm not to be surprised by this, I'm told, because although I have a tumour nesting or nestling there, it is without territorial ambitions, in fact it might still be nesting or nestling while I die of something else, or a combination of something elses, or in an accident, or unlawfully, at the hands of another. In other words, one way or another, it's here for life. As am I, I suppose. But my point is that while I am decaying within and without, and quite right too – it's nature's way, after all, the way of all flesh – I am most of the time unaware of the decay, though there are the hints, of course – the days when the bladder seems to fill even as I'm emptying it, the wheeze and double whistle in the chest, the faintness that follows climbing stairs, but on the whole, apart from a developing sense of decay and imminent death, nothing much has changed in

THE SELF ITSELF

since the moment in my pram, in the garden of Mallows, in Hayling Island, one afternoon some sixty-seven years ago, when I suddenly shook and bounced within my harness and caused the pram to stir – whereupon something in me sprang awake! might perhaps be the right phrase, sprang awake in the act of understanding the connection between the movement of my body and the movement of the rectile – rectile? What's a rectile? Do I mean reticule? Yes, but vehicle would be the better word – the connection between the movement of the body and the vehicle containing it – how much grasped in that slip of a second – how you could change the shape of the universe, get a move on, hustle, rock and tremble through life, through the garden, anyway, a few feet, it may have only been a few inches, for all I know now, that first time, but that they became feet, and then yards, and then quite a few yards, and then more than that, I know for a fact because I was told about it when I was old enough – from the initial suspicion that somehow the pram with the baby in it wasn't quite where it was when last seen – a large pram of the period, of course, highly sprung, probably brakeless, easily mobile, left with the baby in it for the usual half an hour or so in the afternoon, while Mummy was doing what Mummies did in those days, which precluded keeping an eye on the baby, and Daddy was in his surgery, accepting a chicken for his latest diagnosis, if his patient was one of the impoverished of the parish, or dispensing manly medical sympathy to one of the island's younger matrons, and brother Nigel perhaps toddling about the kitchen where Nanny was having her tea and a gossip with cook – while all those people were doing those sorts of things, the pram with the baby in it, the rocking, bouncing baby, was trundling along the garden path to somewhere quite a long way from where it had been when last seen. It was a complete mystery to the adult intelligences, how had he done it, if it was he who had done it, but if not he, who then and why? So the next afternoon they (Mummy and Nanny?) planted the pram in the usual spot, and stood over it, watching. The baby lay there smiling or snivelling up at them, until it struck them that they should try observing the baby when unobserved by the baby, and they withdrew behind bushes and trees etc. and thus witnessed the swaying of the pram, then the juddering of the pram, then its slow, unsteady progress along the path, the movement accompanied by a low humming and keening sound from within that reminded them more of a dog than of a human, and which they found alarming. On the other hand the mystery was solved, because the simple physical facts were easily understood, although in fact full of the deeper mysteries of self, self-discovery, will, solitude, and the need to make a noise when shaking and bouncing in a pram. Jouncing was the word they used for it. I was a jouncer therefore.

MY BATTLE WITH THE WAVES

So. To the left of the hotel, if you are facing the sea, there is a small cove with a shed in it. From this shed a pipe stretches into the sea and pumps water out into something or other behind the shed, a cistern, I think, though I've never seen it. The shed and the pipe and the cistern, if there is a cistern, belong to McGill University, in Montreal, their Marine Science Department. My father went to McGill, which is why I always read the sign carefully, though I know it by heart, when I clamber around the little cove to the public beach next to it – I've taken to swimming there because the hotel beach has developed a high ridge close to shore, when you walk out to sea the ground gives under you, and you have to fling yourself forward and swim before you intend to. I like to have a cigarette as I wade out, smoking and contemplating the various mysteries of life – e.g. where does the sea come from? Why does nature exist? What's that scuttling over my feet? – and it's no fun, plus it's very unsightly, to be caught by a wave with a cigarette between your lips – wasteful too – but the worst part is getting out. It's difficult to get a grip on the ridge, which consists of sand and pebbles, your foot slides down the slope, you topple back into the sea, start again, trying to get out between the incoming waves, which bide their time and then, when you've convinced yourself there isn't one, erupt under you as you place your foot halfway up the ridge again. The year before last a visiting friend of ours, an elderly lady from New York called Bumma, got caught by a brute of a wave – she was virtually alone on the beach, there was no one to help her as she was tumbled and rolled around, sucked back by the undertow, then, before she could regain her footing, rolled and tumbled forward – Bumma was lucky not to have drowned, really, in what would have been a foot or so of water. I kept thinking of her when I was trying to get out the other afternoon, and suddenly hit upon a scheme – a rather daring scheme, basically derived from judo, or ju-jitsu – you use the force opposing you to your advantage – i.e. when a man throws a punch at you, you duck, catch his arm and pull him forward using his own impetus as a lever, then step out of the way as he flows past you and crashes to the ground, where you can kick him at your leisure – I've seen this done often on screen, most notably by a one-armed Spencer Tracy, in *Bad Day at Black Rock*, when he annihilates the brutish two-armed Ernest Borgnine by employing exactly the method I've described, though being Spencer Tracy he doesn't kick him when he's down, he lets him get up to throw another hay-maker. Spencer has to go through the whole process three times, his trilby remaining on his head, by the way, throughout – it's a very exhilarating scene, and now I've got the film recorded I can, and sometimes do, play it over and over again. So. So why Spencer Tracy flinging Ernest Borgnine all over the place? – it's in a diner actually and at the climax through a screen door – Oh yes, conquering the ridge – my plan was to *use* the waves to carry me over the ridge by surfing them – I am actually rather good at surfing, can do it without a board, and lo! there I was on the other side of the ridge, the beach a mere few feet away, all I had to do was scramble to my feet and take a step or two. I'd made it to my knees when the wave I'd surfed in on surged back, taking me with it and peppering my legs and stomach with pebbles, sharp stones and what felt like fragments of broken glass, and then, like poor old Bumma, I was rolled, tumbled, etc., but unlike Bumma I was watched from the shore by a dozen or so guests at the adjoining hotel, lolling on their beach-beds and certainly smiling, in some cases laughing as if I were a floor show – this went on for several minutes. Once or twice I struck out to sea, a dignified, classy crawl, as if I were engaged in a complicated exercise I'd designed for myself, a sort of combat course. I suspect I would still be there, either being rolled around with sand and stone and sea, like a maritime version of Wordsworth's Lucy, or right out in deep water, pretending that that's where I prefer to be, or drowned, if Victoria hadn't come looking for me, sized up the situation in a blink, walked into the water, stretched out her hand – which I took as if intending to shake, but allowed myself to be drawn by it up to safety – extraordinary how much power, I almost wrote brute power, is contained in her slight and graceful form – I've long accepted that she's stronger than me physically as well as morally, but then she's much younger, hasn't got a paunch, doesn't smoke, so she jolly well ought to be able to haul me out of the sea.

SWIMMING WITH A WALRUS

Anyway, the above should make it clear why I now go to the left of the hotel, past the cove with the McGill Marine Science shed in it, and scramble onto the public beach, which has only a small ridge, and furthermore soft pebble-and-shard-free sand – altogether a much better swimming beach, in fact, and much more fun, as the local people swim from it, you see them in large groups, almost like congregations, which they may well be, on outings from the nearby churches, of which there are dozens, of all known, and some (to me) unknown, denominations – portly matrons in one-piece swimming suits with vivid sunsets stamped on them, supple young men, sinuous girls, middle-aged men with angry, Rastafarian locks, families dunking naked babies into the water – and here and there the English, sitting stiffly on boulders and tree stumps if they're middle-aged, or sprawling on the sand with tattoos on their arms and bottles of Banks beer in their hands if they're young, offensive to the eye, let's face it, as offensive as I am in my drooping trunks, pendulous this and puckered that – but I don't have to see myself, do I? And within seconds I'm in the sea, splashing along, ducking through the waves, spouting water out of my mouth something like a whale. This morning, before breakfast, the beach was empty except for a stocky man in his fifties, balding, pink and blotchy, with a small white moustache – he was just wading in as I arrived – he looked so formal and ill-at-ease as in he plodded, up to his knees, up to his waist, scowling blankly – I surged into the water within his sight-line, I hoped, I certainly made enough noise, splashing and whooping, to let him know that there were people for whom the sea is a welcoming place. I dashed and splashed about, dived under, stayed there as long as I could, then surfaced beside a pair of feet sticking straight up out of the water, ankles pressed neatly together, pink soles turned outwards, toes curled. He was doing a handstand. I could see right down to his head between his hands on the seabed – he brought his legs down and somersaulted to the top, not exactly gracefully, but he wasn't ungainly either – his head appeared above the surface, eyes blinking, little white moustache dripping – he looked like a sea creature, a walrus. He stared at me vaguely, scarcely taking me in as he went under again, curling himself into a foetal ball and then rolling on one side, then the other, then a back-somersault, a quick surface, a walrus blink, and down he went again, to celebrate the feel of himself in the sea, this man I had pegged as an office-bound goblin, living behind life's wainscoting.

A GLIMPSE OF A LOST CIVILIZATION

A boat arrived, full of schoolgirls, about thirty of them, between nine and fifteen, I suppose, all wearing traditional brown uniforms, their hair in pigtails, children of a sort I haven't seen in England since my own childhood. They leapt squealing and laughing off the boat into the water, carrying their shoes and socks in their hands, and scampered onto the beach. A young woman, presumably the teacher, got off last, her skirt hiked up. She splashed after them, calling out instructions which she really didn't expect them to follow, but at least reminded them that she was there. They poured up the beach and into the changing rooms in the small park, a sort of compound that also has a café, benches, swings, little shops. A few minutes later they poured out again, into the sea, heads bobbing, screams, shrieks of laughter, splashing each other, ducking each other, an absolute rough house of girls at play, but not a swearword to be heard, nothing bad-tempered, ill-natured, brutish about these children, and it struck me with a pang that such a sight and such sounds would be impossible in the England of today, and will soon be just a folk memory among the elderly, for what authority would dare to allow thirty children to go on a trip to the beach, to plunge into the sea, with only one teacher to supervise them? Indeed, what authority could muster thirty children who would play freely and joyfully, without bawling out obscenities and threats at each other – and at the teacher, probably. When you live in a barbarous country, it's nice, if painful, to spend a little time in a civilized one, to remember what we once were, to think what's become of us.

FROM INFANT GENIUS TO INFANT PERVERT

But what was admired in the Hayling garden in daylight, indeed interpreted as the early manifestation of an original mind, possibly of genius, became regarded as something other, possibly a perversion, when practised at night in an unmoving bed. The bouncing and jouncing and above all the weird canine keening could be heard all over the house, and all through the night, and persisted through my teens and twenties, actually until I got married at the age of twenty-nine – it was worse than snoring because it seemed entirely wilful, even though I was unconscious, or could be assumed to be – my face buried in the pillow, and my body sliding and humping. But if my face was buried in the pillow, how come I was so audible? And how come, at least in my earliest

years, I didn't suffocate – I could have been an early example of
what used to be called cot death but is now frequently, after
confidently delivered though hopelessly flawed medical evidence,
misdiagnosed as murder (a number of mothers wrongfully jailed,
whole families destroyed, children snatched from their homes and
placed with foster parents or in institutions, irretrievably –
irretrievably? Well, yes, we know we might have made a mistake,
say the social services and government ministers responsible, but it's
too late now to correct it, for the children's sake they must stay
fostered or institutionalized, besides no smoke without fire, even if
we're the ones who lit it you can't expect us to put it out, we're
comfortable with what we've done and compassionate and caring
with it) – so with the hypothesis that I died in my cot because my
face was sunk into my pillow while jouncing, and then with a time-
jump of those sixty-seven years, it's easy to see how the course of
our lives might have run differently, Mummy's would have run in
jail, Daddy would either have remarried or sacrificed himself to
clearing Mummy's name, Nigel would have been fostered or
institutionalized, and I, well, I would have been dead, of course,
officially the victim of infanticide (unless they could pin it on the
nanny), but in fact the victim of a jouncing habit that led to pillow
suffocation – but what pillow? Surely babies don't have pillows. If
they lie flat on their stomachs – a clear impossibility, actually, given
that babies' stomachs are round, inflated – I've just been upstairs
and tried it on the hotel bed, I lay with my cheek, right cheek as
I'm a right-hand-side person, pressed flat against the mattress, it felt
so easy and natural that I began to slip away for a moment, the
great soft belly of me cushioning the middle of my body, in fact
becoming a functional asset instead of the pendulous
embarrassment it is when I'm upright and in company – and not
only when I'm in company, I'm embarrassed by it when I'm on my

own, sometimes I stand still in the middle of my study and try to suck it in – I'll try now, I'm in the bar but nobody's really looking – no, nothing stirred except the ghosts in my chest, the effort has left me short of breath, so let me go back to it as it was when I lay down a few minutes earlier – how did I describe it? As a cushion for the middle of my body – so must a baby's be, when it's not full of wind, so must mine have been whenever I was a windless baby, but just now, when I lay on the bed, I felt no impulse to jounce and bounce and fill the hotel with my keening.

A PEACEFUL AND REASONABLE MAN GOES SLEEPLESS

The thing, though, about jouncing in my bed, post-perambulator, and all through my growing up, is that it brought out the worst in my parents – Daddy, after all, needed his sleep, and when we moved to London, into 47 Oakley Gardens, in Chelsea, he had to be up and off to his pathology lab early in the morning, and also needed energy for his romantic enterprises later in the day, furthermore he liked his sleep, not only was he relaxed and nourished by it, but was addicted to it as a kind of pleasure, or was it vice? He liked to be in bed early, and stay in it until the last possible minute – he took his breakfast in it, along with his post and the newspapers, and he was very uxorious, a very uxorious philanderer, so what with one vice and another, one pleasure and another, you can see that he spent quite a lot of his day, as well as most of his night, in bed, and when he was in bed at night he liked his sleep, drowsy, toasty, in Mummy's arms, she in his, zzzzz – and I disturbed all that, the sound of my bed jumping up and down, my child's voice keening, clattered and sliced into his slumber, their slumber, and drove him quite wild with rage, though he tried, being by nature a reasonable and peaceful man, to bring the rage under control and to devise reasonable and peaceful solutions to my problem, though it wasn't in fact my problem, after all I wasn't waking myself up, in fact I was probably jouncing and keening myself into deeper and deeper layers of the unconscious, into sweet and holy spaces or places – or perhaps not, who knows where you go when you're asleep, whether you're jouncing and keening or as still as a corpse.

ANOTHER USE FOR A HAIRBRUSH

His first solution was to ask me, and then, a few nights later, after I'd evidently though not consciously turned down his request, to command me, to sleep on my back. I remember lying rigidly, eyes closed, trying to lower myself into sleep by an act of will, a kind of reverse levitation. My next introduction to consciousness was when he rolled me back onto my back with whispered imprecations, dark words I couldn't understand that for all their intensity were designed to be inaudible to Mummy in their bedroom next door, and perhaps to me, too. Whatever they were, their meaning was inescapable. He believed, even though reason and peaceableness must have argued against it, that I was doing it on purpose and that I was a deliberate and premeditating jouncer. Well, possibly I was. I certainly came to believe that I was, and fought against the deep, corrupt desire to roll onto my side, then onto my stomach – one turbulent night he ran into my room and unleashed a powerful but soft, because unshod, kick at my ribs. From the next room came Mummy's, my Mummy's alarmed and imploring response – 'James! James, darling!' – to his disowning me, so to speak, with 'Will you shut up, you little bastard!' That he should have come to this! He got his foot out of the blanket, threw it over me, and left the room, a little click, a solicitous little click of the closing door, as if being careful not to wake the sleeping child. I heard their voices murmuring away, mainly hers, consoling – I'd recognize the tone now, though I didn't then – she knew her James, he wasn't a man to kick his sleeping nine-year-old, even with a naked foot, for the mere pleasure of it, this was a James who had been driven to desperate measures, a James beside himself. James, peaceable and reasonable and at one with himself again, devised a practical scheme to prevent me rolling on my stomach in my sleep – a hairbrush tied through one of the buttonholes on my pyjama top.

TROUBLE WITH PYJAMAS

One went to bed in suits, in those days, a thickish jacket and a thickish pair of trousers particularly thick at the waist, because of the thick cord that went through it, the ends of which one tied in a burly bow at the front, navel height. It's a wonder, really, that we didn't wear shoes in bed – oh, and the gap at the front of the trousers that wasn't a gap but folds of cloth that you somehow had to pull apart, a fumbling and desperate business when you were in urgent need – sometimes it was simpler to pull the trousers down and pee over the top, the dangers of this procedure being manifest in smells and stains that mother drew to your attention – 'Really, must you be so lazy!' and one couldn't explain the difficulties to the mother, how in the cold, especially, it was like a tight little knot that tucked itself tightly into somewhere between one's legs, one's numbed fingers needed time to locate it, and then it had to be plucked at and coaxed and stretched like a piece of sensitive elastic, and this after one had fumbled through all the folds of cloth to locate the naked groin, let alone the tightly infolded little knot – so you see, Mummy, so much easier to pull the trousers down so you could actually see where it was, and if one bent one's knees and pushed one's groin – or would that be loins? – forward, one could mainly miss the crotch in one's pyjama bottoms, it would only be the last little bit, the dribble that sometimes, inexplicably, becomes a spurt before becoming a treacherous dribble again, dribbling down into the crotch and causing that stain.

SOUNDS FROM THE NEXT ROOM

So I went to bed with the hairbrush dangling from the buttonhole in the pyjama top, lay rigidly on my back, eyes closed, and woke to Daddy's brawling hands, rolling me back on my back, pulling my pyjama jacket into position – it had become twisted around to the side so that the buttons ran from my armpit down. The hairbush lay away from my body, pointlessly attached. On some occasions, worse occasions, the pyjama jacket was completely discarded, lay on the floor even. These were the signs, were they not, of a deliberate, wilful determination to sleep on my stomach and jounce keening through the night, in complete disregard of the father's need for replenishing sleep? I think that during those nights, many, many nights, I became quite simply the enemy, as a screeching cat or a perpetually barking dog becomes the enemy, first the enemy to sleep, then the enemy to self – in this case to my father's self. I expect he wanted to kill me, from time to time, as he lay beside his wife in the darkness, listening to my private night life expressing itself in what, now I come to think of it, must have sounded like an infant parody of the sexual act, the bouncing bed, the twanging springs, the animal keening, at a consistent, monotonous level of a climax impending but never achieved – an eerie, haunting parody of his own noises after lunch, say, in the bed in the flat of his secretary, little Mrs Rolls, or in the bed next door, where his wife, my mother, lay beside him but around whose body his arms – ah, but that was love, I heard it, not in the dead of night but as I lay awake before breakfast, the hairbrush replaced and resting on my stomach. I listened to the real thing, the noises of love, not keenings but murmurs, grunts, laughs, little cries suppressed but still trembling into screams choked off –

TIME ZONES

1) Today

It's 3.30 in the afternoon here in Barbados, 7.30 in England, specifically in Brighton, where the curtain is going up on *The Holy Terror*, an old play of mine. I say the curtain is going up, perhaps now has gone up, but I know so little about the production that I don't know whether there is a curtain. If there is, though, it won't be going up, now I come to think of it, it will still be down and Simon Callow will part it slightly as he steps onto a bit of forestage, to confront his audience, which is not the audience in the theatre but the audience in the play, composed of members of the Women's Institute in Chichester – it might be Cheltenham – the audience in the theatre is characterized and addressed, in other words, as if it were a small clutch of middle-aged, middle-class provincial women. When it was done in New York, nearly twenty years ago, the preview audiences enjoyed this device, cheerfully assuming the role assigned them, but the critics hated it, which is why there weren't any post-preview audiences.

I suppose I should try and write down the history of *The Holy Terror* – no, actually, I shouldn't, it's all in a preface I've written for a collection of my plays, I'll look it up and stick it in here when I get back –

2) *Two Months Later*

I'm in London, where it's extremely cold and unpleasant, transferring to this computer the yellow pads, which, I must say, are frequently difficult to read because of illegibility, stains, etc. I've just got to the sentence where I told myself to stick the preface in – quite easy, really, all I have to do is to look through my computer files for my prefaces, find the one for *The Holy Terror*, copy it and paste it

HERE:

I wrote the first version of *The Holy Terror* in 1986. It was called *Melon* and, like *The Holy Terror*, was about a successful publisher who advocates promiscuity for his wife and himself, then has a nervous breakdown when he decides, against all available evidence, that his wife is having an affair with one of his best friends – which best friend being the conundrum that finally drives him mad. *Melon* was produced at the Theatre Royal, Haymarket, and played to good houses, thanks mainly to Alan

Bates, whose performance as the brute Englishman with the chaotic soul was so dazzling that it flattered the text, and perhaps it was the discrepancy between the story that the play told and the story that Alan told that made me feel, every time I sat through it, that the play didn't quite work. One day, long after it had closed, I found myself first thinking about it, then fretting about it, then sitting down to rewrite it, and finally, after drafts and drafts and more drafts, I was in possession of a new play that was so different from the original that I changed its title to *The Holy Terror*, which opened at the Promenade theatre in New York, in a production that you would have described as eccentric if you hadn't known that the director was a drunk. He drank quite a bit before each day's rehearsals, and quite a bit after them, and more than quite a bit during them, while never losing the conviction, however many times he stumbled down the aisle and tumbled over the seats, often with a lighted cigarette in his mouth and another, also lighted, in the hand that wasn't holding a glass, that he was in full command of his faculties, and that his genius for cutting through to the heart of the matter had never burned more brightly – thus when he had trouble moving the actors around the furniture, he cut the furniture, and when he had trouble deciding between lighting effects, he cut the lighting – on the press night, the audience found themselves confronted by unnerved actors performing on a mainly empty set, and in the house-lights only – the actors could see from the stage, for almost certainly the first time in their careers, the critics' faces, or more likely their heads, the tops of them anyway, as they bent angrily over their pads in order to avoid the actors' eyes, which were enlarged by panic and loathing. The director himself, frightened, triumphant and drunk, was also fully visible and all over the place, now at the backs of the stalls, now at the head of an aisle, now in the dress circle – if I'd been one of the actors I'd have stepped off the stage and murdered him, the news of which might at least have marginalized the review in the next morning's *New York Times*. Of course the producer, who was devoted to the play, made periodic attempts to fire the director but was thwarted by the director's agent, who pointed out that the playwright had director approval, and as the playwright and the director were one and the same it would be a question of asking him to fire himself, which he was unlikely to do, as he got on so well together. *The Holy Terror* lay dormant until about a year ago, when it was picked up by a London management. There are plans to produce it in the spring of 2004, with Simon Callow in the lead.

3) Two Minutes Later

There. Now I'm back to transcribing from the pad again, with a smear of what looks like bird-dropping coming up – ah, the birds in Barbados, darting onto the table, pecking at my hat, dipping into my drink. What is it, under the bird-shit – the word? Rehearsals is the word.

REHEARSALS

began a few weeks ago, but I decided not to attend them. Alan – with whom I still associated the leading part – had died a few days before, on Boxing Day, and I didn't want to hear his voice echoing in the lines, even though, as most of them had been rewritten, he'd never actually said them. Of course I knew that Simon Callow, an old and dear friend of mine, and an actor of great and distinctive talents, would very quickly make the lines his own. But I thought that even if I didn't bring Alan's ghost with me, I'd be haunting the production myself, the older playwright impersonating the twenty or so years younger one, the consumer of Diet Coke passing himself off as the gulper-down of champagne. I did, however, go, by invitation, to what I assumed was to be a read-through at Sadler's Wells, and found myself on the fringe of a little mob waiting in the reception area outside the rehearsal room – they were the producer and some of his staff, publicity people, make-up people, the wardrobe mistress and so forth along with representatives of the provincial theatres we'd be visiting. Inside the rehearsal room were the director and cast, not about to begin the read-through, the producer, Howard Panter, explained to me, but about to end it. 'I'm sorry you couldn't make it,' he said. 'I could have made it,' I said. 'But I wasn't asked.' 'Ah!' he said. 'The door's open. We can go in.' We went in. The director, a jovial-looking, plumpish, youngish man, whose name I've forgotten, stood at the head of a table and talked to his seated cast of six in a low, excluding voice. He saw us finally, with a little start of delight, and invited us to sit in a semicircle around him and greet and meet, or was it meet and greet the cast, himself and each other. 'I am Simon Callow,' said Simon Callow, 'and I am playing the part of Melon,' etc., a bit like an AA meeting, really. We got to me by way of the wardrobe mistress and several representatives of the provincial theatres – 'I,' I said, 'am the reason we are all here this afternoon.' Yes, I actually said that. There was a ripple of sycophantic laughter from one of the provinces. 'Well, not the only reason surely?' the director said, with a surprised smile. 'Yes, the only reason,' I said. Yes, I actually said that, too, and it was pretty well all I said, apart from a brief discussion with Lydia

Fox, who is playing Melon's sexually generous secretary, on the subject of whether her character would be wearing the underclothes that young women wore in the 1970s, when the play is set – what about a girdle, for instance? She'd heard that girdles were very good for showing off your bum. I said I'd heard that too. We said a few more things along those lines to each other, she's very easy to talk to, very pretty, with a laughing, freewheeling conversational style. When she was taken away from me by the costume designer, I went over to Simon Callow. We generally have long and boisterous conversations together, but this time we really had nothing to say, he was for the trenches, as both captain and foot soldier, and I for – well, immediately for Barbados, so I gave him a hug, hoped he'd have fun in the coming month of rehearsals, and that was it, I left.

I MUST UNDERSTAND THAT I AM DEAD

How sour this seems in the remembering, no, in the telling, though I do in fact remember it sourly, and did in fact feel sour at the time – there's something about not wanting to be where you're not wanted or not expected or have not been thought about, especially when the occasion is the read-through of a play, and you're its author – but perhaps they thought I was dead, a dead author, a safely dead author. On the other hand there'd been phone calls, emails, I'd even had a meeting with the director, an hour long, in which he'd told me about his production of *Beauty and the Beast* at Stratford, and his plans for a family holiday in Egypt, so they all knew I was alive at least to that extent, that I could talk on the phone, receive and answer emails, present myself physically to the director, so there it was,

I had to face it, I wasn't dead, I was merely negligible, a man for a meet and a greet but not for a read-through – in the old days, I told myself and now tell myself again, it wouldn't have happened, I wouldn't have let it happen, I'd have made them read through the read-through again and again and again, until they collapsed with exhaustion and dehydration, and then I'd have done such things that the earth would tremble at, and then I'd have, I'd have – but what in fact did I do? I stood around looking surly, that's what I did, brightening only when engaged by an attractive young woman in a conversation about attractive young women's underwear, and then tramped off full of grievance and relief, yes, that's the point, relief, and really I didn't think there were intended ill manners on the management's part, just the usual office negligence, and probably there was nothing intentionally unwelcoming in the director's welcome, just the usual director's nerves. I also knew I would have hated the read-through anyway, it would have made me doubt the actors, doubt the director, above all, doubt the play – and beneath all that I knew I just wasn't up to it any more. When it came down to it, what was I but a dead author, at least as far as *The Holy Terror* was concerned?

OR AUTISTIC

I'm in the bar at my table at two in the morning, only Rollocks, the waiter, in the bar with me – he is laying the tables for breakfast, strolling in his measured way from table to table, occasionally looking towards me to check whether I want another Diet Coke – I don't – the truth is I don't really want to be here. Last year and all the previous years I would come every night and write and talk to

Rollocks, now I stay on my balcony, reading or writing or looking towards the sea, or sometimes looking down into the bar, where I can see Rollocks moving between the tables, and I feel a yearning to go down, but I don't, I stay up there and watch Rollocks moving between the tables. Is it possible to become autistic, or do you have to start off that way? Well, I believe that all day I've been something that corresponds to my understanding of the word autistic – it's as if I've had no inner context at all, no points of reference, a sort of blankness and not a comfortable one. I'm quite unhappy in this, but don't want to talk to anyone about it, not even Victoria, to whom I tell everything, almost everything, certainly more than she actually needs to know – but this is something that she probably does need to know, that her husband has plodded beside her to bar, restaurant and beach, indeed swum beside her in the sea, sat opposite her at the lunch and dinner table, and internally there's been no flicker of life at all, his mind a *tabula rasa*, slightly soiled.

A GOOD DEED PUNISHED

Can I, in all conscience, keep my table at the bar while I have lunch at a table in the restaurant? Yesterday I decided I couldn't, and surrendered my bar table to a lanky North Country couple – he has buck teeth that fix his mouth in a permanent grin of seeming good nature, she is blonde, with a handsome, beaky face and long legs made longer by high-heeled sandals – both wear sunglasses which don't suit them, they make his face seem all teeth, and to hers they give a hooded effect, like a bird of prey. They accepted the table gratefully, as if with a full knowledge of the ancient tradition that it was mine by right and their tenure was at my convenience. When I returned from lunch they vacated it immediately, with a flourish and some jokes about having been honoured, etc. So that was OK. Today at lunch time when they came to the bar I repeated the offer. When I came back after lunch they were sitting with their heads bowed, stubbornly unaware of my hovering presence. I thought I'd give them a few minutes, but when I came back they were just as they had been, heads bowed. Victoria took me for a walk to calm me down, and I was calm when we came back, until I saw that they were still there, heads bowed. Victoria took me for a swim, and when we got back, there, with heads, etc. – I walked around the table at a slight distance and, though their heads were still, I could see their hands moving and hear little clicking sounds, like false teeth – I moved closer to make absolutely sure, and yes, it was true, they were playing Scrabble, sitting at my table, the buggers, playing Scrabble. So here I am now, looking down at them from our balcony – I notice that she has a long, straight back, and he too sits very upright, both of their postures speak of intense concentration, which is I suppose needed when playing a game for halfwits, you have to keep the other half of your wits at bay, if they joined up you'd surely knock the board and the pieces of the alphabet to the ground – not that I've ever actually played Scrabble, I have no patience with indoor games that involve spelling or knowledge or indeed thought or intelligence of any kind – but the fact is, as I look down at them with scowly eyes, I suspect that they make a more attractive, more elegant spectacle at my table than I do, when I sit there writing, my jaw jutting out, cigarette on the go, a study in ill temper and bad living.

LIKE SON

Actually, I've just realized that it's not true that I've never played games that require thought or knowledge. I used to play chess *en famille*, not with Mummy, of course, she thought it was strictly a man's sport, unlike hockey or cricket, at both of which she'd excelled, along with the standing broad jump and the high jump, but chess, she said, demanded the male mind to grasp its intricacies, she couldn't hope even to set the board, the pieces themselves made her female – or was it feminine? – mind reel, just trying to work out what their shapes meant, but she used to stand, smoking in admiration whenever a combination of the males in the household were bent in archetypal male postures over it – elbows on knees, chins in palms, foreheads furrowed, rather like slightly different versions of Thurber's version of *Le Penseur* – though when Nigel and I played in our pubescent days, our games usually climaxed in our rolling around the floor, with our hands locked around each other's throats, kneeing, punching, kicking, sobbing (me), shouting (him), until she had to come in at the run and separate us with her own more authoritative violence, precisely aimed kicks and clips – 'Can't you two ever play without fighting – and over chess, of all things!' she said. 'Chess!' As we grew older, we played alternately with Daddy, who was, Mummy told us, very good at chess, his natural game, because it required thinking. And he seemed to be very good, beating us within a few moves, again and again. I went from accepting this as quite right and proper, in the natural order of things – I think I'd have been quite fearful if I'd won – if I could beat him what manner of father was he? How could he be trusted to look after us, bring us up? – but soon enough the gorge began to rise, feelings began to stir similar to the ones that had stirred years before when Nigel won – his honest, pleasant, thoughtful face as he mowed me down in game after game, the gentle peer over the rims of his spectacles, the Scots undercurrent underneath the Canadian accent which ran below the English one – 'Mate, I think, old boy.' 'What, you've

won again!' came the cry from the passing Mummy, and if I said
something primitively spiteful – 'Oh, any fool can beat me' – the
triumphant, 'Oh, don't be such a poor loser, the world hates a
poor loser.' I tried cheating – nudging a piece into a different
position when he was reloading or tamping down his pipe –
though I'm not sure I gave myself any real advantage, because I
never worked out the consequences properly, probably nudged
myself into worse positions – I don't know why I did it, really,
perhaps just the thought that cheating gave me a kind of
psychological edge, I could do things that would never cross his
mind. And then at a certain stage, when I was about fifteen or
sixteen I should think, I began to study the board with real
concentration, practise moves on my own, in fact began to get a
remote glimmering of how to think a move or two ahead, work
out what could be predicted, or at least sensibly guessed at. As I
got better, our games got longer – he was working through two
bowls of a pipe rather than half a bowl – and there came an
evening when I had him. I saw as clearly as I've ever seen anything
that if I moved my knight, bishop, whatever, he would be check-
mated. 'Mate, Daddy, mate, I believe,' I would say, and keep the
tremble out of my voice. 'What!' she would cry. 'You've beaten
your father!' or with luck, 'You've beaten your own father!' – 'I'm
just going to have a pee,' I said. I remember it quite well, the
peeing, washing my hands, looking at my face in the mirror, a boy
on the threshold, a boy who beat his Daddy, his own Daddy – I
went in, sat down, 'Whose move is it?' though I knew perfectly
well it was mine. He was relaxed back in his chair, feet crossed at
the ankles, eyes miles away. 'Oh, yours, I think.' I bent to the
board, made to pick up the assassinating piece, and saw that it was
a square or so away from where I had left it. Furthermore, his
queen wasn't where I'd last seen her. I lifted mine eyes unto the

father. He was still in his trance, lost to the trivialities of the chess board that is life. 'Cheaters never prosper,' I might have said, Mummy-style, but I didn't. I moved my piece, in due course lost the game. 'Well done, Daddy!' I said, losing gracefully for once. 'It was closer than you realized,' he said. 'There was a moment there when you nearly had me.' But I had had him, hadn't I?

THE JOUNCER EXILED

But I wasn't writing about Daddy cheating at chess, I was writing about – the hairbrush, yes, Daddy and the hairbrush, tying it to my pyjama top – well, then, it didn't work. I went on jouncing, keening, until Daddy desperate, Mummy desperate on his behalf, hit on the solution. They transferred me from the top of the house and the room next to theirs, down three flights of stairs, to the bottom of the house – into the dining room, in fact, which therefore ceased to be the dining room, which was moved next door, in the form of the dining table and dresser, to what, until then, had been a sort of sitting room but mainly the father's study, which, in the form of a large roll-top desk with many compartments and drawers, was moved upstairs to the room directly above the new dining room, which remained what it had always been, the main sitting room, but now with certain odd study-ish aspects to it. There was something about this move – it had, I suppose, a whiff of punishment and exile to it – that Mummy found distressing. 'You're quite comfortable down here, aren't you ?' I was perfectly comfortable in that I was comparatively private, and needed to be in that I had discovered Hank Janson and my sex life was becoming tumultuous. 'Well, at least you're not in the basement, darling.'

THE GIRL IN THE BASEMENT

Of course I wasn't in the basement, the basement was damply uninhabitable, though in fact inhabited by a succession of au pairs who were brought in as cheap nannies to look after baby Piers. The first one was Scots, recently out of jail, come to us while on probation. I suppose she was in her early twenties, young certainly, with a pretty face that had something aged about it, her cheeks were full and her lower jaw often moved about as if she was eating when she wasn't – the effect, as she showed us, Nigel and me, of having over-sized false teeth – when she took them out her cheeks sank and her jaw tightened up, and she put on sixty years, just like that, a shocking transformation that we kept asking her to perform for us – the first few times she turned her back, as if to remove an intimate garment, but as she became used to showing us her new face, old face really, she let us watch the process – hooking her fingers to the back of her mouth and levering her dentures forward until they protruded, then a little shake of her head and they would drop into the palm of her hand, it had the ceremony of a conjuring trick about it, though it rapidly lost its mystery. Elizabeth's mystery was her crime. Mummy told us – 'But you're not to mention it to her. Never. Never.' – that she'd been an accomplice to a man who was still in jail. 'It wasn't really her fault, he led her into it, you see. She was just weak, that's all. She's a good girl at heart.' Or so she had to believe, because in another telling she would be entrusting her baby son, and the moral welfare of her ten- and eleven-year-old boys, to an ex-con, still on probation – so of course she was a good girl, really, though of course she wasn't, at least in Mummy's terms, because she was seeing men not only on her afternoons off but her afternoons on, when she was meant to be wheeling Piers about the Embankment – I would go with her sometimes, and she would turn the pram over to me, tell me in her soft Scots voice that she'd be back in half an hour, she'd meet me by the bench, and off she'd hurry – she was trim and athletic, and walked very quickly, also eagerly, her blonde hair bobbing – and then more than half an hour later I would see her coming towards me, while I could see behind her a man going away, but turning to look – and I think, in spite of the teeth and the slight deformation on the lower part of her face, she was attractive. I know that I liked being with her, even when she behaved treacherously, as when she'd been given money to take us to the cinema to see a western and we ended up at a film with lots of kissing and crying, with Lana Turner in it instead of John Wayne or Alan Ladd. Her explanation that the film we'd been promised had been showing at a cinema now closed because of the polio epidemic, we knew was a lie. She put on a lot of make-up for these cinema outings, lashings of lipstick, as if preparing to meet the characters on the screen, and while watching them she was quite oblivious to us, and remained oblivious, in a trance, all the way through our tea at Lyons Corner House, where she would sit curled on her chair, smoking in a special way, long inhalations and then the smoke issuing like a secret out of the side of her mouth. On the other hand she would forfeit her share of the tea money, so we got an extra bun or two with false cream on top. She also played cricket with us in the basement, along the long damp hall, and if the parents were out in the evening we would go into her small damp room off the long damp hall, and she would give us a cigarette. And of course she doted on Piers, loving to hold him up and show him off to briefly infatuated passers-by on the street.

MY FIRST KILL

We went back to Hayling Island one summer, Mummy and I, because I'd been ill and needed sea air for my convalescence. The father and Nigel stayed on in London, Nigel because he had to go to school and would come down later, the father because he had to go to work. Elizabeth took Piers to stay with an aunt of hers, I think it was an aunt, anyway an older woman who had been approved by her probation officer – 'So she'll be perfectly all right, and she loves babies, Elizabeth says, so Piersy will have the time of his life,' my mother said. We stayed in a boarding house not far from the house we'd lived in, Mallows. The landlord of the boarding house I only remember now from Mummy's subsequent anecdotes – he was small and bald and complacent and common, and used to say – Mummy would repeat it, flourishing her cigarette extravagantly so that, while she didn't become him, she somehow made him become her, a kind of reverse mimicry – 'Be they dukes or navvies, I lets 'em all muck in together.' He made it sound like a policy, she said, often put to the test. I had brought an air rifle with me, a birthday or a Christmas present. One morning after breakfast I took aim from my window and shot dead a little bird with a yellow chest. I went down and picked it up. It was still warm, its yellow chest now scarlet. I attempted a swagger, a huntsman with his first kill. I showed it to Mummy, who admired my marksmanship, then to our host. 'You don't go killing my birds,' he said. 'People come from miles around to stay here especially for my birds.' In fact, I was relieved, but when I explained to Mummy why I was no longer killing birds she was indignant. 'I've never heard of anything so stupid,' she said. 'I mean, what's the point of giving you an air rifle if you're not allowed to shoot things with it?' But really, for her, it was a social thing, that a son of hers should be reprimanded by a common, etc., while for him it was a manly thing, I think, disguising as a commercial objection his revulsion at the little swine's mindless murder of a pretty bird.

A SUICIDE PACT

Towards the end of our stay the seas were very high. People stood on the beach and gaped up at great walls of water that seemed to grow and grow, waves mounting on waves, and then the white combs cascading, one after another. There was nothing for it, Nigel and I decided, but to surge in and ride them, yes, we'd ride them on their white rims right onto the beach, where we would lie broken and dead until we were tugged out to sea, then hurled back on the beach, tugged out, hurled back – this wasn't actually our plan, but would certainly have been its conclusion. We ran back to the house, and caught Mummy in a state, in something of a state, having just put down the telephone. We asked her if we could go for a swim, the waves were enormous, and we tried to describe them – 'Yes, yes,' she cried. 'For goodness' sake don't bother me!', consigning us with a flourish of her cigarette to our death by drowning. We made to dash off for our swimming trunks, hesitated. 'You haven't seen the waves, then?' Nigel asked, whose idea of a future had clearly depended on the request refused. 'No, of course I haven't, I haven't been out, how could I possibly go out!' She gestured at the telephone. 'Why not?' asked Nigel. 'Elizabeth's run away!' It was an exciting thought, like one of the films she took us to – I could see her in the fields, down roads, in her slacks, her brown slacks, down alleys, then in a bar or café, a passport in her hand, eyes veiled, smoke curling. 'Where to?' Nigel asked, as Nigel would. 'How the hell would I know? She's run off, so how would I know where the bloody girl's gone to?' There was another question lurking, an urgent one, that I couldn't put my finger on. 'And did she,' Nigel asked, 'take Piers with her?' Yes, that was the question. 'We don't know. We don't know where Piers is.' So I saw her running with Piers, pushing him in his pram across fields, down alleys – then there was the man, of course, a smallish man, in a shiny suit and scuffed, frequently polished shoes, hair combed back, also shiny, a peaky little face, a Woodbine between his fingers, the whole of him half-turned on the Embankment, looking after Elizabeth as she ran towards me as I waited with Piers in his pram by the bench. 'We don't know,' Mummy said. 'We don't know.' She was almost in tears, her face working and ugly, it was a shock to see her like this, stricken, frightened.

GREEN FLASH

I stopped doing this to go for a little walk on the path that separates the lawn from the beach. I wanted to sort out what I could remember about Elizabeth's vanishing, Piers's whereabouts, there was a whole business to do with telephones, there was a shortage of telephones at this time, whole sections of the community depended on the tall, red telephone boxes, press the 'A' button – if you hear a voice at the other end of the line saying hello and announcing its number – ours was Flaxman 8595 – you are connected, if it rang and rang and you didn't hear a voice, press the 'B' button and get your money back, either two fat pennies, or a neat little sixpence, or a neat but larger shilling –

The memory of the red boxes with their heavy doors, the

ponderous contraption with its A and B buttons, fills me with a melancholy yearning for the days when husbands and wives, parents and children were completely absent from each other for long reaches of time. Now of course they travel in each other's pockets and handbags, whole families scattered around the globe can be in touch with each other by pressing a button, and so – what about the adulterers, how do they cope, have they learnt to lie regularly, almost from minute to minute? 'Yes, yes, I'm in the car, just got to pop down to Ealing to fetch some papers, then up to Hampstead to drop them off – yes, I'll phone you as soon as –' and so forth, while proceeding towards the act, or retreating from it, or even – who knows? – during the act itself, while for their ancestors one lie would do, if one was needed at all – and it was probably only half a lie, a lie of omission, in that he had been to Lord's, had seen some cricket, and the act itself so squeezed in between the beginning of one innings and the end of another that it was almost forgotten. Only really stupid people, or exceptionally unlucky people, or people who needed to resolve the problem by getting caught, got caught in adultery back then, but now – well, I don't know – are moral comparisons possible? Is an adulterer who doesn't really lie because he doesn't really have to superior to an adulterer who is forced by historic circumstance, the invention of the mobile telephone, to lie with almost every other breath?

So I pondered as I walked the path between the lawn and the sea. There were still quite a few people on the beach, about twenty at least, unusual at this late hour. They were standing in clusters or lying on their beach-beds, and there was an odd air of expectancy and tension as they gazed towards the sun, which was at the sea's rim, seeming to hang there, static, as it in fact slid down, diminishing. There was a sudden furnacy glow all around it, and to its left, associated with it in some way, but not attached to it, a bright green dot appeared, a small but complete and brilliant dot. Everyone on the beach cheered, a couple of old chaps threw their straw hats into the air, young people clasped each other in jubilation. I held my own hat aloft and cried out, because they'd seen it, we'd seen it, I'd seen it, the famous green flash, that was already gone while we were still celebrating its arrival, the sun gone with it, and the sea and the sky darkening – you could say it was something, 'quite something' as Harold would say – I mean, there I'd been patrolling along the path, turning my head idly towards the beach and wondering what they were all looking at as I ruminated on red telephone boxes, buttons A and B, with consequent thoughts on contemporary versus old-style adultery, and there it was, the green flash, an inexplicable phenomenon – I felt quite puffed up with the privilege and honour of it. I wonder what Victoria will make of it when I tell her, she looks for it most evenings, has done since she first came to Barbados as a little girl, when she and her mother sat together staring towards the sea, the dropping sun, waiting, hoping, although I expect what they were hoping for was more than a green dot. It may be called a flash, but really, as I say, it's a dot, a speck, a small splodge even, not at all what you imagine from the vocabulary, or from the hat-throwing, the cheering and cuddling which greeted it.

NIGEL'S QUESTIONING MIND

But now back to – let me look – Elizabeth, the day she vanished, with or without Piers is the unanswered question that was ravaging our Mummy's face, mouth twitching, eyes brimming with tears, perhaps from the smoke, as she was also coughing, perhaps from emotion – where was the father during all this? Yes, where was he, at the height of the drama? And how was it the mother didn't know where Piers was, or at least whether Elizabeth had run off with him or left him with her older friend or relative, who had, after all, phoned up to announce Elizabeth's disappearance – had Elizabeth's older relative or friend simply forgotten to mention Piers's whereabouts, had Mummy indeed forgotten to ask, so full of expostulations over the girl's behaviour, that damned girl's behaviour, that her baby boy had simply slipped out of her mind and it wasn't until she had hung up that she'd suddenly remembered?

Why didn't she ring back and ask her? – this from Nigel, naturally.

Because the bloody woman hadn't got a phone – she'd made the call from a box, she had no idea when she'd next phone, and –

But Nigel had moved on. 'Why don't you phone the police?'

Yes, yes, phone the police, I said, because it seemed to me a terrific idea, terrific and terrifying.

'The police!' she said. 'What do you mean, the police!' The idea of the police, at any time, under any circumstances, except to patronize when asking directions – 'Oh, Constable, Constable, can you tell me, pray, the quickest way to Brompton Cemetery?' 'The quickest way, you bet I can,' said PC Gus/And pushed Mama underneath a bus. – in the middle of one of Mummy's expostulations in response to one of Nigel's lethally simple-minded and sensible questions, the telephone rang, Elizabeth's older friend or relative in a red telephone box to report that, by the way, baby Piers was safe and sound, she was sorry but she couldn't look after him, he would have to be collected tomorrow at the latest. Thus ended our holiday, and our only return to Hayling Island.

MALLOWS REVISITED

Until fifty years later, about ten years ago, when Victoria and I drove there, from Chichester, where I had a play on. It was a lovely afternoon, a childhood afternoon, the sandbanks warm in the sun, the sea slapping, gulls drifting – we walked along the beach and I pointed to this and that, slightly haphazardly, I suspect – the pill-box probably hadn't been exactly there, perhaps a hundred or so yards further along or further back, and perhaps the squares of cement embedded between the thick mats of grass weren't the remains of the American barracks, and I took the wrong track across the dune to Ferry Road, but it brought us out near enough to where I'd guessed it would, a short distance from Mallows, with its well-remembered lawn, and the swampy patch beyond it, which we used to cross on planks to reach the road – and yes, there were actually some planks down, though not the same ones, obviously – and there, behind the trees, would be the lawn, and beyond the lawn would be Mallows. There wasn't a lawn behind the trees, and there wasn't Mallows. There was just a fringe of grass that girdled a little cluster of bungalows. A man came out from the nearest, to see what we wanted, were we lost? No, not really, I said, just looking for a house called Mallows, to show my wife. I must have lost my bearings, it's been nearly half a century after all. Oh no, he said, I had my bearings. This was where Mallows had been all right, until fifteen years ago, when they'd knocked it down and put up – he pointed to his home, and the other little homes that crouched there.

AN EXAMPLE OF LIFE'S UNFAIRNESS

I'm sitting at the table on the balcony of our room, writing this. Victoria is still lying on the sunbed, still reading yesterday's papers – yesterday's were Sunday's, so there are heaps of them. Above us the fan is whirring, and in the nearby trees the cicadas are at it, making their noise, ghastly and mechanical. How could something that sounds so mechanical come from a living creature? In a minute I will take two strong painkillers – co-proxamol, actually – to muffle it, but first I shall tell Victoria – let her finish her article. She's finished. Turned her head to me. Smiled. I told her. She refused to believe it.

'But didn't you hear the cheering from the beach? Over there. Directly in front of you.'

'I heard some shouting.'

'It was cheering. We were cheering ourselves for having seen it.'

'But I've watched every evening, every evening except this evening. And here I was reading a newspaper – and you're saying that just there –'

'Yes. Just there. On the other side of your newspaper.'

'And you've never even looked, have you? Not once.'

'That's probably it,' I said. 'The law of undeserved rewards, something like that. But really, you know, it wasn't a flash. More like a dot. A splodge.'

She brooded for a while and she said, 'Well,' she said. 'Well, well,' and went in to have her shower.

I've just taken two co-proxamol. The music from the restaurant has started up. I can see people walking to the bar, others walking along the path by the sea, all dressed for dinner. Underneath the music, I can hear the cicadas, shrill, mechanical, urgent, purposeless – but why do I think they're purposeless? They may be full of purpose. But if so, for what?

for lucky!

WAS IT DIVINE INTERVENTION?

Who knows what might have happened that afternoon if Elizabeth hadn't run away. Would Mummy have given us permission to swim? Yes, of course she would, she always did, and why not? We were very good swimmers, she would have been pleased on our account – 'What fun!' she'd have said. 'Huge waves! How thrilling! You can do some surfing! I might come down later and do some myself.' So we'd have to have gone the next step, put on our trunks, thrown ourselves against the great falling walls of water, been dashed to death on the beach, or swept out by the powerful undertow and drowned. It's possible that the more sensible of the adults would have tried to prevent us going in, but it's equally possible that they wouldn't – this was in the late 1940s, after all, a time of restraint and politeness, when such people as elderly, middle-class Hayling Islanders might have considered it ill-mannered to interfere with two boys seemingly intent on drowning themselves, and some of them might have found it an enjoyable spectacle. I suppose it's possible that Nigel and I would have had the sense, when it came to it, not to go in, but I doubt it. Once we were in our bathing trunks, and seen to be in them – a matter of a dress code, really. No, what saved us was that call from a red telephone box somewhere in England, made by Elizabeth's older friend or relative, who on her previous call had announced Elizabeth's flight but forgotten to mention that Piers hadn't gone too – and so we didn't change into our bathing trunks, go down to the beach and get drowned, we stayed with Mummy while she talked of Elizabeth's moral character, and how Daddy had always said that there was something about that girl he didn't trust – whether this was part of a plan, God's plan, or fate's, or nature's, that one or both of us were being saved for a great task, still uncompleted, as far as I know –

A PERFECT SHOT

Well then, was the same true for the baby in Battersea Park, about three years later, sitting so stiff and upright in his pram that he must have been harnessed – but why 'his' and 'he'? – it might have been a girl, but I've always assumed a boy, so – *his* pram, therefore, he sitting bolt upright, unattended, about twenty yards from where Nigel and I were playing cricket, just the two of us, but with a proper bat, three stumps with bails, and a hard ball, without a seam, called a 'compos' because it was made of compressed rubber, bouncy and bullet hard, hard enough to kill, certainly hard enough to kill a baby arranged bolt upright in a pram when savagely hooked with a proper bat straight at the baby's skull. It was a terrific shot, pow! shoulders open, right leg stretched forward, left heel rotating as I swivelled my body and opened my shoulders and swung my proper bat across the line of the ball pow! and connected in the centre pow! straight and true towards that thinly membraned head, as if to a target – now I wasn't exactly, not consciously, aiming at the baby's head, but there was definitely a connection between my eye and the ball and the baby's head that had to be completed by the bat in my hand, like an electrical circuit – no, there was intent too, that's the most difficult bit to explain, I, I, the I that I live in, the I that is I, didn't intend to hit the baby's head, would I truly believe have died rather than hit the baby's head, but my eye, my instinct, my reflexes intended the ball to hit the baby's head – or maybe the baby's head was where the ball would go if I hit it perfectly, and that, yes, that was what I intended, the perfect shot to that particular ball, so a born sportsman, you see, Mummy's genes – it seemed to go on and on, the compos, to be speeding through the air without actually progressing until it struck the baby's head, killed the baby, a deep dent in the side of the skull, blood and matter, the ball imbedded –if a thin metal strut, part of the hood, hadn't been raised – that's all, not the hood itself, but a thin strip of metal was what the rifled bullet of red rubber struck, and off which it shot, deflected, past the baby's face, over the pram and on to the grass beyond it rolled, and rolled and rolled –

'Run!' we shouted. 'Run, run!' and we ran, ran, leaving the stumps and bails, though I clung to the bat, all the way to the Albert Bridge. We mingled with the pedestrians, a couple of inconspicuous boys wasting time on their summer holidays. Of course, there was no need to run, no one had seen what happened, not even the baby himself, who was still sitting bolt up while we ran – well, if he was harnessed he'd little choice, and where was his mother, nanny, au pair? – no question of it being man in those days – was she having a gossipy stroll with a friend, a tryst with a boyfriend or lover, had she forgotten the baby completely? – anyway, nobody had seen what had happened, nothing in fact had happened, I had *nearly* killed a baby, that's all. *Nearly* killed him. So the world was unchanged. We could have gone on playing, but making sure to hit the ball away from the baby, or picked up the stumps and put them down in another part of the park, or even thanked God for our luck and gone safely home, to look for something else to do. But we ran. I suppose we were running from the horror of what had nearly happened, indeed logically should have happened, guilty of killing a baby – instead of nearly guilty of killing a baby, or should that be guilty of nearly killing a baby?

A TROUBLING SIGHT

I saw a woman sitting on the sand under the trees facing the wrong way – i.e. with her back to the sea. She was in her fifties, at a guess, plump, quite short, with frizzy grey hair showing under her straw hat. She was reading. All perfectly normal, really, except that there was something wrong – it could have been to do with the contrast between the parts of her body that were tanned and the white parts, or the unfortunate design of her swimsuit. Anyway, from where I stood it seemed as if her buttocks began directly under her shoulders like one of the freaks in that famous film of Tod Browning, called, well, *Freaks* actually, isn't it? It did occur to me that this might be one of my hallucinations, in which case I'm branching out, I've never hallucinated deformities before. I stood there with the water up to my ankles, hands behind my back, pretending to gaze in a generally vague and benign way on the people lying on their sunbeds, most of them elderly, most of them overweight, but with the light dappling down on them through the high trees they still made quite a pretty sight, sort of French and impressionist, and none of them looked grotesque except the woman with buttocks under her shoulders – or were they breasts on her back? – to whom my eyes kept reverting with more and more revulsion – and then a man came up to her, elderly and scrawny, wearing a baseball cap backwards on his head and an indecent scrap of bright red bikini between his legs, what they call a thong, I suppose. He was carrying a large blue towel which he flung over her. He helped her up, then flourished the towel away, as if finishing off a conjuring trick, and there she stood, a normal woman with normal legs, only a trifle short, with a normal length of back and neck. They walked off towards the bar, she trudging purposefully up the slope of the sand, he skipping friskily behind her, his aged genitals bouncing in their little crimson sac. I must keep an eye out for them in the restaurant, at lunch and dinner, an ear out too – I'd like to catch them in conversation. Now back to baby-killing – why? Yes. Why? Leave it for a while – perhaps tomorrow – go for another swim now, collect Victoria – where's Victoria?

AN ENCOUNTER AND A PHONE CALL

As I was going into the hotel lavatory just now I had a feeling that something older and scalier than myself was going to come out, and it did. It looked down at my feet. 'You're going barefoot,' it cried in astonishment, in American. 'I am,' I said. It pointed down at my feet. 'And you've got five toesies!' 'Ten,' I said. 'I've got ten toesies.' 'So you have!' it shrieked. 'So you have!' and went out. Some form of dementia, senile dementia, I suppose – what can it be like, to live in that sort of consciousness? Or half-consciousness, or whatever it is? – but he seemed merry – does that mean he felt merry? Well, we shall find out as Larkin says in which poem? 'The Old Fools' is it? Now I must go up to our room and phone Harold.

I spent at least fifteen minutes failing to dial correctly – getting the code to England wrong, even getting the number for getting out of the hotel wrong, forgetting to put in the 7 for our bit of London, and then, then when I got all those parts right, misdialling once or twice – 'The weather's lovely here,' I said. 'Good,' he said, as if surprised that I could think he might think it mightn't be. I told him we'd got the table. 'Ah,' he said. 'The same one?' The very same one, I said, that we always sat at. He sounded pleased, pleased and relieved. I also said we'd checked out their accommodation, that it was top-notch in every respect – I did actually use the word top-notch, sometimes when I talk to Harold I find myself using unfamiliar words and phrases. He liked this one, and repeated it. 'Top-notch you say. That's terrific.' 'Well,' I said, 'looking forward to your being here, have a good flight, love to Antonia.' 'Love to Victoria,' he said, and we hung up. I didn't warn him that I'm going to get him to read my new play while he's here, I want him to come light of heart, believing himself on holiday, free of obligations, then wham! I'll shove it at him, 'Mind having a look at this, Harold? No rush of course.' We'd better check out their room – we should have done it before I phoned, but I'm sure I didn't lie, their quarters will be top-notch, all right, all the quarters here are top-notch – top-notch, what a word!

THE BEST MOMENT OF MY LIFE

Twice guilty of nearly killing a baby, the second near victim being baby Piers. Baby Piers, I can't work out the chronology now, but I think he must have been born after I was moved downstairs into the dining room. I can't remember where he started off – perhaps in a cot in the parents' bedroom – but by the time he was crawling he was established next door to them, in my old room, from which every morning he would crawl to the top of the stairs, then manoeuvre himself down them in traditional baby style, bumping from step to step, three flights, on his bottom. He would then crawl to the front door, pick up the morning's post, post it through a gap in the floorboards, where it lay undiscovered until our father, perplexed and possibly even mortified by receiving nothing but medical journals for about a month, launched an investigation. Then he'd crawl into my bedroom, the door of which I left open for him every night when I went to bed, climb onto the bottom of the bed and bounce on my feet until I woke up. I was already half awake, actually, because I always knew he was there and would kick him gently up and down in harmony

with his bouncing, gave him a little extra propulsion so that he
went a little higher, and a little higher, and I laughing drowsily
with his gurgles and cries of joy, higher and higher I kicked and
he bounced, until one morning I gave him a little too much extra
propulsion and my kick bounced him off the bed – was there
intention, was there intention? Well, there was something –
malevolent, yes, there was something malevolent working in me
through the drowsiness, not an impulse to hurt but to do
something unexpected, that would change the mood and rhythm
of the game, I wanted to surprise him and shock him, this
trusting, devoted two-year-old whom I adored, to make the game
suddenly my game and not his. He landed on the wooden floor on
his head. It made a sound, soft but distinct, Piers's baby skull. He
lay there still, his face a white I'd never seen before, his eyes closed.
I picked him up, put him on the bed and begged him to wake up.
Nothing happened, no colour in his cheeks, his eyes sealed. I ran
around the room crying and pleading with God to bring him
back, for Mummy and Daddy to come in and make him all right.
I picked him up and clutched him to me. He was soft and dead
in my arms. I put him down on the bed – I think that what was
going through me was this – that I loved him overwhelmingly,
more than I had ever loved anyone, and that I'd killed him and
would have to be punished, but that the punishment didn't matter
as the world was no longer the place it had been moments before,
moments before it had been a glorious and comfortable place and
there was nothing I could do that would ever get me back into it,
I must now go upstairs with dead Piers in my arms and present
him to Daddy and Mummy, and the new world of punishment
without Piers would begin. I remember quite clearly how I bent
to pick him up from the bed just as he let out a mewl, and he
opened his eyes, blinked, saw me, and gurgled. Oh, the smell of

him when I had him in my arms, the sweet soft life in him, it was without doubt the purest flood of emotion, the least complicated, the simplest flood of gratitude and love –

AFTERWARDS

Five or six years later, when we were in Halifax, Nova Scotia, we quarrelled so violently that he seized a carving knife and threw it at me. No, threw it close to me. I can't remember what the quarrel was about, but whatever it was, I was entirely in the wrong – how couldn't I have been, as I was sixteen or seventeen, and he was six or seven, and from my point of view he was mine to control, and from his, he wasn't? 'He threw the carving knife at me!' I said, when the mother came to find out what all the noise was about. 'He could have killed me! Yes, you could have killed me, Piers!' He said he hadn't thrown it at me, he'd thrown it at the floor. 'Well, nearly killed me!' I said triumphantly. 'There! He admits it, Mummy!'

TOMORROW

the Pinters arrive. I shan't give Harold my new play immediately, let him have a day or two of rest and then slip it into his unsuspecting – I was going to write innocent, innocent hand, but what would an innocent hand look like – small, chubby, unmarked, nail-less, useless? – what could Harold possibly do with a hand like that, an innocent hand?

JAMES DAVIDSON SEAGULL

It's a most beautiful day, the small boats are humming across the absolutely still Caribbean, a couple of waterskiers are criss-crossing each other in complicated patterns, oh, one's just come a cropper, a young woman, a second ago all poise and grace as she rode on her skis, arms stretched out, head back, hair flowing, the next a grotesque flurry of upturned legs, the skis sticking out of the water like a compass – she's all right, though, she's waving to the driver, a slim guy in an orange shirt with Rastafarian locks and shades, he's circling around to her – meanwhile a gang of little birds are hopping about my drink, a virgin sea breeze (cranberry and grapefruit), one has hopped onto the rim of the glass, jerking its head now one way and now the other, seeing what's in front of it out of the corner of its eye – I think I have to go on doing what I'm doing, to give it a chance to dip its beak – no, well yes, that is he dipped his beak two or three times without making it to the liquid, gave a couple of panic-stricken twists of its head, flew off – I wonder what sort of bird it is, dun-yellow-chested, dark grey plumage – smaller than a sparrow – a kind of martin, I suppose – it has a blue band around its left leg, just above the claw – strangely large claws, parrot-like, out of proportion to its body – the band looks as if it's made of rubber or plastic, put there by an ornithologist, I suppose, who wants to keep tabs on its movement – yesterday Victoria pointed out a dove with three blue bands, two on one leg, one on the other, making one imagine it'd been specially tagged, like a criminal. I wish I knew more about birds, most of all I'd like to know how much consciousness they have, or is everything they do programmed, I think I once read, like computers. They often look, when they're on the ground, as if they've been wound up, hopping stiltedly this way and that, but in flight they're a different matter, actually not very different with these small birds, martins and sparrows, they zigzag in spasms, as if in response to abrupt electronic impulses, but seagulls now – my father said once, when we were all sitting on the beach in Hayling Island, 'I wish I were a seagull' – what made it surprising was that it was apropos of nothing, a sudden utterance, as if his soul spoke. But why, Mummy asked, why would you want to be a seagull, James? Is it because they fly so beautifully? James said yes, he supposed it was that, the way they swooped and soared, the freedom and majesty of the flying, the ease of it, just cresting on the winds, their wings spread – also they can be quite vicious, attack people, he said, as if it were a continuation of the thought rather than a qualification, so perhaps he was interested in that aspect of them too, he envied them their temperaments as well as their flying skills – I thought of that conversation a few years ago, when we were visiting my brother Nigel and his wife, Barbara, at their summer home in Pictou, Nova Scotia – Victoria and I went most afternoons, and in appalling weather, grey skies, squally rain, an edgy wind, to a very long, dark-sanded beach, on which there were washed-up tree trunks that the gulls squatted on, shrieking angrily – a couple of times when I came out of the sea, cold and frankly rather miserable with it, two or three of them rose from their logs, soared upwards, dropped, or rather lurched, down until they got to face level, just a foot or so in front of me, then up they'd go, soaring, and back they'd come, jolting at me and shrieking their shrieks. The second time it happened I broke into a run, lumbering across the ridges of sand, shouting swearwords at them. We thought they were probably protecting something, their eggs, their nests, but really they gave the impression that they didn't like humans, or more particularly me, as I was the only human going into and out of the sea, their sea, and it was noticeable that

Victoria, sitting dry and fully dressed on one of the tree trunks, was never abused or threatened. When we told Nigel about it he said yes, some people had actually been attacked at the beginning of the summer, a man's scalp had been pierced and a woman had had her eye plucked out. Can he have said that? Eye plucked out? Well, Nigel, being Nigel, would never have said it if it weren't true, but on the other hand I'd never have gone back to the beach, possibly gone to a beach in Nova Scotia ever again, if I'd believed that a gull had plucked out a woman's eye – so conceivably I've made it up, but attribute it to Nigel as a way of transforming it into a fact. But I still don't believe it.

WORDS IN MY EAR

I was just about to write my first sentence of the day without any idea of what it would be, when somebody moved behind me, bent into my ear and muttered, 'I think it's wonderful.' I recognized the voice, of course, and the face when I turned to look up into it, and even knew what he was talking about, but still I went into light shock, stomach jumping, brain dead. 'What?' I said. 'What?' 'I think it's wonderful,' Harold said again. 'Oh,' I said. 'Oh, good.' 'We'll talk later,' he said, 'when you've finished –', gesturing down at this my pad, then went to a nearby table at the bar, where I can see him now if I shift my eyes to the right. I've shifted my eyes to the right – Antonia's just joined him. She's wearing a very pretty straw hat, she's smiling as she sits down, he turns towards her with what I can see is one of his loving growls, and no wonder, she looks beautiful. They make a very dramatic pair, the blonde and dark of it, a completion of opposites. Victoria and I adore seeing them dance at the end of the evening, neither of them capable of free movement at the moment, Antonia's knee is bad and Harold is still frail, still recovering from cancer and the treatment for it – so they pick their way carefully from the dinner table to the dancing area, arrange their arms around each other and then, his knees bending and straightening, her feet twitching, they sway together in the gorgeous Barbados night, to the band's quite ghastly music – wonderful. Yes, that was also the word Harold used of my new play, *The Old Masters*, which I gave to him only last night – I didn't think he would get to it so quickly, there being so much dreaming and lolling about to do in Barbados before one settles to a specific chore, if one ever does.

WHAT WAS HE TALKING ABOUT?

I call it 'my new play' but actually what I gave Harold to read was the latest, though I hope to God final, version of a play I've been working on for a long time – how long? I can't work it out, but say at least two years – and a version of which has already been published under the title of *The Pig Trade*, and has nearly been produced on a number of occasions, most notably at Bath, with Peter Hall directing and Corin Redgrave and John Wood playing the two main characters, Berenson and Duveen – but things fell apart for reasons too complicated and depressing to be worth remembering, let alone writing down, especially on a lovely morning in Barbados, with Harold waiting a few tables away to discuss how wonderful the new version is – or perhaps I misunderstood him, he might have meant something entirely different was wonderful, for instance that the view (it is) or the day (it is) or that IT – existence itself – is wonderful ( ) – he might not have read the play yet, might even have forgotten that I gave him the play. I've just shifted my eyes to his table, Antonia is expounding something to him in a learned manner, he's concentrated on her, nodding, in a way that suggests his mind is completely uncluttered by such debris as a play, read or unread – now he's laughing, and – Now concentrate! And explain why you did a new and final, you hope final, version of the play you now call *The Old Masters* but used to call *The Pig Trade*. The reason that I did a new and I hope final version of the play I now call *The Old Masters* but once called *The Pig Trade* is that some many months ago I sent *The Pig Trade* to a friend of mine, an American director called Nicholas Martin, who last year did a terrific production of a very, very old play of mine called *Butley* in Boston, with Nathan Lane, who is a very old friend of mine, no, perhaps only an old friend, as he's fifteen years younger than me, playing Butley. I hoped to interest Nicholas Martin in doing an American production of *The Pig Trade*, hoped indeed he might do it in the theatre that he'd done *Butley* in, the Huntington, one of the loveliest theatres I've ever been in, and by far and away the most comfortable. Well, there was a silence, one of those silences that playwrights are familiar with (this one is, anyway) and to which the word ominous is usually attached. So a long, ominous silence before he phoned and spoke with characteristic briskness, characteristic politeness, the truth as he saw it – he didn't think *The Pig Trade* would work in Boston, not on his stage, anyway, the stage of the Huntington theatre, it was too character-driven (i.e. no discernible story, at least not enough of one to motor the play along) and as for the epilogue, he said Jesus! in a tone that made it impossible to take for admiring, because he meant of course 'Christ!' – I said I was grateful for his frankness, because I was in fact grateful, or at least there was gratitude mingled in with all the other reactions, such as shame, rage, kill kill kill Nicholas Martin! Once you get to a certain point in your career as a playwright people are reluctant to tell you anything unpleasant and useful, preferring instead to honour your reputation by fobbing you off with compliments, and the truth is that however much you want the compliments you need the truth more, and you always know you're getting it when you feel, along with all the sensations listed above, a cold stab of mortification, right into the heart of your vanity.

FATHERING AN ORPHAN

It took me a few days before I could face reading *The Pig Trade* again. When I did, I sped rapidly along, not allowing myself to become too mired in the character-driven, under-plotted middle, drew a breath when I came to the epilogue, and in I went – 'Jee-zus!! Christ!' – how could this be? How could I possibly conclude a play, after a long, too long, scene between the two main characters – a kind of clash-of-the-Titans scene – with an interminable scene between two minor characters, on whom I actually proposed to bring down the curtain, leaving the two major characters, the leading actors, in the dressing room, no doubt glumly hoping that the audience would remember them when they came on stage to take their bow? Only Shakespeare could get away with such slapdashery, and he wouldn't have spent months labouring over it. Perhaps that's another definition of genius. It doesn't waste time when doing things badly, it does them at the double.

I rewrote *The Pig Trade* with the intention of eliminating the epilogue. In the process I found myself rewriting almost the whole play, and the stretches I didn't rewrite I cut. What I had when I finished was the same story, the same characters, and an entirely different play about which I felt less queasy. The queasiness will certainly return, doubled or trebled, if it ever gets onto the stage, but one mustn't count one's chicken, for the moment I'm queasy-free, and will show myself as such when I talk to Harold – well, at least I shall be able to say that I'm pretty sure it will work on the stage, that whether people like it or not they would have a whole creature, complete in itself, to like or dislike. One can't really hope for better than that if one's a playwright, in my experience – well, yes, one can, there have been a few occasions when I've finished a play – there's been a sort of click that goes right through me, a click of everything, with the last line written, falling into place, of everything being absolutely right, no, perfect is the word, of the play being perfect, and again it's not a question of its therefore being perfect for other people, audiences might in fact hate it when it's put before them in its perfection, but that isn't the point, whether it's liked or not, the point is that there it is, inviolable, intact, unchangeable, quite distinctly itself and quite distinctly apart from me. I've had this clicking experience four times – with all the other plays I've sometimes had the echo of a click, which is really, I suppose, merely the memory of the experience, and which signifies that though it isn't perfect I can no longer make it any better, time to let go before I begin to make it worse, knowing that I'd always be attached to it in an unhappy sort of way, it would have the status and future of a partial orphan. Why am I going into all this? Because I've never tried to think it out before, so much of my thinking about my work has been obscured by a sense of shame. But this might add a dash of understanding – that I feel the sort of shame that a bad parent, or anyway a failed parent, must feel when he realizes he's sent into the world a child not strong enough to make its way.

A ROW OVER MASTURBATION AND OTHER MATTERS

I've just looked up and to my right. Antonia's gone, presumably for her pre-lunch swim. Harold's on his own, and seems to be slightly winking at me. He's at it now, not the real wink of someone trying to pick me up, but a glittering of the eye, and he's smiling. I've just smiled back. He's given a little wave. I've given a little wave back, and now I'm writing this. When I've got to the bottom of the page I'll go over and sit down and we'll talk about *The Old Masters*, if that's what he wants to do, until our wives come. Then we'll go in to lunch, although it's not 'in', of course, as the lunch room, the dining room, is outside, and the bar where Harold and I are sitting is an extension of the dining room, which has a roof but no walls except at the back, and the sea curves around it, all the way around from the end of the restaurant to the bar, and so, whether we're in the bar or the restaurant, we're by the sea, we can stand up, run across the strip of sand and throw ourselves in whenever we get too excited, the conversation too heated, there have been times when we've got too excited, in my view, when explosions in argument have brought one or the other of us to his feet – actually mainly me – but neither of us – I mean me – I've never run away from the table and across the strip of sand and thrown myself into the sea. We haven't had a row of that sort for a while now. In one sense that's a good thing, because I don't enjoy them very much, although I always enjoy the memory of them. In another sense it's a bad thing, because it means Harold's capacity for explosive anger is currently diminished because of his recent poor health.

As I write this I'm trying to remember what the rows were about. There was one here, in this hotel, a few years ago about Hopkins, whether he masturbated, not Anthony Hopkins, the actor, but the poet Gerard Manley, one of us took the view that he did and one took the view that he didn't, but I have no idea which way round it was, if I ask myself now what view I take, did Gerard Manley Hopkins masturbate or did he not, I think I would say something equivocal, to include the psychic side of masturbation and possibly to exclude the physical side, which is perhaps a definition of 'sprung rhythm' now I come to think of it, and even 'inscape', 'outscape' being actual, down-to-earth masturbation, or seed-wasting, but after all this I still don't know whether I argued for or against G. M. Hopkins as a seed-waster or seed-hoarder. There was another row about Coleridge, a few nights after that, but what aspect of Coleridge? And a real humdinger at a restaurant called Tides, down the road from here, about the charlatan and all-round menace of a psychiatrist R. D. Laing. Pretty obvious what side I took on that. It concluded with me leaving the table, yes, but also saying, 'I'm not walking out, I'm going to have a pee, I'll be right back to finish this off, Harold!' Unfortunately I couldn't come right back, I got locked in the lavatory, an outside affair with an unreliable bolt, I had to shout and beat my fists on the door until somebody at last overheard me. When I got back to the table, about twenty minutes later, the three of them, Antonia, Victoria, Harold, were all sitting in exactly the same positions as when I'd left. There was a bit of a kerfuffle therefore. Victoria drove me to a dump called Olive's for coffee. Nice dump, actually, good coffee. Harold and Antonia suddenly came through the door, embraces and handshakes, ambiguous apologies all round, laughter and so forth and off we went again until the next round – which was about what? – no, no, time to go and join Harold, I've gone past the bottom of the page, I'm in fact over onto and into the next page, and if I don't hurry the wives will be down, and our conversation will have to wait, I'm impatient to have it now, it's only nerves that have kept me at this, so off I'll go – going –

TABLEAU VIVANT

Back. Not straight back. First I had the talk with Harold. Then, when the wives came down, I went off for a swim. Now they've gone to lunch. I've stopped by my table on my way to joining them, to collect my cigarettes and lighter, and find myself sitting down and writing this. Isn't it a bit creepy, though, when I should be with them at the lunch table, to be sitting instead at this my office table, and writing about them? Well, I'm not writing about them, not yet, and what do I mean them, them! Them is, are, my wife, Victoria, and two of my closest and dearest friends, Harold and his wife, Antonia, and there they'll be, no more than ten yards away, concealed behind the curve of the bar, though actually, by swivelling my body around, like this – I can see them. Though they can't see me. At least not without making an equivalent swivel, and why should they, as they don't know I'm here to be seen. So I can go on writing while watching them. Harold is talking to the wine waiter, Sam, who Victoria thinks looks like Eddie Murphy, slightly finer than Eddie Murphy but, as I point out, less comedy in his features, in fact rather a grave face, with the lineaments of Eddie Murphy. Harold's expression is very serious as he looks up at Sam, his finger stabbing at the wine list. Victoria and Antonia are bent towards each other, talking, both are laughing, their straw hats bobbing at each other, Victoria's hat is austere and classical, Antonia's as always is magnificent around the brim, a floral tribute – to what? To whom? Life? Love? Harold, perhaps? – They look very lovely, the two women – the whole tableau is perfect, I'd like to hold them like that for ever, not in a photograph but in the flesh, allowing them to pursue their lives as usual – a strange thought, that we could leave behind in our lives a sequence of tableaux vivants which we could revisit whenever we wished as we aged away – but would we want to do that? What would we feel ten years from now if we were to see us as we are at this very instant? Would it cheer us up, because it's a cheerful scene, or make us cry? So long ago, we'll say, so long ago. And yet there we are, not knowing – not knowing what? Not knowing what's going to become of us – Sam's just caught my eye, he'd bent down to where Harold's finger was now resting, straightened and looked in my direction as if he felt an eye upon him. He's given me a radiant if puzzled smile, I'm actually smiling back at him as I write that I'm smiling back at him, my face turned towards his as my hand goes on writing, which means the words will be sloping all over the place when I look at them –

No, they're OK, there's almost no deviation, in fact if anything they're neater and more legible than the writing I write when I'm looking at it. But I'd better go now and sit at the table, though there's no actual rush, they're just getting up to go to the buffet, and really at lunch we all eat at our own pace, it's a stately scramble, with so many dishes to pick and choose from. When I come back after lunch I'll report my conversation with Harold while it's still fresh. I'm looking forward to doing that, as it's one of the most exciting conversations I've had for years – professionally, I mean, of course. I've had various conversations with doctors about the state of my prostate etc. which I suppose could be described as exciting.

WALK OF SHAME

A very jolly lunch, Harold making public – i.e. to Victoria, he's probably already told Antonia – what he feels about the play. I tried not to bridle (is this the word?) and simper (certainly the word), be dignified and yet casual but probably got caught between the two. There was also the problem of lunch itself. It's a buffet affair, which is OK when you're all going up to pile your plates with shrimp and ham and tuna and whatever else you fancy, but it's not so OK when you're the only one who wants a pudding. You have to walk between the tables and past the many waiters, everybody noticing you, you feel, and then at the counter you have to instruct the very charming and pretty girl called Marsha to slice you just a sliver more of the cheesecake, and a little splodge, what is it, actually, Marsha? Oh yes, meringue – yes, yes, that's fine, and a scoop of vanilla ice cream, please, ha ha – for some reason (obvious reason, I suppose) they give you rather a small plate, the pastry and custard and meringue and ice cream lap over its side, or drip or tumble off onto your foot, as you do your walk of shame, past the other guests and the tall, lean, tight-bellied, though in some cases fat, smiling waiters, to your table. My little but loaded plate always attracts comment from the other three. They ask me to itemize the contents – what's that? Antonia asks with keen interest – oh, meringue, and that – that green stuff? from Harold – ah, jelly – and even Victoria finds it necessary to confirm that the cheesecake is in fact cheesecake – none of it malicious, at least I don't think it is, but still I find myself becoming self-conscious and overly bluff, it's difficult to enjoy eating a variety of puddings when three pairs of eyes, however sympathetic, are trained on you – and more difficult when you're eager to present yourself as a distinguished elderly playwright calmly receiving his meed of praise, when there's also a trickle of ice cream on the chin, a crumb of pie at the side of the mouth – 'Oh yes, well – you're quite right, Harold, it's what I was aiming for, wasn't it, darling?' – trying not to gobble down the praise in the same fashion as you gobble down the pudding, you're afraid you'll accompany every spoonful and receive every flattering sentence with an oink and a grunt –

ARE YEARS OF OUR LORD STILL ALLOWED?

The thing about Harold in the conversation before lunch was that he clearly already loves *The Old Masters*, spoke about it as, in my experience, only Harold can, seeming to know it in all its nooks and crannies, citing moments in scenes and reciting lines, actual lines – this on one reading.

'Look,' he said, 'what exactly is the position of the play? I mean, what's happening to it?'

I said that Greg Ripley-Duggan was the producer and that Peter Hall would direct it, if actors and a theatre were available during one of the brief spells when he was free – Harold said he hoped Peter would work it out, he couldn't imagine anyone better than Peter for *The Old Masters*, 'right up his street,' he said, but if it turned out that he couldn't fit it into his schedule – he indicated himself, with a gesture to his chest. So that's how things stand with *The Old Masters* on this day of January, with Peter Hall to direct it, Harold Pinter on the bench, what day of January? – no, it's February, this day of February, what day of February? Early February – no, still late January, I suspect – that's the loveliest part of being in this lovely hotel on lovely Barbados, with the sun shining, a breeze stirring your greying locks, and the sea, the sea –

I've written away enough time after lunch for it to be digestively safe for a swim, so who cares what day this day is, somewhere in late January, in this year of our Lord 2004 – if years of our Lord are still permitted – well, they are on this God-respecting island, and they are by me, and that's what counts.

NEWS

Judy Daish (my agent) phoned to let me know that Greg Ripley-Duggan had just heard from the artistic director of the Birmingham Rep, to whom he had sent *The Old Masters*, that he would like to put it on their stage – a perfect venue for a pre-London try-out, what did I think? I said I didn't know much about Birmingham, but if they wanted to do my play, that's virtually all I needed to know. There are dates, she said. They only had one to offer in the near future, if we found it unacceptable we might have to wait for a year. How near was the near future? May. May! That was – what – three months near. And not a single part cast. I said we'd better find out if Peter Hall would be free in May.

A MEMORY OF *HIDDEN LAUGHTER*

On the beach I can see Michael Rudman and his wife, the actress Felicity Kendall, who turned up at the hotel yesterday evening. Michael is in baggy blue trunks, slight paunch (nothing like mine), pronounced stoop, Felicity is doing supple things with her body, stretching and bending. Michael and I have dinner together every few months, so we're quite friends, and I once directed Felicity in one of my plays, *Hidden Laughter*, in which she was terrific and in her last scene very moving, I thought – sitting on a swing in a country garden at night, reading out to the local vicar a letter she's just written to her husband, reminding him of the happiness of their marriage, their love for each other, she reads it tearfully, and yet with pride in her own grace as a writer, in her confidence in the strength and honesty of her feelings, not knowing, as she reads and swings and sobs just a little, that her husband has already left her, and that the vicar to whom he's entrusted this news he has also charged with the responsibility of breaking it to her, a moment that will come immediately after she's finished reading her letter, just after the curtain falls in fact. I loved the way she did the scene, so fragile and full of hope, loved the way Peter Barkworth as the vicar floundered in an agony on her behalf, and on his own as the bearer of the news, and yet kept making gestures of encouragement and enthusiasm, complimenting her on her prose, half-rising and then remembering he has to remain seated on the tree stump, to conceal the husband's forgotten briefcase, evidence that he'd been and gone, left her life in a hurry and for ever – and frankly I loved the scene itself, one of the few scenes I've written that I liked to sit through, enjoying it and being moved by it as if it had been written and directed by someone better than me.

I DO SOME GOOD

There are four computers in the hotel computer room, all of them next to each other, and if three people are at it when I go in I become nervous and therefore clumsy, conscious of how their fingers ripple over the keyboard, summoning up images and texts and possibly all kinds of pornography in code, while I jab and poke and keep having to go back and start again – it takes me at least twenty minutes to get to my email, I forget my password or get it wrong, it's easy to do both as it has no connection to anything to do with me, in fact it sounds like a breakfast cereal with an 'i' where you'd expect a 'y' or the other way around. I used to tell myself that this is a generational thing, that if I'd been brought up with or by computers my fingers too would flutter and caress and all those mysterious doors would open on fairy lands forlorn – not that I would want to enter them, unless there are some for straights, as there used to be when Keats – but this morning there were two old ladies and an old gent, by old I mean a decade or so older than myself, so coming up to, possibly gone over into, their eighties. They had headgear on, the man a baseball cap, the ladies the usual straw hats, the old guy was wearing an enormous pair of sunglasses that virtually covered the top half of his face, which was quite small, with a neat nose and appley cheeks, so probably American, one of the old ladies also wore sunglasses, normal size, but with a hearing aid attached, the other old lady was frankly fat, mighty fat, but with evidently perfect vision and a ready sense of humour, her plump fingers scampering about the keyboard and bringing up whatever it was that made her so wheeze and chuckle, chuckle and wheeze, it was very distracting if you were me and lowering yourself into the chair of the only free computer, the wheezes and chuckles and chuckles and wheezes coming from immediately to my right, to my immediate left the old guy, his face so close to the screen that it seemed to be growing out of it, and next to him the other old lady – so it took me half an hour to tap out a few sentences to Greg Ripley-Duggan, after I'd spent nearly as long opening his to me, and then opening one from Peter Hall saying that he couldn't rearrange his dates to fit in Birmingham, it was painful as he was very attached to *The Old Masters*, he wished it and me all the best. So Harold is now the official director of *The Old Masters*. And that's that, really, until we get back to London – Harold and Antonia go next week, Victoria and I the week after. There's something else I want to say, whether *The Old Masters* is a good play or not, it's already done good in the world. Until it came his way Harold was rather – not exactly miserable – but for him subdued, rarely exploding into laughter or anger, with a vagueness, almost an absence, about him. Now he's full of energy and purpose, thinking out loud about the set, about casting, etc.

AN IMPORTANT QUESTION ASKED

All the couples here walk on the paths in front of or behind each other, instead of side by side. The paths are wide enough to accommodate them side by side, but they obviously prefer this single-file system, like ducks. I wonder why? Harold and Antonia do it too, and so do Michael and Felicity, who are going up one of the paths now, Felicity leading, lifting and lowering her head in a busy fashion, Michael stooping along behind her, almost hunchbacked – I asked him about it, whether he had a back problem, he said no, not really, just years of bad posture. He's going to do something about it when he's home – posture classes, I suppose. But what about me and my wife, do we walk in single file?

ROLLOCKS BY MOONLIGHT

Two in the morning. I'm in the bar, a bottle of cold Diet Coke in front of me, Rollocks moving about behind me, setting the tables for breakfast. This is only the second late-night visit I've paid to the bar this year. We've had our conversation about how last year was for each of us – his has been good, he says, on the whole, he's thinking of retiring, if not at the end of this summer, then at the end of next, or possibly the one after – fairly soon, anyway – and we've talked about the sandflies, the mosquitoes, the effectiveness of the repellent I've pasted around my wrists, ankles and neck, the steaminess of the night, the partially obscured moon, the absence of stars – then he brought me one of probably a dozen Diet Cokes he's kept on ice for me since he'd heard I arrived, nearly three weeks ago, and we resumed our familiar roles, he to the tables, I to my pad, where I intend to write about – no, it's no good, I have to go up to my room, the anti-insect paste is no longer working, my wrists and ankles have been bitten, my neck is itching – first I must go and say goodnight to Rollocks, he is standing with his tray clasped to his chest, staring towards the sea, as if he can hear the mermaids singing, each to each – I'll leave him be.

A SONG FOR RONNIE

'But for me the light is growing dim,' my mother used to sing in the kitchen of our house in Halifax, Nova Scotia, as she cooked up the stew into which she mainly avoided dropping her cigarette ash. She'd heard it – country and western, I suppose – coming from the radio one morning, and had taken to it at once, not singing along with it, but humming at it, out of tune, every time it came on, and then giving full-throated, tuneless voice to the refrain – 'But for me-e-e-e-e/The light/Is growin'/Dimmmm –'

The only other creature who seemed to love Mummy's singing as much as I did, though probably for different reasons, was the cat we acquired when we moved from Hayling Island to London just before the end of the war. He was a ginger and white full-grown tom called Ronnie. He was hopelessly dissolute, out all night though returning punctually when a Jenkins delivered the milk at seven in the morning. As soon as Mummy heard the rattles of the bottles on the doorstep she would get up and watch from the bedroom window until the operating Jenkins – either the father or one of the sons, it didn't matter, she loathed them all – had trundled off, and then hurry downstairs to pick up the bottles – simultaneously Ronnie would stroll up the path, and on into the kitchen, where he would sit by his saucer, waiting for it to be filled. He arrived in the household already battered from numerous fights – he'd had half an ear bitten off, lost the tip of his tail, and one or the other of his eyes was usually partly closed. I assume there were vets in Chelsea in those days, but Ronnie was never taken to one, whatever his condition – I don't think it ever crossed our parents' minds that they were responsible for anything but letting him out and in and feeding him, though Mummy liked having him on her lap – she would summon him by singing loudly, in her out-of-tune voice, one of her favourite songs from *Oklahoma!*, and Ronnie would lope into the room, spring onto her lap, and stay there purring for as long as she sang – no longer, though, he'd get down as soon as she stopped, and leave the room without a word, so to speak. Mummy treated the pets with the same casual and affectionate violence that she treated her children – though she once knocked Ronnie, who was getting in the way of her cigarette and her ladle, off the kitchen window into the back yard, quite a drop – in mitigation it should be said that it was a tiny kitchen, room for one only standing up, and for once she was appalled, at least momentarily, if only by the shocked reactions of Nigel and myself, who were playing French cricket in the yard, when Ronnie

dropped yowelling between us – 'Oh, really!' she said, when she'd
had enough of our 'Mummy, how could you!'s etc. 'He's perfectly
all right, he's a cat after all, he knows how to land on his feet – look
at him!' He'd clambered up the wall and was now staggering along
its top as if drunk and about to fall down again –

BETRAYAL

but in fact he was perfectly all right, always – altercations, tumbles,
outright and ferocious combat with other toms, ghastly tussles with
angry and unwilling sexual partners, whose outraged screams rent
the night air – he survived them all, along with the disapproval of
neighbours – a Belgian woman who lived in the basement flat three
or four doors along and had two female greys called Meenee and
Meedee oh, Mini and Midi I realize they must have been now I see
them written down. She remonstrated with Mummy whenever
they coincided on the pavement. They made a striking pair. The
small, angry Belgian woman, who lived in a bundle of shawls and
had a sort of pork-pie arrangement of a hat on her head and
enormous, globular earrings which shook when she talked, would
stop Mummy with a raised hand and a little cry, and Mummy
would stand towering over her with arms folded, the head of her
fox stole with its bright button eyes fixed over her shoulder on the
Belgian woman. 'Yes,' she said, with smiling, middle-class
impatience, 'what is it?', knowing perfectly well what it was.
'Would you pliss,' said the Belgian woman, 'pliss ask your kat to
ztop visitink my katz.' 'I have asked him, several times,' Mummy
said, 'but he pays no attention. Why,' she added, 'don't you ask him
yourself, in your own language? He might understand you.' She
was always lofty when dealing with neighbours' complaints, the

more justified the complaints, the loftier she was, but she was quite right about her inability to control Ronnie, whose romantic exploits she rather admired. Would she have admired them more if she'd realized how closely, in some respects, they resembled those of her husband? – though I like to think that Daddy never made any woman scream in pain and outrage, only with pleasure. Ronnie survived everything – perpetual warfare, public denunciation – he was his own man, fearless and calm though increasingly ravaged – survived everything, except our departure to Halifax, Nova Scotia. We gave him to some friends, who lived not far away, on the Embankment. They'd met Ronnie on a number of occasions, been impressed by his raffish vitality, and took him in with enthusiasm – but he didn't want to be taken in, stood mewing and growling at their front door until he was let out, then made his way back to 47 Oakley Gardens, where he hung about on the doorstep, hurrying forward every time the door opened, to have it closed immediately in his face – he was collected from there and carried back to the Embankment again and again, until one day he wasn't there to be collected. The friends wrote explaining why they couldn't give news of him. They were apologetic, of course, but we understood that it wasn't their fault that he wouldn't become their cat. And I suppose we were philosophical. We told ourselves that it wasn't us Ronnie missed, but his operational base. I don't know what difference the distinction makes, or if there is one, when it comes down to it – it's certainly not one that Ronnie would have bothered to make, I think. All he could have known was that one day his world was there, the next it had gone, and wouldn't come back, however often he hung about waiting for a Jenkins to arrive with the milk, the door to open –

AN IMPORTANT QUESTION ANSWERED

Yes, we walk in single file, Victoria and I, just like the others, sometimes she leads, sometimes I do.

IN MEMORIAM

We began our days in Halifax, Nova Scotia, with a succession of kittens that died very quickly, one from eating something poisonous in the surrounding woods, another, who liked to sleep tucked under the wheel of our car, was run over by my father when backing out of the garage, two or even three others from natural deaths – it became really quite depressing, as if there were a curse on us for betraying Ronnie, anyway it seemed a good idea to switch to dogs, to change our luck – some neighbours offered us a beagle from their new litter, and so Sam came to us when he was still a small puppy, though he never really behaved like a puppy, he was slow, thoughtful, food-directed from the beginning, and just grew larger, without any perceptible maturing, into a dog. I used to practise my bullfighting with him, attaching chocolates to the corner of a tea towel, then swivelling it around my body, Sam lumbered after it, trying to catch one of the corners as I shouted, *Olé, Olé, perro!, Olé,* with a stamp of my feet. Eventually he twigged that he'd never catch a chocolate, but that he'd always be rewarded with one if he kept stumbling around after it – humiliating, perhaps, but I think when it came to food Sam lived below the humiliation line – and anyway, it was better than a sword between the shoulder blades. When he was about three he took to leaving the house after his breakfast and not returning until dusk, keeping strictly to this schedule like a civil servant –

one could almost see him with a briefcase, especially on his return, when he had the air of bearing a heavy load, a day's load, which indeed he was. We discovered that between breakfast and dusk he kept appointments around the neighbourhood and quite deep into the centre of town, receiving at every house he visited a substantial meal. He was a commercial traveller of a pet, really, giving in return – what? Well, just the pleasure of a visit, I suppose, from a friendly dog, a friendly and hungry dog. When my parents moved back to London they took Sam with them. He was quite old by then, older in dog's terms than my mother was in human terms, but he survived her by a couple of years. My father kept him when he went to live in Lyme Regis, but saw him not as a companion but as a burdensome leftover from the days before he was a widower, and solitary. He overfed him from laziness and walked him reluctantly, letting him crap on the pavement and even on doorsteps, and when I remonstrated – 'You know Sam,' he said, 'he goes his own way, as your mother always said.' Sam died shortly after my father married Betty, my mother's cousin. Piers and I carried his corpse on a winter evening through the back streets of Lyme to the Cobb, from which we flung him into the sea, and said a few ceremonial words. Piers had been five or six when Sam came to us, was in his early twenties – an undergraduate at Cambridge – when Sam died, so he'd known him for most of his life. Daddy and Betty went off to the South of France, fulfilling at a stroke Betty's, little Betty's, double dream of living on the Mediterranean, of being married to Daddy. But dreams can be like prayers if too many years lapse before they're fulfilled. Living by the Mediterranean with her husband, Dr James Davidson Gray, the distinguished pathologist, my dear!, became living in a poky little flat in a hideous block on a hill above Menton with a dying man who'd never enjoyed her company – except for short periods in bed, of course, on occasional afternoons many years ago. After his death I invited her to stay with us one summer in the Hotel de dui Castelli, in Sestri Levante, on the Ligurian coast, where I went with my family and usually Piers, every year for about a decade. When she arrived, she was in the middle of a spluttering and coughing monologue that she seemed to have begun on the train from Menton. She was carrying her suitcase. A cardboard label was attached to its handle and on it she'd written in red ink in bold capital letters MRS ELIZABETH GREY. Gray was the name she'd known since she'd first met her cousin's fiancé fifty years before, it was now legally her own, and yet there it was, misspelt, significantly misspelt, because it turned my father from a Scot into an Englishman. Piers and I saw the label simultaneously, and we turned to Betty to say – what? Whatever it was, we couldn't say it – what would have been the point, after all? She never listened, as her husband complained to me when I went to Menton to take him to his last bed, in the Charing Cross Hospital, never listened. But then he never really listened to her either, hearing in her voice, seeing in her gestures, a first cousin's approximation to his dead wife. The fact of the matter is that there was something neither understood about the other – probably Mummy, whose hold on them both was unbreakable – Mummy was the wife of his heart, Betty merely little Betty. So poor little Betty. And poor old Daddy too, for marrying his little Betty, and of course poor Mummy too, for dying before her time and leaving them to each other. Perhaps they separately heard her voice, as they lay sleepless beside each other in their Menton bed saying to her husband, 'Oh, James! Really! That a husband of mine! And with little Betty of all people! How could you, James! What were you thinking of!' and to his new wife, 'Really, Betty! That a cousin of mine! My own cousin! With my own husband too! And after I was dead! What were you

thinking of!' It's all right, Mummy, they were thinking of you –
that was their trouble.

SPIES?

Now this couple, Americans I think, though they're young and fit-
looking they don't seem quite right in the open air, in the sunlight,
there's something depressed and rodenty about them, as if they
belong in the lofts and cellars of New York, possibly they're theatre
critics or in publishing, she's very skinny, black hair drawn back and
down her neck, a long nose that goes up in a point at the last
minute, quite a pretty nose, really, quite a pretty face, but urban-
feral – they're speaking in low voices, almost as if they think I'm
trying to overhear their conversation, which I am, so I must busy
myself over my pad, keep my head down, my pen flying – voices
muttering, hers slightly squeakily, his – Minnie Mouse, that's who
she reminds me of, Minnie Mouse, the dark, lovely eyes and the
chin falling away in little folds – can that be right, that Minnie
Mouse had a folding chin? I don't know any longer what Minnie
Mouse's chin was like, not having seen any of her films for years
and years, in fact all I really remember are her high heels and her
lipstick, and her artificial eyelashes – and as the American woman
over there isn't wearing high heels or lipstick and her eyelashes are
normal I can't in fact claim that she resembles Minnie Mouse –
nevertheless she reminds me of Minnie Mouse – the reason I'm
delaying getting around to the man is that he's got his back to me,
a round head, thick black hair so neatly packed on it that it looks
like a lid, a strong white neck and then a medium-sized man's back,
quite sturdy, he's wearing a shiny blue shirt, obviously new,
probably only just unwrapped, an impression of shiny blue

swimming trunks, could he be wearing a twinset? Matching trunks and shirt? A glimpse of solid thighs, then under the table his feet, in black Speedos – I know they're Speedos, it's written on them – are turned out like a duck's – he says almost nothing, soft little grunts in response to Minnie's squeaky paragraphs. God, I wish I could hear what they're saying, I have the feeling now that they may be academics – he's turned around, Minnie dropped her voice from a squeak to a whisper and around he turned, I can feel his eyes on me, can they know that I'm writing about them? She's staring at me too, I can feel their eyes –

What they were looking at was a pigeon on my table, a few inches away from me, dipping its beak into my hat and attempting to extract a strand of straw – I made a gesture, a fuck-off-off-my-hat kind of gesture – it snatched out the strand, flew off into the rafters of the bar –

'That's nice,' the man said to me, 'helping her build her nest.'

'Him,' the woman said, less squeaky now she was speaking at a normal level. 'The males build the nests.'

'Is that how it works?' said the man. 'Or how you think it ought to work?'

'Both,' she said. They laughed together, and I laughed with them.

'Looks like you've provided for a lot of pigeons,' he said, nodding at my hat, which, it's true, is very tattered, but then it's inherited from my dead friend Ian Hamilton, who wore it to cover the effects of chemotherapy – I brought it with me to Barbados last year, just a few days after his funeral, and I wore it in Italy last summer, and I shall keep on wearing it whenever we're in sunny spots until only the rim is left, and then I might try to have it thatched, or whatever you do to keep straw hats going.

'Yes, it's getting on a bit, this hat. Worn down.'

His eyes were now on my yellow pad, and so were hers. There was a question shaping itself, but she said, 'Well, I guess you don't want to be disturbed.' And he said, 'Yeah, you look kind of busy,' and they both gave me a nice smile, and left me to get on with writing about them, and trying to overhear their conversation, which I will now make myself stop doing. It would be wrong, I think. Still, I wish I knew what they did. Definitely New Yorkers, publishing possibly, or in television – yes, television – they've got up, nodded pleasant farewells, are walking across the lawn towards the beach – she's got a rather loping walk, loose-limbed but not athletic – he's taller than I thought, stiff little strides, almost military – CIA?

PAN, AT THE NEXT TABLE

Anyway, now I'm alone again, the bar is empty again – I'd just written that – the bar is empty again – when lo! an elderly man, by which I mean older than myself, with a nose so bulbous and knotted and veined that if he's not an alcoholic he should sue it – there he is at the table next to mine, he has chosen it out of all the empty tables, there are ten of them, I've counted, just to sit beside me, attracted by the long shapelessness of my own nose, perhaps, or just by a muddled desire to be a nuisance – he's carrying an object the size and shape of a large book that I didn't at first notice which he fiddled with for a few moments and then, just as I turned away, he pressed a knob and a man's voice, plus music, both cackly, burst forth, yes, a radio, the old bugger's got a radio, and he's sitting there, holding the radio to his mouth, like a sandwich, he's got very bushy eyebrows, by the way, thickets, actually, and a beard, also thickety, but just sticking out from the base of his chin – it's the head of a Pan, and he's holding the radio to his mouth no longer like a sandwich, like a flute, with hideous, unflutish noises emanating from it – he's conversing with Sam, the very neat and handsome young waiter, the one with the Eddie Murphy face, which he is bending to Pan's lips, so that he can hear him behind the music, no need – Pan's voice is loud, boisterous, slurred, he's requesting tea – 'Lots of good, strong tea, to wash the alcohol out,' he says, following his words with a coarse chuckle. Sam gives him a polite, blank look. 'I drink lots and lots of alcohol, that's why I drink tea, always a pot or two at this time of the morning. Sluices it out. The alcohol.' Sam nods gravely, goes off. Probably, like most of the waiters in this hotel, he's teetotal. Pan goes on chuckling to himself, changes the channel on the station, is trying to catch my eye, which I keep resolutely fixed on the page as I write this sentence, which will be my last until he's gone, or his radio's off –

The radio is off. He is drinking his tea, and smoking a large cigar. Clouds of his smoke are drifting over me, making me feel queasy. Nevertheless I've picked up my pen, feeling it important to get this down – that there is a very coarse-looking man in his swimming trunks and straw hat sitting smoking a cigar, trying to catch the eye of an elderly, not particularly refined-looking man in his swimming trunks and a straw hat who is, in fact, smoking a cigarette and writing about him, and one day when the elderly writing man is back in London he might take out this pad from his drawer in his desk, leaf through it, come across this account, ponder it, and wonder if the old roué of a Pan with his stinking cigar and nose like a rotting fig is dead – he's blowing the smoke in my direction, quite deliberately, he's picked up the radio, he's turning it on again and he's leering at me, I can feel it – Christ! Ah, he's been joined by a middle-aged man with a boyish haircut. The radio goes off. They are talking in loud voices, blurred laughter from Pan, and the younger man, who is the type – what type? – yes, could be something to do with the *Daily Mail*, for instance, morally seedy, down-at-heel, but lots of money, ill-gained, and a dreary cynicism about the eye – they're talking about his boat, he's got a boat that's passing through, or rather not passing through customs, he's been waiting for days now, ten phone calls a day but still they're keeping it from him, him from it, so perhaps he's in drugs, more likely to appear in a photograph in the *Daily Mail* than work for it, one of those inner-page sort of men, with inset a photograph of his girlfriend, or 3rd ex-wife, he's got up, he's coming my way, coming straight at my table, at me, I'll keep my head bowed, keep scribbl—

FIRST ONE

He's gone. He stopped at my table and said, 'Hello, Simon.' That's what he said. My name. I said, 'Hello,' in a mumble, keeping my head down. 'I admire your discipline.' He sounded faintly lascivious. 'Yes. The way you keep at it.' This too sounded lascivious, more than faintly. 'I couldn't do that,' he said. 'Here you are in the sun, and there's the sea, and you're sitting at a table writing away. I admire that.' I thanked him. 'What are you writing?' I remembered recent phrases – *Daily Mail*, seedy, down-at-heel, 3rd ex-wife, etc. 'A novel?' 'No, not exactly a novel, not really anything really.' 'Well, Simon,' he said, saying 'Simon' with a particular relish, almost satirically, 'you keep at it.' I said I would, or anyhow would try to, and he went off. He was wearing shoes, long brown flannel trousers and a blue shirt, proper shirt, as for an office, looking as if it needed a tie – what is he doing in this hotel, in Barbados? Could he be a policeman, or some combination of journalist and policeman that seems to be the new form, chaps who mobile the *Mail* even as they're slapping the cuffs on, at 6 a.m., the television cameras in place, but he can't be here for me, surely, his conversation a sinister introduction to the main event – my arrest tomorrow at just two hours after I've gone to bed, but I can't think of anything I've done recently, and would he get the money to fly out from London to arrest a man of sixty-seven who hasn't recently committed a criminal act?

THEN THE OTHER

And now here is Pan, for God's sake –

He had the cigar in one hand, the radio neither off nor on, but spitting and humming slightly, in the other hand. And his chin, his beard resting almost on my shoulder, which put his nose almost in my ear – he spoke pleasantly through his nose into my ear – this hotel, he said, was one of the nicest he'd ever been to, the staff were so charming, he said, and the guests, the great thing about them, he said, was that they were all friendly, but never intrusive, never intrusive, he said pleasantly into my ear, his beard scraping my shoulder, as the fumes from his cigar drifted across my face and the radio hummed and spat almost in my armpit. 'Don't you find that?' – a young lady turned up, attractive, with curly dark hair, bangles on her wrists, a silver chain around each ankle. 'Ah, there you are,' she said. 'I knew I'd find you in the bar,' and gave me a smile, as if she'd known she'd find me in it too. 'I've been having tea,' he said. 'And talking to my friend. And waiting for you.' He clamped the cigar in his mouth, put the radio into one of her hands, looped his arm around her waist, lurched her off towards the swimming pool, or perhaps its shrubbery.

AT LAST

Now he's gone it's the most beautiful morning again, and I would be tranquil, I really think I would be, if I weren't convinced, beginning to be convinced, that I'm the victim of a conspiracy. Is it that people can't bear the sight of an elderly etc., sixty-seven etc. sitting at a shady table at the sea's edge on a sunny morning in Barbados, working – or not even working, just writing, and not even writing to any particular purpose, merely moving his hand, which happens to be holding his pen, across a yellow pad with long pages with lots and lots of lines on it with lots and lots of spaces between that have, naturally, to be filled. What else can I do in life but fill these spaces?

But does the sight of me doing it provoke people into feeling that they've got a duty to stop me? I've been doing this very thing, on this date, at this table, for eleven years now, every year on 20 Jan at this hour, this very minute, in fact, I could be seen at this very table, in this very chair – nonsense, not this very chair, every couple of years they change the chairs for chairs of a different style, progressively more uncomfortable. When I started out the chair was a miracle of comfort, a firm, weather-proof armchair, more elevated than you'd expect in an armchair, that seemed to settle you over the table into a natural writing position, but also allowed you to collapse backwards for thought, vacancy, erotic meditation, then a slight adjustment, almost unconscious, and one was at it again, the shifts between inertia and activity unnoticed by myself –

recumbent, erect, active, a full page, recumbent, erect, active, a full page. This year we still have last year's chairs, wrought-iron, gardeny sort of chairs, with thin white cushions that keep you in a stiff, upright position, oddly unsupported, and you can't help seeing your hand, the pen, the movement across the page, every single word you write as you're writing it – Alan. Yes, there it is at last. Alan.

HIS DEPENDABILITY

We were here at this time last year, when he phoned to say he'd been diagnosed with cancer of the pancreas and the liver. His voice was robust, cheerful, just as it was when he was talking about the usual sort of stuff we talk about, a new role, a new film, a new illness – he'd had a lot of unexplained illnesses recently – he'd had a hip operation, his stomach had been bad, his knee hurt, sometimes shortness of breath – but he'd taken them in his stride, little spells in hospital, a long one for the hip because the operation had gone slightly wrong (botched, he wondered), but he had been unremittingly robust, cheerful, the sense of the comedy of it all pervading – the comedy of getting older, of people's reactions to his illnesses, the expressions they adopted, the tones they assumed – so was his tone when he was talking now – then – a year ago, about his cancer of the pancreas and liver. The trouble was, he said, that he'd known from all the other illnesses that there was something more, something more wrong with him than a dodgy stomach, a difficult knee, occasional shortness of breath, something else had been going on all the time, and actually he'd thought so all the time, but he'd been in New York, playing in *Fortune's Fool*, a complete triumph, he'd been the toast of Manhattan – funny, if you change that only slightly to in Manhattan he'd been toast, a phrase I loved when it first turned up in the sort of movies I used to love – 'Make a move and you're toast!' – well, he wasn't toast in Manhattan, he was the toast of Manhattan, winning all the acting awards – and the thing was, it was his show in more than the star's normal sense, as he'd done the play first in Chichester, where it really hadn't been much good, a plodding and ponderous fable, badly lit and erratically acted by the supporting cast, although he himself, at the ebullient centre, had been Alan enough to give the evening a charge – but really, it had floundered along, and he'd been depressed by the impoverished lighting, the helter-skelter staging – but on the other hand his son Ben had been in it, for Alan a great thing, perhaps the greatest thing, to be on the stage with his son, it justified the enterprise, it justified going on with the enterprise, it justified the long struggle to take it to New York, to play it in first for a long period outside New York – I got gloomy reports from people who saw it in its early days, in one town or another – things were changed and then changed again, the staging was still all over the place, but his co-star, Frank Langella, was sympathetic and great fun, his director was old but sympathetic and great fun, and Ben was having a great time, learning more and more as he got better and better, and Alan knew, he just knew, that by the time they got to New York it would be a triumph, and so it was, a triumph, he was the toast etc., and yet the things that were wrong with him got worse, the knee, the stomach, the fatigue, whenever he went on stage he was exhausted, couldn't understand, went to a New York doctor who did a series of tests, gave him some pills that settled his stomach, but said, 'When you get back to London you've got to have all this checked out. Don't leave it.' So when he got back to London he left it, didn't have anything checked out but his hip, and even with all the complications of that, he didn't have himself checked for anything serious. 'But why not?' I asked, after a dinner, as we went to his car, a large and ridiculous car, built for cross-country driving, that sort of thing. 'You keep saying you feel awful, you think there's something really wrong with you, so why the hell don't you!' He said he would. We had the conversation several times, with the same firm conclusion – he would, yes, he really would. Well, of course he was a diabetic, had been for nearly twenty years or so, and partly assumed that his diabetes might be behind it all. He was used to being very insouciant about his diabetes, rolling up his shirt in a restaurant, crouching slightly so the syringe couldn't be seen as he plunged it into the side of his midriff, pulling it out, slipping it back into his pocket – the whole business completed in a matter of seconds – but really behind the diabetes he now knew there was another illness, showing itself in different guises and glimpses – but he was in all respects such a sturdy man, his body sturdy, the will and spirit within it sturdy, the whole of him rooted in a sure sense of himself and his place in the world – it was this that made him so complete a presence on the stage and screen, and yet gave him freedom and brio in his acting – though he was so quick from one thing to another, from tenderness to savagery, from contemptuous wit to unfathomable pain, the centre always held, Alan was always there, however dangerous or defeated his mood, the final dot of him was intact, so that audiences, thrilled and sometimes nearly unnerved, felt finally safe in his company. I suppose that's what they loved about him, really, that he could take them into anarchy or despair without loosening them from their trust in his kindness, it was visible in his eyes, even at their iciest you could feel it there, and you knew that you could depend on it, an essential part of his kindness was its dependability.

HOW HE DEALT WITH THE LIGHTS

Also his dependability was practical, you could count on him in a tricky situation, on the stage as in life. I remember him making his entrance as Butley, hungover, a wreck, lurching to his desk to turn on the lamp that was scripted not to come on, had never come on before, not in the dress rehearsals, not in the two weeks of performances in Oxford, not in the four or five previews, but at the Criterion, on the night of 14 July 1971, the official opening night with a full house and all the critics in, it came on. Harold and I, director and writer, standing at the back of the stalls, looked at each other, aghast, then looked towards Alan, who, we supposed, would be looking aghast at the lamp. He scarcely gave it a glance as he Butleyed to the other desk, and the lamp which was scripted to come on and therefore, I assumed, now wouldn't, not only came on, it came on while Alan was still reaching for its switch, but went off again the instant he touched it. I'm no longer clear about what Alan did next, actually I don't think I was clear at the time, whatever it was it couldn't have made any logical sense, but it made complete emotional sense and sense therefore to the audience, who laughed in sympathy with Butley's evident frustrations, even though they seemed to be mysteriously, even magically, created. But my real memory of the incident is not what Alan did, nor my momentary panic, but my underlying confidence, shared I believe with Harold, that whatever he did it would be the right, the perfect, thing, because he was so right and perfect in the part, so founded and centred in it that his any action became the right action by virtue of its being his, and because he was Alan, in whom one had a perfect and complete trust, on and off the stage.

HIS LAUGHTER, ETC.

There was a scene in rehearsals that he was unsure of – he hadn't got the feel of it, his tone was wrong, something he couldn't quite catch in the meaning of the lines – each time he got through the scene he would turn enquiringly to the director, who looked at him with a blank, though friendly, smile, then turned his attention to something else. Finally Alan asked him – could he please have a comment straight out, whatever struck the director would be welcomed, however trivial, he just needed a note, any note, he badly needed a note on how he was doing this scene. The next time he did the scene, he turned eagerly towards the director, who almost succeeded in failing to catch Alan's eye, but couldn't avoid his eyebrows, fiercely raised in interrogation. He stood for a minute, broodingly, as if sorting through note after note in his head, then swiftly raised his right thumb then turned away, to the other actors. Alan, telling this story, one of his favourites for illustrating the general uselessness of directors, would bend so far forward with laughter that his forehead would actually touch his knees, and he would actually have to mop the tears of laughter out of his eyes 'Oh dear!' he would say. 'Oh, God,' and as like as not he'd jerk his thumb up again, and the laughter would start again – any meal with Alan would contain as much laughter as speech. But when I think about it, what could the director say that would have been more eloquent than a raised thumb – obviously what he meant by it was that Alan's acting of the scene was true and honest and right, words which would also apply to the way he tried to live his life, and why not a raised thumb to that too, especially if it would have caused him to laugh so much that his forehead met his knee? It was his merriness, I think, that marked him out from anybody else I've known – his laughter made you feel instantly better. A generous, forthcoming laugh that demanded company, so that sometimes you laughed not because you found it, whatever it was, particularly funny, but because Alan's laugh had somehow got into you, yours fed on his and his on yours so you ended up like children, clutching at each other, the initiating cause often forgotten – 'But why did we, what were we –? Oh – oh yes!' and like as not, off again. It's terrible to think I shall never hear it again, and that it's nowhere to be heard – his laughter on screen is not the same thing at all, of course, being an organized and probably in some cases frequently rehearsed laugh, although what you do get on screen, in his eyes, is the mischief and the appetite, the exuberance –

HIS CLAUDIUS

in Zeffirelli's *Hamlet* is the most sensual, the most appetitive, the most louchely endearing – during an early scene when he's trying to lecture and cajole Hamlet out of his woe etc. a servant on the other side of the room brings in a tray with a flask of wine and some goblets on it, Alan's Claudius, attempting to be doleful, measured, earnest, catches sight of the tray, scampers across the room, fills the goblets to the brim, turns to Gertrude with lascivious delight – his wine in his fist, his woman before him, his crown on his head, what more could a man want? Except to be rid of the spoilsport, killjoy nephew – you can see too, for once, what's in it for her, what fun she has with him in bed, what a rollicking place he's turned the court into, a playground – it's as if Falstaff had come to Elsinore, where he'd been tracked down by a poisoned Hal – Alan would have been a great Falstaff, the wit, the relish in life, the sexiness that would have embraced Hal as well as Mistress Quickly, I used to nag him to do it, and he would pretend to ponder it, but really his vanity got in the way – the problem was the fat, he couldn't bear to play a fat man, however nimble-tongued and quick of wit, however gorgeous in his pomp, broken in his fall – really, he still saw himself, until quite late in his career, too late in his career, as a leading man, romantic – to his inner eye lean and svelte and dashing when in truth he was big-boned, stocky, a heavy mover, though his energy also made him quick when he wanted to be – but his natural tempo was slow, his natural walk an amble – his energy distracted the attention from his shape, as did the marvellous eyes, the handsome mouth, the line of the cheeks, and the exuberant head of hair – but it grew on a round head, set on a bullish neck, and physically he was a peasant, a Derbyshire peasant, and his hands were agricultural. His consciousness of his body made him shy of exposing it professionally, though he famously exposed all of it in the film of *Women in Love*, but that was when he was young, and besides the camera and the editor could redefine, above all select – later, and especially on the stage, he was careful – in *Melon*, for instance, he hid behind the furniture when stripping down to his underwear, and pretty well stayed there, almost crouching, until the end of the scene – his no-nonsense, let's-get-on-with-it exchanges with the girl he was about to fuck seeming more like bombardo – bombardo? Is there such a word? I must have meant bravado, or did I mean bombast? Well, both of them combined give my meaning – his bombardo perversely made him more attractive, it created a tension between his desire and an innate modesty, possibly prudishness, that made him irresistible, so the girl, instead of being swept along by the force of his brute male assertiveness, succumbed to his sweetly boyish bombardo. I tried once or twice, out of a sense of duty to my own text, to get him out into the open, but he invariably said it was no good, wherever he went he seemed to end up behind the desk or the chair, and added that he wasn't a young man any more, there was too much of him, he was bloody well going to keep most of it to himself, they were already seeing more of him than was good for them – or him. But, as I say, the truth of it is that though he was in fact bulky, he never seemed it – his intelligence transformed him, gave the illusion of his being light-footed, mercurial – sometimes you scarcely noticed the movements that carried him from one side of the stage to the other, as if his mind and the meaning of his lines had taken him there without help from his body, but in repose he was a massive presence, nothing to do with his height or weight, but of density, really, the bulk of him somehow compacted, concentrated in the audience's concentration – Alan alone on stage at the end of a play, motionless, was volcanic. He was also beautiful, I think, in the way that no artefact can be beautiful, because he was breathing, dying.

HIS INADEQUACIES AS A HATER

He was a great mimic, a great creative mimic – in the course of an evening he could give you a whole novel full of characters, waiters in restaurants, agents, publicists, the nurses and doctors during his last weeks in the hospital, and earlier, in his palmy days, his mother-in-law, whom he adored, and not simply for the comedy she provided him with – and that was it, every character was suffused with his own delight in their being, so that they were always presented in all their vivid absurdity without malice, with a kind of love, and a gratitude for giving him so much pleasure in their creation. Correspondingly, he was not much of a hater, although capable of explosions of anger and contempt, mostly against directors, but he would usually append a coda of forgiveness and the suggestion that it was probably his own fault really. Once, though, when he was coming to the end of his chemotherapy, he went abruptly, without warning, into a low, muttering but precisely articulated monologue of loathing for a famous director. He went on for quite a long time, and when he finished he sat in silence, his head lowered. I waited for a burst of laughter or the fabulous smile, but neither came. 'There,' he said eventually, 'there. I've said it at last. And I don't feel any better for it.' I think he was in part speaking about his illness, about which he scarcely said a bad word, seeming to accept it as a mysterious visitation that probably made sense if one understood the real order of things, rather than as a betrayal of his body, or as an outrage against perfectly reasonable expectations. Shortly after he'd been moved back into the London Clinic for the last time, he said that if he was going to die soon, it was all right – 'I've had a very good life. I've done everything I want, really. Yes, it would be all right.'

WAS HIS A GOOD LIFE?

For Alan, the birth of his twin sons, Benedick and Tristan, was life's greatest gift, its blessing. Tristan died in a freak accident in Tokyo at the age of seventeen. At his funeral Alan spoke of his memories of the twins' growing up, of the differences and similarities in their natures, of the promises for both the future had seemed to offer, he spoke calmly and gently, seeming almost at ease, until suddenly, mid-sentence, he stopped, his face seemed to fall apart, his mouth hung open, his eyes started, as he gaped into the horror of where he was and why he was speaking. He blinked, looked towards Benedick, gathered himself and went on. I've always thought that giving that address was the bravest and noblest thing I've seen a man do. Two years later his wife, Victoria, wasted to the bone with grief and bewilderment, drifted to Italy, to a hotel where she, Alan and the twins had gone one summer. For her it was a place of special memories, memories of herself as a young mother in her prime, of a dashing film-star husband, of two beautiful sons who were also *enfants sauvages*. She arrived at the front desk so enfeebled that the receptionist immediately phoned for an ambulance, she was taken off to hospital, where she died the next day, of malnutrition, dehydration, extreme self-neglect, in fact – but how had she managed the journey? How had she found the strength even to contemplate it, let alone complete it? In his funeral address Alan spoke of her with such tenderness and understanding that he sounded at moments almost parental – the truth is, I think, that he was born to be a father, not a husband, and his marriage was really a sort of flawed adoption. He was honest and sad about the ways in which he'd failed her, but then she was always, in a friend's phrase, a reluctant incarnation, and I doubt if anyone could have given her what she needed in life, or even known what it was. His own death – his own death –

BOTH ALIVE AND DEAD

I've been trying to remember the film of *Women in Love*, whether I like it. I know I wrote down its title the other day, presumably in some context to do with Alan – well, I haven't seen it for ages, doubt if I'll ever see it again, or any film with Alan in it – such a disturbing part of modern life, you can find yourself watching an old film with great pleasure, a film you saw and loved in your childhood, take one of my favourite films of all time, *Shane*, with Alan Ladd as a gunslinger who rides away from his death-dealing past into a valley where circumstances compel him, against his will and for the sake of peace for people he has come to love, to deal out death again, and then ride on to oblivion. I have watched certain scenes from the film probably more than thirty times over the last fifty years, I was seventeen, in my last year at school, when it came out in London, so yes, fifty years – nobody in the film is over forty except perhaps the villainous rancher, and the old chap, played by Buchanan, is it? Edgar Buchanan – who wants to give up and go away until they burn down his ranch although now I think about it, nobody apart from Brandon De Wilde, who plays the son, he's about ten, I should think, of Van Heflin and Jean Arthur – nobody is much under forty, which is surely unusual for a film, even of that period – but you see them there still, is my point, Brandon De Wilde, Jean Arthur, Van Heflin, Elisha Cook Jr, Ben Johnson, and of course Jack Palance creaking about in black, his every movement measured and unnaturally, almost mechanically, paced, even when he goes for his gun – and of course Alan Ladd, blond in blond, or light-brown, buckskin – and there's the great scene, the open-air party, the settlers celebrating what can it have been? Thanksgiving, I suppose, Shane asking Van Heflin's wife – Jean Arthur – to dance – 'We're leaving Cheyenne-eh oh, eh-eh – We're leaving Cheyenne' – of course I've forgotten the rest of the words, though I remember the tune, I can't carry a tune to sing, but I carry this one in my heart, soul – and Van Heflin leaning on a fence, watching Shane dance with his wife, seeing the attractiveness, the almost rightness of them as a couple, Shane's tenderness and delicacy, his wife's dignified submissiveness. And of course later, when Van Heflin prepares to go to his almost certain death to protect his homestead, his family, he tells his wife that he knows she will be well looked after, as will their son, who idolizes Shane, Shane will be a better protector than himself – well, think of all that now, from now, in these days of cinematic trash, where the foul and vacuous *Lord of the Rings*, with its interminable set pieces, one set piece after another, of hideous mass slaughter, is voted by the nation as the nation's favourite film, and you find yourself asking yourself, what kind of nation is this? What kind of nation? *Shane* seems not only immensely dignified – indeed noble – in its conception, but also immensely innocent in its assumption that there are good people who struggle to live honourably, that a man who has lived badly, like the professional gunfighter Shane, can acknowledge what he has been, and sacrifice himself so that people he has come to love will have what he yearns for, that their future counts for more than his – even Wilson, the dead-souled killer, sticks to a code, or the appearance of a code – he doesn't draw his gun until the helpless Elisha Cook Jr, provoked by Jack Palance's smiling, jeering contempt for his Southern sense of honour, reaches for his gun – to my mind the most terrible moment in cinema – the rain beats down, Palance stands sheltered from it on the porch of the saloon, Elisha Cook Jr stands not many yards from him, drenched, his boots mired in mud, his gun only just out of its holster, still pointing down – Palance's gun drawn so quickly one can hardly see the movement, pointing directly at his chest – the long pause is the rest of Elisha Cook Jr's life, Palance smiling, Cook's eyes bulging – then the shot, Cook hurled backwards from the impact, spread out dead in the mud. This is awful violence, violence with meaning, it makes us know and feel what an act of murder is – in fact, there are only two killings in the film, that one and Wilson's, caused by Shane in the saloon in almost identical fashion, but this time it's Shane who does the taunting, and Wilson's guns which are incompletely drawn – Wilson hurtling backwards, his guns a quarter up, one I think firing uselessly, his thin limbs sticking out in all directions, a skeleton in black clothes, and of course the child watching from underneath the saloon's swing doors, his arm around his dog, sees the two ranchers concealed, one on the landing above the bar, his rifle aiming, warns Shane. A brief fusillade, the ranchers dead – so four killings not two. Shane stands wounded but impassive, then the sudden, completely unexpected, flashy and arrogant twirl of the gun before he drops it in its holster – 'You got him, didn't you, Shane? You shot Wilson!' 'Yes. That was Wilson. He was fast. Fast on the draw', this said almost in a trance, before riding off into the darkness, hunched sideways from the pain of his wound, the child crying out for him to come back, music swelling, child's voice echoing – and so forth. Well, not so forth. Credits, and The End naturally. But what I was thinking about, what I started all this from, was not *Shane*, its plot and its people, but the fact that they're all dead, all the actors, including Brandon De Wilde, who must have been about seven years younger than me, killed in a car crash in his twenties, early thirties, perhaps, and yet there they all are again, and the contradiction that never existed before the invention of movies, of people who are long dead being visibly alive, you can see them breathe, there they are, the characters and the actors, both with futures of life and death unknown to them in the two stories they're in. I'll go on watching *Shane* until nature prevents me, but I think I shall always avoid seeing Alan on the screen, or at least avoid watching him, I've already seen him a few times when channel-hopping, a glimpse of him in a bowler hat, an eyebrow raised, smiling quizzically –

HE IS SPOON-FED

He looked like Galileo, have I said this before? The rim of white beard, his hair growing back to a thick white stubble on his skull, his marvellous blue eyes as clear as they were in his youth, all his natural exuberance distilled into a different sort of energy, to be released after a few moments of rest, but the range of expressions as great as ever, with a new one, sweet and sly as he lay on the bed, his head propped up, studying you, or from his favourite position, a small armchair facing the bed, where he sat in his hospital gown, his feet planted, with the air of a benevolent emperor. He was, in fact, imperial in his dying, deeply happy with what had come to him at the end, his Tony Award on Broadway, his knighthood, all that was his due had come at last. He received his friends until nearly the end, sitting in a chair by the bed, a rug over his lap, full of delight and above all attention. He wanted to hear everything that was going on in our lives, gave sympathy and advice where things were bad, and shared in any pleasures and successes. He was Alan as I'd always known him, the very best of best friends, the one you phoned up immediately when you were in need, the one you hoped would phone you up when he was. Ben came from New York to lodge with him in his room for the final few weeks, sleeping on a camp bed so that he was available at night, tending him like a nurse and son, spooning food into his mouth when he resisted eating, getting him to swallow by cajoling and teasing. Alan adored this reversal of roles, describing how he'd used similar tactics when spoon-feeding Ben and Tristan, and then going into imitations of his father, at the end of his life, assuming a quavering and tetchy tone – 'Take it away, it's disgusting, disgusting, I can't eat it, who are these people anyway, call themselves nurses, call themselves doctors!' – and then spluttering with laughter, Ben laughing too as he slipped another spoonful down. They touched each other a lot, Ben patting Alan's head, Alan stroking Ben's cheek, as if they were the same age. Mates.

HIS LAST DAYS

I used to have the taxi stop on the Marylebone Road, at the top of Marylebone High Street, and walk the hundred yards or so to Harley Street and the London Clinic. I'd do it slowly, spinning it out, smoking two cigarettes, and then often have one more on the steps of the Clinic, where there would usually be someone smoking, either one of the hospital porters, or a relative or, like me, friend of a patient, and once or twice a patient, I think – we all had pretty well the same manner of smoking, it was a cigarette that mattered, that we couldn't get enough of, but couldn't linger over, short, greedy puffs, then a decisive step onto the pavement, drop the butt, a quick stamp, a decisive step back and into the clinic, then the lift up to the third floor, or was it the second? Anyway, the cancer floor – along the corridor, not bothering to stop at the reception desk because the nurses know you by now, or seem to, and there's his door – the first thing I did on returning to the pavement was to light up, putting myself in touch with the man I'd left on the pavement smoking, as if the visit itself were in parenthesis, that linked up to the parentheses of the previous visits, so that the visits now seem to be a continuum, a main sentence all of its own – I would smoke my way through to Marylebone High Street by the back route, and sit at a pub that had chairs and tables outside, even though we were in December, and Christmas nearer with every visit – I would sit at a table with a Diet Coke and concentrate on anything but Alan, or find a blankness sometimes so successfully that I'd forget what I was doing there, smoking, with a Diet Coke, outside a pub in the cold, and I'd get the next taxi that came along, hailing it from my table. The truth is that, whatever joy there was in seeing Alan, it was also unbearable. That stretch from the top of Marylebone High Street to the top of Harley Street – whenever we pass it in a taxi I look out of the window and measure it with my eye, but even as I register how short it is, I feel the lurch of dread in my stomach and hope I never have to walk it again, never have to stand on those steps again – and there's another thing that comes back to me, that as I approached the clinic I used to look up to the window of Alan's room, imagine him sitting in his chair or lying on his bed, and then imagine myself as I would be in a few moments, in that room that seemed to me from the outside, looking up at its window, so self-contained and far away that I could never be in it.

HE AND TOTO FIND PEACE

So that's how it was all the days in December, leading up to Christmas – Alan dying in the London Clinic, and Toto going mad in Holland Park – I could hear her screams as I came down the street towards the house – not, I suppose, technically screams, but shrill, joined-up yaps that had the effect of screams in that they shredded the nerves and made one think of cruelty, pain and ambulances – such a small dog, and in repose such a pretty one, with alert, intelligent eyes, and affectionate. We'd originally given her as a birthday present to my granddaughters, Maddie and Gee-Gee. Victoria had picked her up at the kennels on her way to London from Suffolk at 3 p.m. on 11 September – in fact, she was drawing up outside the kennel doors as the news about the twin towers came through on her car radio – so in a sense Toto is a 9/11 baby, about whom songs could be written therefore, but her condition that Christmas was actually the result of something far more momentous in her world, an hysterical pregnancy which coincided with her having come to live with us – she gave birth to a small stuffed bear, which she protected with extraordinary savagery from predators like Victoria and myself. When she wasn't crouched snarling over it, she was drooling over it and cuddling it, and then would suddenly rampage around the house screaming the screams I used to hear on coming home from the London Clinic. So the two experiences are intermingled – no, they're not – as I've said, Alan's dying is a long, separate event, and Toto's madness is a long, separate event that happened at the same time, parallel with it, one home and one away – the worst was Christmas, Alan in his coma, Toto in a frenzy because somehow her stuffed bear of a baby had vanished and she decided that she had delivered herself of all the presents under the Christmas tree and crouched, snarling, among them – this meant that no one could approach the tree without being threatened – a mad dog is a mad dog, however charming to look at and sweet her nature, and her shows of teeth, saliva dripping from her muzzle, were terrifying among the pink and gold and silver and scarlet packages – when she went on one of her looping, screaming runs, we tried to gather up the presents, but either she would be back before we'd done or, if we shut her out, she would patrol the hall screaming – so when it came down to it there was nothing we could do but leave them under the tree and let her embed herself. Eventually the stuffed bear was found on a high shelf in the kitchen, and was placed on the floor some way from the presents, Toto ran to it, buried her face in it, licked it, stroked it and rolled it about, then carried it gently down to the basement and put it to bed – and so, apart from sudden rushes upstairs to check briefly on her other family, under the tree, and other rushes through the flap and screaming circuits of the garden – which led to a petition from some of the neighbours asking us to confine her to the house, her garden screams were too distressing, and set their own dogs off – the situation held through to Boxing Day – we saw him a few hours before he died, when we took Ben some food, as the visitors' cafeteria was closed over the festive season, indeed the Clinic gave off the feeling that it had closed down, the only occupants the ill and the dying – he was still, his arms lying straight outside the blankets, his eyes closed, his chest moving irregularly – we could hear his breathing, shallow suckings in and expulsions after long intervals – he was obviously near the end, and looked ready for it, neat and noble, only the breathing disorderly. Ben white and staring, looked as close to death as Alan – but then he hadn't eaten for a long time, nothing was open in the neighbourhood, not even the pubs. We stayed until Ben had eaten, said goodbye to Alan with a kiss on his forehead, and came home to Toto, running this way and that, screaming. In the New Year we got canine Prozac from the vet. It calmed her down somewhat, and she began to treat the bear as a toy rather than as a baby, knocking it about, throwing it into the air and catching it, until she discarded it altogether – it still lies in her basket in the basement, but she scarcely ever goes down there, now that she sleeps in different spots all over the house in the daytime, and on our bed at night.

DEPARTURES

Oh, I saw Pan this afternoon, sitting in the reception with his suitcases, waiting for the taxi for the airport. He looked subdued, no cigar, his hands folded in his lap. He was dressed in a blue blazer, cream-coloured slacks and sturdy brown shoes, for London or Manchester, wherever. His nose seemed to fit in better when he was wearing his usual togs, it could go almost unnoticed in the Garrick Club or the MCC. The young woman with bangles and chains was attending him, but not departing with him. She was wearing beach clothes and hotel slippers, and kept going to the desk to ask about his taxi – 'Mr Prynne's got to be at the airport by three, at the latest' – there's something solemn and poignant about these departures in the lobby, the piled-up luggage, the cold-weather clothes, somebody at the desk worrying about the taxi and the flight – flamboyant Pan with a cigar becomes passive Mr Prynne staring down at his mottled hands. I wonder if Pan and the young woman are lovers, and Mr Prynne is going home to the wife and children, grandchildren? Well, the day after tomorrow it will be our turn, Victoria's and mine, to sit beside our luggage in the lobby, waiting to be returned to the fitful fever, all that, and people who are staying on will observe us and try not to think that one day soon –

PART TWO

PART TWO

IT TOLLS FOR SIMON

The Holy Terror in Brighton, then. How did it go? Be honest. Well, I registered only two things – that the audience was having a good time, and there was something about the play that didn't ring a bell, or rang the wrong bell – I can probably put this down to jet lag, and the intense yearning for Barbados, the sun and the sea, that always immediately follows on leaving them, I really was scarcely able to listen and watch, understanding only that the sets were very complicated and seemed to rattle on and off stage like bumper cars, which I found exhilarating, and that I loved the sheer exuberance of Simon Callow's performance, his conspiratorial relationship with the audience, who liked him even when he was abusing them – oh, yes, that was one more thing, the audience – the theatre manager told me when I came in that the audiences are terrific, he's getting lots of feedback, telephone calls, letters, the box office is jumping, nothing like it for a long time, people are really excited by it, he said, best of all they're passing on the excitement so that the houses are not only full, they're full of people who expect to enjoy themselves, and consequently do – so that was all right, though it was before I'd actually seen the show, and so before it rang – or tolled – the wrong bell. Simon and I had supper, I talked enthusiastically, while admitting that I had nothing useful to say – after all, it would hardly have been useful to say it was all fine except that it rang, or tolled, the wrong bell, and I don't know which or what bell, still don't, would it? I'll go and see Victoria, chatting about it out loud may stir up some thoughts or memories.

She was asleep, with George on one side of her, Toto on the other side, my side. I rolled Toto onto the chest at the foot of the bed, lay down and set about whispering stuff into Victoria's ear – 'There's something wrong with the play. I don't mean the lines, none of them sounded as if they weren't by me, I vaguely remembered all of them' – whispered stuff like that, which she seemed to find rather soothing, anyway she didn't spring awake as she usually does when I interrupt her sleep with a sentence, and when I finally realized 'It's the wrong play. They're doing the wrong play!' she murmured something that sounded approving or grateful. I rolled Toto back beside her, and now I'm here at my pad trying to work it out. Actually, they're not exactly doing the wrong play, they're doing the wrong version. There are two published texts, and they're delivering the earlier one, which was six or seven drafts away from the later one, the one I'd assumed they were doing.

I don't quite know what to do. After all, they've learnt the lines, have already performed for ten days in Brighton, can I simply phone Simon up in the morning and ask him to start rehearsing a different text, which would certainly involve changes in the actors' moves, and might involve changes to the set, adding new bits to bump in, while bumping existing bits out altogether? Does it matter that they're using the wrong text? If the Brighton audiences are happy with the wrong text why not leave it alone? Of course this wouldn't have happened if I'd been invited to the read-through on the first day of rehearsal, can I take satisfaction from that?

I've just phoned Simon and told him the situation. He took it with astonishing resilience, seeing it, not as a calamity, but as an opportunity to do interesting work on tour. I've sent him the authorized, let's call it that, the authorized version, and during the coming weeks, in places like Woking and Milton Keynes, charming ones like Bath, he and the other actors will, without benefit of the director – he left after the opening in Brighton to do a seventeenth-century Spanish play in Stratford – put in scenes from the authorized, cutting roughly equivalent stretches from the version they've spent weeks rehearsing and are now performing – an epic task, really, involving long hours and no doubt embarrassments on stage, when actors will suddenly find themselves living in one text with an actor who is living in the other text. I'll have to go and see it, not at Brighton again, too soon, and not at Woking, I went to Woking once, no need to go again – Milton Keynes, then, I've never been to

MILTON KEYNES

with its wide desolate boulevards, its noisy ghastly mall, a town designed for a future that it's somehow missed, so it's both aggressively modern and hopelessly out of date. The theatre, naturally, is vast and ugly, inside and out. I forgot to ask how many seats but I'd guess, at a minimum, twelve hundred, it probably does lots of pop shows, that sort of thing, anyway the audience was there like a rash, splotches of them sitting together, then an acre of space, more splotches, although if you'd joined the splotches they might have made up a decent little house. The show looked small too, as the stage was big, the surroundings cavernous, but I concentrated as keenly on the play as if I'd written it myself, admired the work that had been done, noticed the differences in the text and came out feeling that I'd had exactly the same experience as at Brighton, which I can now remember more clearly than immediately after Brighton. When I had dinner with Simon I told him confidently that he was growing in command – as he was – as the other actors were – worried a little about the set, but had nothing to say about the play at all. And Simon –

THE PLURAL OF PIERS?

Simon. It's odd to be writing my own name when referring to somebody else. I remember having dinner with Simon at a restaurant a year or so ago, and introducing him to the *maître d'*, also called Simon, so there were the three of us, Simon and Simon and Simon. When I was growing up my name was an agony to me, in fact I didn't meet anyone called Simon until I was at Cambridge. It was the same for Nigel and Piers, we all blamed Mummy for our names, we were victims of her affectation, we believed, Piers especially, who had to go to schools in Canada with a name that to infant Canadians was precious and effeminate and couldn't even be abbreviated. Now of course they're all very common names, there are probably whole nurseries of Simons, Nigels and – I don't know how to write the plural of Piers – is it the only Christian name to end in an 's'? I can't think of another one – Thomas, you fool. There are bound to be others – all right, is it the only monosyllabic Christian name that ends in 's'? Bess. Tess. But they're abbreviations, and a double 's' isn't the same as an 's', but still, to be safe – is Piers the only monosyllabic *male* Christian name that ends in 's'? Charles and James, you fool. Safe from what?

UNLEARNING EXPERIENCES

Tomorrow is the first night of *The Holy Terror*, at the Duke of York's. I've been to four consecutive previews, including tonight's, which is the last apart from a matinée tomorrow, which I shan't go to – I've never heard of having a matinée before a first night, can it be a good idea? If it goes badly they'll be depressed, subdued, come on stage in the evening, for the crucial performance, and act without conviction. On the other hand, I suppose if it goes well they'll be confident – too confident?

But what can I say about the four previews? Only that although all four were well received by the audience I came away from each one with the feeling that I'd had exactly the same experience as at Milton Keynes, which had been like the first experience in Brighton. Half a dozen identical experiences then, three in completely different places, all with different texts, lighting, sound cues. I can't make out what this means, it may just mean that the play hasn't got into my system, in the way that my plays do when I worry and fret through each rehearsal. It may also mean that I'm still going through an autistic phase, I've got an idea that I've already described this, when nothing seems to make much impression, or matter much – although I want the play to be a success, quite positively want that, and just as positively want Simon to be a success in it – I've always admired his gifts, as an actor and as a writer, and I consider myself lucky in our friendship. I can't bear to think of him coming a cropper on my behalf, and also – and also – well, it seems to me that his talents, his relish for life, his love of his friends all come from the same source – of course they do, how could they possibly come from different sources? What am I trying to say? First-night nerves, I'd assume, if I were nervous.

MY NEW SHOES

I was wearing a pair of new shoes, black and soft, a bit like moccasins, that would have been comfortable if there hadn't been an odd sensation, that they were full of water – it was air, I suppose, but every step I took made a whooshing sound inside my shoe, I couldn't actually hear it, but I felt it, whoosh, whoosh, whoosh, whoosh, as I walked along St Martin's Lane to the Duke of York's, for a quick visit to the actors, about an hour before the curtain went up. Whoosh, whoosh, as I went down the stairs backstage, into the dressing rooms. I decided that these shoes, never before worn, would never be worn again, they seemed to be whooshing even when I was sitting down, talking to the actors with chuckling optimism about the night that lay before us, and were going whoosh as I walked to Sheekey's, around the corner from the theatre, and met Victoria in the bar. I told her about the shoes. She looked down at them, and said yes, there was something odd about them, they didn't look quite like shoes, didn't quite go with my trousers, so perhaps my trousers were odd. My trousers were at least comfortable, I said, inasmuch as I wasn't consciously wearing any, whereas I couldn't keep my mind off my shoes, even when I was attempting to raise the morale of the actors, which was worryingly high, perhaps it would have been wiser to lower their morale a bit, blessed is he that expecteth nothing – I went on to talk about the play, telling her that it was an old play, nothing to do with me any more, really, apart from the fact that my name was on it, and on the posters outside the theatre, and probably up in lights above the title.

We sidled back to the Duke of York's, acknowledging but not recognizing people on the pavement, then into a private room where there were about eight people standing right in the middle of the room, holding glasses of wine and champagne. I sat down on a sofa that was in a corner, and Victoria stood in front of me, as if to guard me, not a gallant arrangement, but these occasions bring out both my defenceless side and her protective nature. A man and a woman detached themselves, came over to us, the man someone I know but my mind blanked out, I couldn't remember his name or a thing about him, but it didn't matter because his intention was to introduce me to the woman, whom he ushered around Victoria and arranged in front of me with a sweeping gesture – 'Behold!' his gesture seemed to say, 'Behold this woman!' And I did behold her, and lo! she was passing comely, and passing compliments too, although they weren't compliments about any of my theatrical works, they were about other things I do, in another life, – but you can't be choosy with compliments, I've discovered, you have to take them while you can get them. 'But you don't want to talk to me on an occasion like this,' she said, with a pretty smile, wished me luck, and returned herself to the centre of attention in the centre of the room. 'She does a quiz show,' Victoria said, 'she's famous for being clever and rude.' I said that I was glad she hadn't been rude to me, it would be a bit much to have someone being rude to you before the curtain went up on a play that virtually nobody in London had yet seen – or at least that virtually nobody had yet seen in London, well, that a few people had seen in previews in London, but if she'd been one of them she'd hardly come back for a second helping on the off-chance of a chance to be rude to the playwright – Victoria explained that she hadn't been in the slightest bit rude, evidently hadn't seen the play as she'd said she was looking forward to it – I agreed that if she'd already seen it, she'd know better than to look forward to it. Victoria terminated the exchange by pointing out that we now had the room to ourselves. 'Why?' I said. 'Where have they gone?' She said that as the final bell had rung, she imagined they'd gone to their seats. We should go to ours. We sat down at the back of the dress circle of what must be the prettiest theatre in London. There was a strange fretfulness in the atmosphere – there wasn't a buzz of anticipation but of impatience, fidgeting and sighing, noisy mutterings and angry sniggers – when Simon started the play by stepping between the curtains and addressing the audience as if it were composed of the ladies of the Chichester Women's Institute, a silence descended, not a silence of concentration but heavy, inert and rancorous – it really was most peculiar, and deeply troubling for a playwright who has always longed to be taken to the bosom of first-nighters, as they are mostly critics and determine the future of the work in question. Now it's true that there were spots of attention and even laughter, and even appreciative laughter, so somewhere down there in the stalls was a small alternative audience. I reminded myself that we've opened in an almost empty city, half-deserted streets, muttering retreats, etc., possibly everybody in town was now in the Duke of York's – all the critics and theatre journalists summoned back from their Easter rituals, egg hunts with the children, maypole and fertility dances, to cover a play that they could detect from its title, or had been told by relatives in Brighton, Woking or Milton Keynes, was a bad play, which it may be, and anti-life, which in fact it isn't, although I admit it's not a play that is 100 per cent unequivocally pro-life, rather it's a play that advises you to be careful where you tread, there can be an empty space where you're aiming to put your foot next, it's that sort of play, equivalent to a health warning on a packet of cigarettes – well then, consider my own reactions to health warnings on cigarettes, yes, consider your own reactions to health

warnings of any kind, they're very similar to the reactions of last
night's audience to your play, perhaps that's the explanation then –

At the interval we went back to Sheekey's, sat in the bar, at the
table where we'd sat earlier, when we'd discussed my shoes – now
it was the play, but the vocabulary was very similar – whoosh,
whoosh, flop, splat. A couple burst into the bar – it's the only word
for it – burst in, walked to the end of the counter, hopped angrily
onto high stools, and slapped their programmes down – no, she
didn't, he did, but it was in its emotional content a simultaneous
gesture, her hand was on his knee as he slapped the programme
onto the counter, not once but three times, punishing it, was what
he was doing to it – now Sheekey's is close to a number of other
theatres, so I hoped this couple had come from one of those, we
couldn't actually see the front of the programme, at least not until
he raised it, and showed it, with a contemptuous gesture, to a
sympathetically enquiring barman, and then we knew that they
hadn't come from one of those but from ours, which wouldn't be
ours, we were already surmising, for very long.

I BECOME CHILDISH

We left Sheekey's, heads again bowed for anonymity, discovered
that though we were a couple of minutes late we were in fact early,
inasmuch as the pavement was crowded with people who clearly
felt no need to get back inside the theatre – from what I could see
of them as I peeked past, they were having a better time – i.e.
animated and gesticulating – where they were than where they'd
been, and would have to be again about three minutes ago. I
imagine they were critics, comparing notes, as I've oft heard tell
that now and then, when they really all agree that they're on to a

bummer, they cluster together instead of keeping a fastidious and ethical distance from each other. I suppose it's a kind of herd instinct, really, perhaps a celebration, demonstrating to the world that whatever their individual differences, they tap in, at the profounder aesthetic levels, to a collective consciousness – well, whatever they were up to, I didn't like the look of them, there's one in particular that I seem to have known all my life, I mean as far back as the day I was born there was this face, that tone – reviewing my emergence from the womb with a lumbering melancholy, a shake of the ponderous head, he always makes me think of a nappy, a full nappy, as if he's just over-eaten, and is pausing briefly on the way to the potty – this is just childishness, I'm being childish, he's merely doing his job – his big jobs – ha ha – stop, stop – though it's grotesque to think that he's already written his review, that in a few hours it will be steaming away on people's doormats –

AN ADULT AGAIN

well, back to getting off the pavement into the lobby of the theatre, through that, down some stairs to the private room, which was stuffed with people, so many that it was difficult to get the door open, all of them with glasses in their hands, all of them throbbing with a noisy, ill-judged optimism – these were the producer's friends, backers and so forth, people with something to lose, including their wives if they'd invested her money in the play – we hung about there in a corner for a few seconds, the sofa being heavily occupied, then went up to our seats. It's a general rule that however badly a first night goes in the first act, the second is always a bit better – the actors have got used to the house, the house has got used to not liking the play, everyone is halfway towards going home, or somewhere else where the evening will pick up – a bad evening at the theatre guarantees a good evening in the restaurant, so much to laugh at and be apoplectic about – 'I couldn't believe it, couldn't actually believe it when he began –' 'And that ghastly bit when she –' 'And that line, did you hear that line? and so forth. I've had many happy dinners of that sort, pausing only sometimes to wonder about all the dinners I haven't been at, when my own play has provided the merriment and apoplexy.

AN ENCOUNTER WITH A RABID WOMAN, PROBABLY A CRITIC

The second act didn't go any better than the first, it went a little worse, the ill-feeling was slightly intensified, the spots of laughter more subdued. Perhaps some of the laughers had left, or had been brought around to the majority view during the interval. I actually can't remember the curtain call, so it was probably polite, merely lacking enthusiasm and honesty, like some of my school reports, but I do remember that we were the first out of our seats and through the doors, into the corridor – there was a small woman coming towards us, she must have come up from the stalls, and was probably a critic. I'd arrange to have only a very small photograph of myself, passport size, in the programme in the hope of preventing identification, but this small woman gave me the impression that she'd not only identified me, she knew me well, that she'd hated the play and was enjoying letting me have a glimpse, by baring her teeth, of her review – in all my years in the theatre, years and years in the theatre, in all those many, many years, with no time off for good behaviour, I have never seen a more chilling sight than those bared teeth – although I suppose it's possible that they were false, and a bad fit, that she wasn't a critic and that her intentions were entirely friendly, or that she was on her way to a heart attack, and her teeth were bared in a grimace of agony – but no, there were the eyes too, the sort of eyes that went with bared teeth and a bad review. In seconds we were safely by ourselves, in the private room, and astonishingly, seconds later, we were in the company of a multitude, they seemed to come in from all sides though there was only the one door, and they already had glasses in their hands. The producer bundled himself in, holding bottles of champagne, and talking at speed, loudly – have I mentioned him yet? Howard Panter. I can't be bothered to describe him but he's balding, about fifty, medium height, not portly but looks as if he has been and will be again. When I first knew him he was subject to seizures and so forth, but he is currently robust, last night extra-robust, his voice as I've said loud and jerky and all over the place, as if he were a hyperactive ventriloquist. His movements were jerky too. I can't remember seeing him in the private room before the curtain went up, so he must have braved the bar, presumably because he preferred to mingle with strangers rather than his backers and accountants, shortly perhaps to become strangers too. The reason I ought to have mentioned him, if I haven't, is that he's been a devoted and intelligent producer, attending the play regularly when it was out of town and present at every preview, his comments have always seemed to me shrewd and constructive, and he has faith, and shows his faith – this should probably be written in one of the past tenses – he showed, has shown, had shown his faith – the coming week might sap it out of him – or do I mean zap, zap it out of him? – I suddenly see the little woman-critic with those teeth fixed in Howard Panter's throat, economic throat, as well as in my writer's throat, Simon's actor's throat, all our throats, and Howard's faith, ripped out of him by that Rottweiling little – teeth could be false, remember, incipient heart attack, remember, sad little lady with her dentures on the bedside table, sad little lady on a slab in the hospital – I mean bed in the hospital, slabs are in the mortuary – though these days a bed in one soon becomes a slab in the other, why don't they merge?

We hung about until the audience had left the building, then went up to the lobby, where there was to be a party for the actors, backers, etc. As we came through the door a little group of tightly knit stragglers were heading for the pavement, among them the famously cruel and clever quiz lady. She saw me, her step faltered, she smiled, she raised a thumb so courteously and compassionately that it seemed to jab straight into my kidneys, then the faltering step quickened and she was gone. Victoria and I were alone in the lobby, though we could see people standing on the pavement outside, lighting cigarettes, moving towards taxis. I longed to go out there and light a cigarette, but it was safer, wiser, in the lobby where there would be allies from the company, the producer's family and friends – I wondered whether the director had sent family and friends along in lieu of himself, I gather he'd been seen once at a preview, at a matinée performance when, exhausted by his labours on the Spanish play in Stratford, and the exhausting trip from there to the Duke of York's, he had come into one of the dressing rooms, lain down on a sofa and requested a kiss – 'Isn't somebody going to give me a kiss, don't I deserve a kiss?' When he'd got one – at least I suppose he'd got one, but from whom? – he gave his blessing to the work Simon, the other actors and Howard Panter had done since he'd last seen the play on the first night in Brighton, talked awhile about his life and times in Stratford, departed with soft hugs and squeezes, and was glimpsed no more. The social responsibility for this celebration thus devolved in part on me, but I reckoned that after a few handshakes, kisses and cuddles, whatever was mandatory, we could leave for a restaurant near home, where we'd arranged to meet up with friends. Once we were with them we would be carefree until the morning brought the reviews. Well, not carefree exactly, but we could allow ourselves to relax into gloom among close friends who were more like relatives, without the attendant problems – none of us looked like each other, talked like each other, reminded us of ourselves and our lineages.

A LAUGH SEEN THROUGH GLASS

The actors came in a group, minus Simon. They were flushed with the triumph of getting through the evening without mishap, no fluffed lines, no false moves, no stalled scene changes, a full house, and the adrenalin still up but the panic that caused it leaking away. They said the house had been a bit sticky, but then first nights, London audiences, critics, what do you expect, they'd known worse, though several of them couldn't have, as this was their first West End experience. Simon came into the lobby through the main doors of the theatre – I was having a stilted conversation with a fellow playwright and a titled actor, who were both working hard on their bedside manner, finding ways of reassuring me that the rope was secure around my neck, the trapdoor ready under my feet – the compliments that told the true story were 'brave' and 'bold', as in 'It's such a bold piece of writing and Simon is so very very bold in it' and 'How good that the West End still has brave producers, willing to take risks' – they and Simon embraced *à la mode*, then Simon and I went to a quiet spot and spoke about the audience. There was a fat man in the front row, he said, who stared fixedly at him during the curtain call, and gave him a very personal slow handclap, which he continued after everyone else had stopped clapping – the worst audience, he said, the worst audience he'd ever – absolutely the worst, I agreed, absolutely – and then, for want of a howl or a scream, we burst out laughing – no big deal with me, as my laugh is really a wheeze with cackles in it, but a very big deal with Simon, he has a laugh that could fill, or perhaps empty, a cathedral, it is a cheering noise, it comes from a deep relish of the awfulness of life as well as of its pleasures – with an adjustment of the shoulders, he advanced into the lobby. I extracted Victoria from a quaint young Indian who was dressed in the style far beyond his years and now completely out of fashion, a grey suit, white collar and dark tie, and a large pair of spectacles. He had a pad in one hand, a pen in the other, and held them out to me as if for an autograph. When I made to take them he pulled them back quickly and said, 'No, could you just tell me how you feel?' 'How I feel?' 'Yes, please, how you feel after such a successful night.' 'He's from the *Telegraph*,' Victoria said, smiling pleasantly at him. 'Ah!' I said. 'Ah! Well, we'd better be off, better be off, eh?' and went out onto the pavement. Through the doors we saw him stepping quickly towards Simon, whose head was thrown back in a laugh we couldn't hear, reminding me of the Munch – visually there's sometimes little to choose between a soundless laugh and a soundless scream – the interesting question is what would Simon have seen, if he'd seen but not heard himself laughing that laugh.

HOW DID WE GET THERE?

I don't remember how we got to Kensington Place, the restaurant in Notting Hill, I might ask Victoria tomorrow, when we're both fully awake, or perhaps ask her when I go to bed, which will be some time around 6 a.m., from the feel of me. One of her many accomplishments, and one that is crucial to the smooth working of our marriage, is that she is willing to have, seems even to enjoy, conversations, some of them quite complicated, at whatever hour I come to bed, however deeply asleep she might have been the second before I ask a question, frequently factual – e.g. When exactly did we go to Spetses for the first time, was it in August, you can't remember the actual date can you, was it a Monday? I seem to have got it into my head it was a Tuesday or Monday? etc. – and she will provide answers one after the other, most of them correct. Or I make a statement, an emphatic statement – e.g. – I can't think of an example of any of these emphatic statements right now, but they're usually to do with the state of the world, education, literacy, that sort of thing, and involve the usual adjectives – loathsome, disgraceful, revolting, so forth – but when I get in beside her tonight, I shan't ask her how we got from the Duke of York's to the restaurant, because by then I will have forgotten that I want to know, and will need to know something else entirely, or will make an emphatic statement about first-night audiences and theatre critics, she won't even have to wake up to deal with that, her response will be automatic, having been given so many times before. Anyway the only reason I found myself wondering how we got to Kensington Place is because I can't remember, and the reason I can't remember is because it isn't important – but the thing is, the thing is, it's now become important because I can't remember it – if I worked it out logically I'd say we took a taxi, how else? I'd certainly remember if we walked, or went by tube or bus, because it would be difficult to believe, in fact I wouldn't believe it, I'd think I was the victim of false memory syndrome, that someone had artificially implanted in me the idea that we'd walked or tubed or bussed from the Duke of York's to Notting Hill –

HOW WE GOT THERE

Hah! Got it! We had a hired car, of course we did, Philip drove us, as he always does on such occasions, he was wearing his semi-official chauffeur's uniform, a very natty dark suit and black tie, but no cap – the suit and tie establishing to the world at large that he is a professional driver, the absence of a cap signifying that he is also a friend to the occupants of the magnificently upholstered back seat – it has an armrest with a hole in it for your glass, or in my case a can of Diet Coke, it has an ashtray that is grand enough for cigar stubs, and it has tinted windows so that not only can the world at large not look in at you, you can't look out on the world at large, which is frankly very irritating, but it's a beautiful car, so spacious that it must have been designed for celebrities who, in the way of celebrities, don't want to see – what is there for them to look at? – or be seen – no, that can't be right, celebrities surely want to be seen, that's why they become celebrities, so it must be that they don't want to be seen when they're doing certain things in the back of a car. I'll ask Philip if there are in fact two windows, a removable tinted window over a transparent window, so that when the celebrities have finished doing their certain things they can show themselves off – wait a minute – why then are the tinted windows in place whenever I'm in the car? Could it be that he's ashamed of me? It's true that I often look quite scruffy and I chain-smoke – so he doesn't want an elderly, scruffy chain-smoking man to be visible in his car – but then that wouldn't apply when Victoria's in the car, she's always elegant, he would be proud to have her in his car – that's unfortunately put, he'd be glad to show her off, yes, that's better, to show her off in his car – silver, sleek, expensive-looking car – what make is it, I wonder? Yes, that's the question I'll put to Victoria when I go to bed, what make is Philip's car, and she'll say, 'But you've been in it lots of times,' and I'll say, yes, I know what it looks like, both on the outside and the inside, but I've never noticed the make, and she'll say, 'Oh, it's a Mercedes,' and she'll be right, because I've just realized that it is in fact a Mercedes, Philip's referred to it as such – 'Yes, I can take you,' he'll say. 'I've just got my Mercedes back from the garage' – so now I know, no point in asking her – Philip, by the way, is not ashamed of me, he's not trying to prevent people from seeing me in the back of his car, he just assumes I don't like being looked at, especially when I'm smoking, and he doesn't think I want to look out of the window because I'm either bending my head towards Victoria, or, if I'm alone, I'm reading or thinking or fidgeting, and of course, of course, I always lower the window – I nearly said wind down the window, but these days you press a button – so it doesn't matter if it's a single tinted window, it's only closed when you're very cold – Get to Kensington Place, for God's sake, why not?

BREAKDOWN

Why not? Well, not because I can't remember it, but because I prefer not to. It wasn't unpleasant in itself, how could it be with such company, Judy Daish, my agent for twenty-five years or so, a great beauty with many sympathetic features – kind, generous, thoughtful and I would say caring, if I could bear the word; and then there was her new chap, Gordon, just come into her life, actually almost the first chap I can remember with husband status, he's charming, with flowing brown locks and a toothsome smile, and says intelligent things in a murmuring voice – and then there were William and Caroline Waldegrave, Victoria's oldest friends, now old friends of mine, William was a politician, an MP and minister in Thatcher's government, he seemed destined for great things until his party killed its queen bee, and the hive went to hell, is perhaps a lazy way of putting it – anyway William left politics, or the other way around, and he is now in banking, his formidable and kindly intellect engaged on matters that can't be as destructive to the public good as what goes on in Parliament, especially in these days, when governments pretend to believe that they have an obligation to protect the citizen from himself (and herself, needless to say, needless to say) – nanny state is a term frequently used to convey its moralistic, dependence-making, interfering nature, but it's an inadequate one, as nannies also make you feel safe, or should do, and the government of today is determined to do the opposite – the terrorists are coming, the attack is inevitable, London, Huddersfield, Sheffield, Little Sodsbury, who knows where or when, but come it will, we can't prevent it, but we can make your life complicated, anxious and miserable by implementing regulation after regulation that will help to guard you from the terrorists and their attacks, from which no one can protect you, which are coming because they're inevitable – here is a list of things you may not do, tomorrow will bring a list of other things that you may not do, eventually you'll have forgotten how to do them and even why you wanted to do them, and in the end, by the time we've finished regulating you, you should come not to mind the terrorists and their attacks, which are coming, from which no one, especially us, can protect you, because your lives will be so cabined, cribbed and confined that you might as well give them up to people who think it a duty and a pleasure to take them, so be supine in the name of Western civilization, our values are that we don't have any, our future is to pay for our past by surrendering – surrendering – actually the thing about William, which is what I was talking about – writing about –

A GOOD TIME IN NOTTING HILL

There is also his wife, Caroline, who is beautiful, kind and good, what more need I say? Why am I saying it, anyway? The point is that with such company, in a familiar restaurant where the food is fine, better than fine, it should have been a good and fine evening, especially as the other four, the Daishes and the Waldegraves, were in excellent spirits, had enjoyed the play, were convinced that the audience had enjoyed the play and that we could anticipate nothing but good news in tomorrow's (today's) papers – Victoria and I tried to explain the real facts of the matter, that the audience had hated the play, the reviews would stink. This disagreement sustained itself for about ten minutes in a low-key kind of way, subsided, bobbed up, subsided, other matters were discussed, food was eaten, wine was drunk, one bottle of Diet Coke followed another, the mood became jolly, vibrant, Judy and Victoria climbed onto the table and danced a samba to stamping feet and handclaps – five Russians – four girls and an elderly woman – joined in. Gordon grappled with a waiter who tried to prevent Judy and Victoria from taking off their skirts, William stood on his chair and called for UN intervention, Caroline made friendly gestures through the window to passers-by on the pavement, coarsely misinterpreted – so inevitably, in the jolly hubbub of an evening in Notting Hill, the agony of the Duke of York's became a thin and inconsequential memory – and here I am at seven in the morning, with nothing much on my mind but the reviews that the producer and most members of the cast will have read, and Victoria and I have no intention of reading. Time for bed, dozy-dead, head I mean, dozy-head, time for bed, hozy-dead.

CONGRATULATIONS ARE IN ORDER

I've just about got up, and am shortly going back to bed. Judy phoned at some hour or other, not long after I'd gone to sleep. I heard the ringing in Victoria's study, then Victoria's voice, a long pause, then in she came. She said that Judy said that our policy of not reading the reviews has again been completely vindicated. So a triumph, really, for practical wisdom, is one way of looking at it.

SIMON INTRODUCES SIMON TO TWO-BEERS

Home from dinner with Simon. We went to a dining club I'd never heard of, down an alley off St Martin's Lane. It really seemed to consist of a steep, narrow stairway, with several landings off which there were rooms of different sizes. We ate by ourselves at the top, in a medium-sized room, deliberately underlit. There was an attractive waiter, an attractive waitress, both attentive without being much present, who brought us food – but from where? I have no idea where the food came from, but it was OK, or would have been if I'd had an appetite. Simon, hungry after a performance that had been doubly draining because the house had been so small – he could have counted it, he said – was shell-shocked, was the phrase he used, shell-shocked. The laugh, though, was miraculously there, and we had some fun even when he quoted from the reviews. He tactfully refrained from quoting anything about the play, confining himself to himself. They were so wounding that I once or twice suspected that he was making them up, or was engaged in some weird auto-therapy, or like a medieval monk thrashing his naked self for the good of his soul. But they were all true, he assured me, and I suppose it was his actor's gift – or curse – that had enabled him to commit them to memory verbatim. There were a couple of sentences from a woman in one of the heavies, with a name like a beer – no, like two beers – that were so vile that he gaped at me after saying them, as if not quite believing what he'd just heard from himself. I gaped back at him, equally incredulous, then we both burst out laughing, it really did seem inconceivable that anybody would want to have their name attached to such words. Actually I pointed out, possibly correctly, that if Simon had been Simone and the critic a man, she could probably have sued him for libel, or had him prosecuted under some recent legislation – there was bound to have been some – for sexual abuse, harassment, stirring up sexual hatred, whatever. But Simone was Simon and two-beers was a woman, so all he could do was to quote her, gape, laugh and – no getting away from it – suffer. How could he not suffer, having to go on stage with those words boiling in his consciousness, feeling sure that everybody in the audience had read the review and had also committed it to memory, in fact were only there because of the review, were savouring it as they watched him perform. One of the advantages of being a playwright is that not only can I stay away from the theatre, I don't have to leave the house even, or I can go about in taxis or walk quickly with my head lowered, deny my name if questioned, claim that there are, in fact, two Simon Grays at work, one of whom wrote flops (him), the other of whom churned out turkeys (him), and that neither of them was me –but actors can't, or won't, at least not 99.9999 recurring per cent of them, jump the sinking ship, it's not in an actor's soul, while a playwright – well, that the playwright is the sinking ship, is perhaps to put it too solipsistically – but I had the feeling that while Simon would stand on the prow, hand to forehead in final salute, he would be relieved when the waters closed over his head.

IS SIMON AN ASSASSIN OR A HOMEBODY?

We sat on quite late, then went down the narrow steep staircase out into the alley, and walked down St Martin's Lane to a minicab rank opposite the Arts Theatre. London had that eerie, empty feeling it always has at the tail end of a long public holiday, almost seeming to be at peace with itself, though there were little packs of drunks wheeling about, shouting menacing words into the night sky and half-trying to collide with us on the pavement. They were quite easy to avoid, as their movements were uncoordinated and they were too full of booze to be more than blustering, unfocused belligerence. I assumed that they were English, this being nowadays characteristically English behaviour, home and away, but some were Slavic or Russian, Simon thought. I noticed that as usual he was carrying various briefcases and packages – it's an odd thing that whenever I meet Simon, in whatever circumstances, he is always thus loaded down, and the contents of the packages are impossible to identify with the naked eye, they are shapeless and cumbersome, perhaps laundry, and little packages of luxury foods, treats for his two handsome boxers, Biff and Roxie, a new tablecloth and napkins, or fresh socks for his partner – as well as scripts – and almost certainly the manuscript of his current work in progress, a further volume on the life of Orson Welles. I could always ask him, I suppose, I don't think it would be impertinent, but it would ruin the mystery, if it is indeed a mystery, which it probably isn't – my own guess is completely against mystery – napkins, socks, Orson Welles. Of course, the truth might be more glamorous, a gun – a length of rope with a noose at the end, a bottle of poison, parts of a chainsaw and dossiers on the London theatre critics containing detailed studies of their day-to-day movements and photographs of their loved ones.

HE HAS IT COMING

The odd thing is that, apart from Simon and its effect on him, I don't find myself caring very much. I really don't believe this is hard-won maturity, or a lack of imagination about the content of the reviews I haven't read. Mine were obviously as bad as Simon's, or worse, so what really is going on here? Is it another manifestation of the autism I sometimes suspect is taking me over, a diminishing capacity to respond adequately to situations to which I know the adequate response – play opens, bad reviews, failing box office, play closes, career on the ropes again = deep depression, acute self-loathing, fear of others, possibly hallucinations again. I think, though, the truth is that it doesn't matter because it doesn't matter, that's the truth. Or isolate the bit that does matter, Simon's distress, and abstract it – consider it – it matters, his distress, because you care for him and you're sorry that your play's the cause – but you don't care about the play because you don't care about the man who wrote it, he was twenty years ago and is now a stranger to you – the work's his work, the reviews are for him, let him suffer them, after all he's still quite young, in his late forties, he can take the knocks, pull himself together, go back to the old Olympia portable, begin writing something else – what did he write next? – oh yes, *Hidden Laughter*, that went OK, a good run – eight, nine months – so he's got that to look forward to, along with alcoholism, stomach operations (well deserved), three weeks on nil by mouth (do him good), insolvency (that'll teach him!), Victoria, a happy marriage – all that he's got to look forward to – so let him get on with it, take the rough with the smooth, dream, fret, have fun, etc., back there twenty years ago. I'm here, at home in my study, writing this, Victoria's in bed with George and Toto beside her, all three asleep, Errol's asleep under the table in the hall, and Tom – where's Tom? In the kitchen, on the counter, where I've just put her, her nose in a bowl of those nutritional nuggets that look like mouse droppings, which later she'll probably drop onto the carpet outside the bedroom, where it will look like cat crap. So, all present and correct. All present and therefore correct.

A PENULTIMATE PHONE CALL

The producer, Howard Panter phoned this afternoon to apologize for the reviews. I said I couldn't see how they were his fault. He said what he really meant was that he was sorry people had written such things about me. I said it was OK, thanks, because I didn't know exactly what they'd written and had no intention of finding out. He sounded surprised, slightly disbelieving, also grateful as he wouldn't have to waste pity he needed for Simon and himself, his wife and his backers. He then told me in a reasonably clear, firm voice about the advance. None and falling. The size of the audiences. Almost none and falling. Then we talked for a while about how unfair it all was, how foul for Simon, who had worked so hard, so devotedly. Occasionally he laughed, not entirely hysterically – one of the other nice things about Howard is his sense of the preposterousness of life, and particularly of the business he's in – it sometimes occurs to me that he's in the right business but the wrong branch – he was apparently a superlative stage manager in his youth, has once or twice lit shows when something happened (the sack?) to the lighting designer, no doubt there are many things he could do, most ably, why then suffer the agonies and calamities of a producer? Not a sensible question, really, it's like asking why someone likes being a boss, or goes gambling. Actually, I suspect he was really making a penultimate phone call. In a few days he'll make the ultimate one, announcing the closing of *The Holy Terror*.

SIMON UNBOUND

I went in tonight, and was surprised to see a number of reviews and quotes up. I didn't read them but assume they were favourable – they wouldn't display unfavourable ones outside the theatre, after all – at least I hope they wouldn't – unless of course Simon has ordered them there, as *aides-mémoire*. I thought his performance was extraordinary, as if all the critical hostility had liberated him from inhibitions – no, that can't be the right word, his performance was always uninhibited, but previously it had had an element of strained-for uninhibitedness and therefore an element of disorganization about it. Last night it was completely free, yes, that's the word, and it was also completely under control. A real man, not a magnificent performer, was going through all these self-inflicted ordeals. The house was small, of course, but it too was both free and under control, and made it clear that it was having a good time. A charming and attractive novelist introduced herself to me at the interval, said how much she and her husband – a publisher – were enjoying it, couldn't believe it was closing tomorrow, then said a few words of the sort one likes to hear on these occasions about reviewers. I shook my head sorrowfully, not saying much, but adoring her, of course. I must try and get hold of one of her novels. At supper afterwards Simon was serene, really, like a man who has just realized that he has not only survived but been strengthened by a brutal operation. He mentioned that nobody from the management had been to see him since the first night. But then, we agreed, that's life in the theatre. Perhaps it's life in life, too.

WHEREABOUTS?

I went out. I'm just back. I don't have any sensation of having been out, in fact the only evidence that I've been out is that I'm still wearing my raincoat, which might of course mean, not that I've been out and come back, but that I've put on my raincoat, saw this pad on my desk, sat down and started writing. Well, the evidence for having been out would be in my memory, that's the only place I could hope to find evidence – check my shoes, they're dry, check outside, it's not raining, check my pulse, it's still pulsing, so not dead then, check my . . . what next?

Reconstruct. If I concentrate I'll remember a) whether I went out and b) if I did, where I went to.

What I normally do at about this time, five in the afternoon, is walk up Holland Park Avenue to the Renaissance café, sit at a table on the pavement, order a small espresso in a large cup with hot water on the side, so I can adjust the strength to my pleasing. I smoke a few cigarettes, sometimes read a newspaper or the *Spectator*. Then I order another espresso in a large cup with hot water on the side – in fact, this has become such a routine that it's not surprising that I don't remember it – a routine not only for me but for the young waiters and waitresses at the Renaissance, I just show myself at the door, when I see that one of them has seen me I sit down, and a few minutes later he or she puts my order, that I no longer have to order, on my table. The clammy truth is, though, that I simply do not remember doing any of that just now – can't remember walking up Holland Park Avenue, or back down it, leaving the house or entering it, walking down the stairs to the front door, up the stairs from the front door, I only remember standing in my raincoat, looking down at the pad on the desk, and sitting down to write this. Concentrate. Concentrate. I know. I'll see if I can pick up a clue from the animals. Will they show by their reactions that I've already been out, therefore why am I doing it again?

Toto is asleep on the sofa in the sitting room, lying on her side, her paws tucked in. She is completely absent in sleep, nothing of her stirs at all, no sign even of breathing, her eyes are open but seem completely sightless. I whispered her name, very softly, 'Toto, Toto,' and I thought her muzzle twitched slightly, but I wasn't sure, if it did it was more a wrinkling than a twitch. George is asleep on the sofa in the sitting room – that's confusing, but only because of the words, we have two sitting rooms that open into each other but don't make up one large room, the double doors between them, although wide open, still divide them – so Toto in the back sitting room, by the garden, George in the front room, by the street, both of them in exactly the same sleeping position, but George with her eyes shut and her upper side, the side she isn't lying on, heaving gently – I didn't say her name, because I thought it might wake her, and why should she be woken when she's asleep, possibly happily? There was no sign of Tom – there's usually very little sign of her, as she likes to hide away from the other three, who get on so well together – but she's old now, a little old lady, probably up in the attic room, her favourite spot, sitting neatly, her paws in front of her and nearly crossed, they're so close together. She's become very demanding, I should note, after nightfall, when only the two of us are up and she feels it's safe to roam – then she comes calling on me, if my study door is shut she scratches at it and then makes soft thumping sounds, as if she's butting it with her head – as soon as I let her in she makes a noise, somewhere between a growl and meow, and turns and walks out of the room, and down the stairs, stopping, looking over her shoulder to make sure I'm following her – then into the kitchen – she stands waiting for me to pick her up and put her on the counter, then she walks in a wobbly but eager fashion to her saucer, which, if it's empty, I fill with those nutritional nuggets – I leave her there, go back to my study, and about half an hour later she's at my door, scratching and butting, and down we go again. Sometimes we do this six or seven times, until five or six in the morning, when I go to bed, and I do sometimes get very fed up with it, seeing it as mainly an exercise in power on her part. I mean, there she is, elderly, indeed quite a bit older than I am in her terms, and frail, and refusing to go outside in London – though she does in the country, stays out all night, slaughtering away – but still she commands this younger, more robust and higher – no, better say taller, to eliminate any hint of evolutionary vanity – creature to do her bidding, up and down, up and down I trek, grumbling at her and complaining but nevertheless onto the counter she goes, upstairs I go, then scratch scratch, butt butt, and downstairs we go –

ON THE SCENT

Errol was sitting by the front door, looking important, and as if he
wanted to go out, but when I opened the door for him, he turned
around, walked past me into the kitchen and waited pointedly by
his bowl on the floor, but I wasn't having any of it, because
something had clicked that promised to sort it out, whether I had
been out for a walk or not – first what clicked was a deduction –
or is it induction? – that Errol wasn't waiting by the door because
he wanted to go out, but because he'd only recently come in, and
being Errol, and somewhat lazy and comfort-seeking, hadn't come
very far in and furthermore was warming himself up from being
out by sitting by the nearest radiator in the hall, and this deduction
or induction having clicked into place cerebrally, what further and
positively clicked was the actual memory of Errol coming out with
me when I left the house, and Errol coming in with me when I re-
entered the house, they weren't visual memories, and not specific,
but I felt both experiences in my body, I remembered in my body,
my nervous system, the very recent sensations of going out and in
with Errol, and so I've established I've been out all right. Which
means, for a start, that I can take my raincoat off, as I don't need
to go out again, I've had my walk and my two coffees at the
Renaissance – and now that I know this I find I can taste the coffee
down there in my stomach, taste the memory of it in my mouth,
and furthermore, from the sudden rawness in my stomach, I'm sure
I had not two, but three, as I sometimes do when I'm trying to
think about something, or just feeling relaxed and enjoying the
pavement life – and then comes the reminder, in the form of
stomach rawness and a sudden burp of coffee-flavoured air, a touch
acidic, up the various tubes of my stomach into my mouth, that
three is one too many, one and a half too many I suspect – anyway,

the fact is that I am now receiving positive information from various sources that I have actually been out, and if only I could remember being out, the stages of it, some incident during it, I could put the matter to rest – why should I care, anyway? the important thing for me is that I have to go out every day, preferably when it's still light, breathe in the fumes and pollution of Holland Park Avenue as an alternative to the fumes and pollution of my study, have two or three coffees to upset my stomach, and then come home again. As long as I know I've done it, why really does it matter whether I can remember having done it? I never remember posting a letter, haven't for years, I only know that I've posted it because it's no longer in my hand or my pocket, and come to that why does it matter whether I've posted it, as these days it has only a limited chance of arriving, at least at the address I wrote down on the envelope, and then when and if it gets to the postmen – no, they're not that any more – then when and if it gets to the people who carry the post bags, no, they don't carry them any more and they're not bags, either, the post is wheeled about the pavements in little wagons, from which, one gathers from a recent newspaper report, passers-by help themselves – and why not, as they're left unattended while the postman is at somebody's door, his back turned as he puts somebody's post through somebody else's letterbox.

A SHORT STATEMENT ABOUT THE NATURE OF THE UNIVERSE

The thing to take in is that there are billions upon billions of subjectivities, which represent themselves to you as objectivities and which, when I'm alone in my study, as I am now, can be thought of as one massive objectivity, which we call the world. Sometimes the world is only me, at other times everything except me.

GIVEN THE ABOVE

Yes, it does matter that I don't know for certain whether I went out or not. It's not something I should guess at, or have to work out from clues deduced or induced from the demeanours of our animals. Not knowing might mean that there's something going wrong with me, or my memory – not *or* my memory, I am my memory, therefore –

Here's what I'll do. I'll go out again, clock what's going on on the pavements between here and the Renaissance, note which waiter or waitress sees me at the door, which one brings my coffee, study every passer-by, keep on full alert as I walk home, and I'll – what? Yes, I'll check on the animals, their position and state of consciousness when I leave and register any changes when I come back, then straight up here and put it all down immediately.

I'm off now.

THE ABDUCTION OF TRIXY

And now I'm back and I'm buggered if I'm going to put down anything about being out. I remember it all quite clearly, every moment of it, it was all quite usual in the usual boring way, which is to say that it was all quite interesting in the usual interesting way – there was, for instance – oh, the bag lady, for instance. She stands outside Tesco's, holding out her tin cup in which she hopes you will put either money or cigarettes – I generally put in cigarettes, as I fear that she might spend the money on something that could harm her – when I put the cigarettes in her cup she says, 'Thank you very much, I'm really grateful for that,' and she says it in a dead little mutter, so that it in no way sticks to you, it's as if she doesn't see you, only the cigarettes going into her tin – the fingers around the tin, showing through half-gloves, are darkly stained with nicotine, the fingernails filthy – her whole outfit is a shamble of layers of clothing, but you can't tell which is on top of what, cardigans, sweaters, scarves going in and out of each other like wrapping cloths. She has a face that has sharp life in it, the dark eyes under the half-lowered lids move watchfully, you can see that she makes identifications, categorizes you in ways which aren't only commercial. We sometimes have conversations, it used to be about her dog, which I liked a lot, it was scrawny but not ill-fed, obviously devoted to her, and turned its face up and seemed to be listening to the conversation. We would talk for a while, she quite animatedly about her comings and goings, the dog looking up and listening, and I mainly asking questions – then I'd give her the cigarettes and her voice would change completely, and out would come the dead little mutter about gratitude, as if the moment we moved into the transaction we ceased to be two people who'd been talking, I became an unobserved giver, she a mechanical beggar, receiving. The little moment was quite unpleasant, really, the point of course being to remove embarrassment from the exchange, but actually importing something sullied and dishonourable into it – though I have no idea how either of us could have handled it any better, and it's preferable to her more intimate moments, as when she mutters out of the side of her mouth, as I pass her by, 'You look lovely with your hair like that' – this, I should say, when I've just had it cut, not styled or fashioned or *au bouffant* or whatever the phrase is, I get it cut twice a year, once in December or so, for Christmas, and once in July or August, the effect of it being traumatic both for me, because I feel vulnerable around the back of my neck and at the tops of my ears, and for those who are fond of me, who tend to rear back when they first see me, and to say things like, 'It's taken ten years off you', though what they really mean is that there's much, much more face than we're used to, possibly too much much more – but Annabelle, let me call the bag lady Annabelle, so that I don't keep calling her the bag lady, when she says, 'I like your hair that way', it makes her sound like something from the olden days, when ladies of the night spoke similar words under the street lamps, though of course the effect is unintentional, because Annabelle's a perfectly respectable bag lady, though more ambiguously so now than when she had the dog in her arms or at her feet – the dog, a terrier-like bitch, I can't remember her name, let's call her Trixy, was stolen from her by a smartly dressed middle-aged woman with a foreign accent. She approached Annabelle one morning and praised her for having such a loving and beautiful dog, and then the dog for being so loving and beautiful. She asked to be allowed to hold her and then asked whether Annabelle had had her spayed. Annabelle replied that she'd often thought about it, but really she never seemed to find the time, and probably didn't have enough money. 'Oh,' said the lady. 'How sad. How sad for you and for Trixy. Would you like me to arrange it for you? I know a vet who will do it cheaply – it will cost you nothing, I will pay whatever small sum – and Trixy will be back with you this afternoon, shall we say three, no, we shall say four o'clock, to make sure Trixy is fully recovered from the anaesthetic, so I will see you, we will see you at four o'clock here, on this spot, on the pavement', and away she went, bearing Trixy to her home, perhaps by way of the vet and perhaps not, depending on whether she wanted Trixy to have puppies or not. Her motives were probably clear to herself, she was saving the dog from Annabelle's seemingly louche and feckless lifestyle, and the question as to whether Trixy was content to live in Annabelle's lifestyle probably never occurred to her – or it may have, she may have considered all the moral pros and cons and come to her decision regretfully, as God is sometimes said to come to His. Annabelle put little posters up on the trees along Holland Park Avenue – 'Missing! Trixy was last seen in the company of a well-dressed lady with a foreign accent' sort of thing, and added at the bottom of the poster that she and her granddaughter were missing the dog very much. The granddaughter came as a great surprise to me, I had never thought of Annabelle as a likely mother, let alone grandmother, though once you accept the former, the latter is a perfectly reasonable proposition – and she does seem to have a partner – could he be a husband? – a man of the same indeterminate age as herself, with lanky legs, a narrow face, and long flaxen hair which he sometimes wears tied back in a pigtail –

IS THE GRANDDAUGHTER A BORE?

He has a touch of the dandy about him in a tattered sort of way, and likes to stride urgently along Holland Park Avenue, or lie on his side on the pavement, in front of what was once Harts and is now Tesco's, holding out a tin cup that you have to bend quite low down to, to put money in. He's an artist, when he's at work he sits cross-legged, doing light, lyrical but – to my eye – slightly insipid watercolours of beach scenes and woodland glades. He and Annabelle meet up from time to time and talk to each other.

Sometimes they exchange coins, and one or other of them will go into the telephone kiosk opposite the Renaissance and behave mysteriously with the telephone and the coins, squatting with the telephone in hand, but not talking into it. I avert my eyes if they do it while I'm having coffee at my table, I feel that whatever they're doing, though highly visible through the windows, is also private and probably illegal. On the other hand they may simply be calling the granddaughter, squatting to get down to her size as a way of feeling closer to her – in which case, why not talk to her? Could it be that she's talking to them and they find her too boring – as children often are – to listen to, and so they squat there, holding the telephone away from themselves, until the money runs out. No, I'm sure the kinder explanation, that they're doing something illegal, is the likely one – I just can't work out what it is. But why am I on the subject of Annabelle and her partner? – oh yes, to prove to myself that I went out – I shouldn't call her Annabelle and him 'her partner', he should be dignified with a name too, something Jamesian and floral to go with the aesthete in him – in summer he likes to wear shirts with roses and daisies on them, I seem to recall – rather than a name that represents the grubbier side of his personality, as represented by his appearance. I'm referring here to the nails on the fingers that clasp the cup, the texture of the ponytailed hair – so what about Hyacinth, as in Hyacinth Robinson, in *The Princess Casamassima*?– Hyacinth and Annabelle, yes, that makes for a pleasant-sounding couple.

MIDNIGHT

A feeling of inertia – a lump of flotsam, or is it jetsam I feel like, what is the difference? There is a difference – is flotsam what floats on the surface, and jetsam what's been tossed away, tossed into the waves to be washed this way and that? 'Flot' Old English for float, possibly, while 'jet' from the French *jeter*, to throw – well, that's me, that's what it feels like to be me, something thrown on the waters, a floater and a bobber – but thrown by whom? Fate? Circumstances? The ambition of others? My own ambition, which is what? Well, nothing more, really, than to sit here, doing this.

2 A.M.

I've just dropped my cigarette onto my shirt. I do this more and more, most of my shirts have brown streaks on them, or neat little holes – neat because I rub away the charred edges, in the hope that the neat little holes will appear deliberate, a fashion statement, but really I know, without Victoria having to tell me, that they look as if they've been made by dropped lighted cigarettes. Most of my trousers are similarly marked. Smoking is such a complicatedly dirty habit, staining and soiling and altogether ruining one's garments as well as one's body, and causing so many expenses in such a variety of ways that if I were sensible I would welcome its being banned, but I've only to read a letter in the papers from an anti-smoker or see a couple of them on television to feel that I should regard all stains and holes as wounds won in a fight to the death, though I admit that I'm frightened that one night I'll doze off, well, not exactly frightened, worried, merely worried, that one night I'll wake up in flames.

DAWN

Well, say I could go back, where then, and when? I suppose to Halifax, Nova Scotia, when I was eighteen. I'd stay there for a while, in fact for a decade or two, anyway long enough to learn that I didn't want to leave – but then it would have left me, wouldn't it? Gone on to become what it is today, a pleasant-looking town but where women (men too, I imagine) are forbidden to wear perfume in public places because, like cigarette smoke, it may cause offence to others, and with a beautiful harbour so polluted that you aren't allowed to swim in it. When I was eighteen I used to swim in the harbour every day in summer – the beach was only a hundred yards away, you opened the front door, crossed the road into the woods and followed one of the paths down to the sea – there was a deep shelf, so you could dive straight into the water, which was never warm but always so clean and fresh. Now humans endanger their lives by going into it, fish die in it.

PART THREE

MY PROJECT

Various things are going on that I ought to try writing about, but I always forget – not forget that they're happening or have just happened, but forget to move on to them. So now's the time, why not? Put down a sentence that will get you going – put down two sentences would be even better, because there are two distinct things – a) my book, *The Smoking Diaries*, is about to be published and b) my play, *The Old Masters*, is in rehearsal. So get down to it. Start with b).

HABIT BREAKING

The rehearsal room is in a church hall off Kensington Church Street and is actually within walking distance of here – not that I've actually walked it, Victoria drives me, or I take a taxi. It's a large, handsome room on the first floor and I can smoke in it. I sit on a chair beside another chair with an ashtray on it, and watch the actors, watch Harold at a long table directing the actors, watch and watch, sometimes saying something, but not often. I've grown out of the habit of attending rehearsals. When Harold and I first started together, on *Butley* in whenever it was, the summer of 1969 I think, he would encourage me to speak freely, which I began to do, and continued to do through the next five or six productions, more and more freely, in fact, even though I noticed that he would occasionally engage in a brief, dark-cheeked and scowling tussle with his patience, but always hearing me out, thinking about what I had said, then agreeing or disagreeing, and on we'd go – but when we got to the seventh, think, think – *Butley, Otherwise Engaged, The Rear Column, Close of Play, Quartermaine's Terms, The Common Pursuit* – that's six, the seventh – yes, it was the seventh, *Life Support*, I was in hospital while he was in rehearsal, and when I got out I was too ill to see the play until late in its tour, at Bath, I seem to remember. The next play we did was about three or four – no, I must check this, for the moment just say several, several years later – *The Late Middle Classes*, when I was almost but not quite well, but found myself not going into rehearsal much. A few times I started out for rehearsals, which were in Watford, but turned back quite early in the journey, though if I actually got as far as Watford Station I usually went on to the rehearsal room, where I sat awkward and tongue-tied, and left as soon as I could. So what started as an enforced abstinence through illness turned into a habit, really, and now emotionally I'm in the habit of not going to rehearsals of *The Old Masters*. This habit I force myself to break every single day. I cajole and bully myself out of the front door and into the car or taxi, and usually I ask Victoria or the taxi driver to drop me off a little way from the church hall, so that I can pretend to myself I'm not going to go in. I do now and then walk past the entrance to the driveway, walk around and around and up and down for a while – the weather has been lovely since the first day – smoking and thinking that I'm thinking, but really what I'm doing is not going in yet. In the end I never get in before three or four in the afternoon, and so only have to sit there through a couple of hours or so, which is still too long, by a couple of hours or so. It's not that it's boring, or that I'm inactive – I have to do cuts, some of them quite large, and a few small rewrites, there's always something going on to watch and think about and

I do my best to do all that's required of me, but the difficulty is that – that – the truth is that I'm not really very interested. Not interested enough. Although there are many passing pleasures to be found in

HAROLD AND CO.

observing Harold's powers of concentration, for instance, and the clarity of his intelligence, his quick sympathy with the actors as well as the command of his presence. He says he's exhausted the moment he leaves, and quite tired in the morning when he gets up, but the moment he's there, in the rehearsal room, he feels galvanized, enjoys every minute – 'every bloody minute' – scarcely notices the time passing. The day's work over, the adrenalin drains away, and he feels tired and elderly again. Then of course it can never be dull watching actors like these at work, the cunning and expertise of Peter Bowles, the complete originality of Edward Fox – he is, in a sense, perfectly miscast, Berenson being a man of great mental agility with a tongue to match – 'If a panther could speak, he would speak like Berenson,' someone who knew him well said of him – emotionally mercurial, in all his aspects vain as well as arrogant – Edward is temperamentally the opposite, well, he has, like all of us, his own vanity and arrogance, but his thought processes as revealed in rehearsal are eccentric and seemingly spasmodic, his speech made up of half-sentences, strange, almost goofy smiles, uneasy gestures and brooding silences. Probably the only thing he has in common with Berenson is his size and his neatness of presence – what he is creating isn't in accord with historical reality, inasmuch as we have it, but a character unique to Edward and yet of absolute integrity within the terms of the play –

unlike Berenson in almost all his aspects, he will give us the equivocal moral being that Berenson was – well, that my Berenson is – and a bafflingly perverse opponent for Duveen, as unlike Berenson as a character as Peter Bowles is unlike Edward as a rehearsing actor, Peter being methodical, detailed, openly fretful, his eye alert to contradictions in the text, his manner apparently easy and generous but also dogged, in fact positively stubborn – a question once raised is a question that he will make sure is returned to and returned to, however eager Harold and the other actors are to press on, until it has been solved to his satisfaction – which is when he has more than a sniff of how he will say the lines in performance weeks from now.

Peter and Edward treat each other with great respect, equal beasts of a different species, but have in common a care for outward appearances, even in rehearsals. Most actors in rehearsal turn up in loose-fitting old clothes, comfortable shoes. Peter and Edward, tall and dark, small and blond, are always immaculately dressed, formally dressed, in much the same style – tailored jackets, creased trousers, dapper shoes, shirt and tie, frequently waistcoats. Yesterday afternoon they both had neatly folded handkerchiefs protruding from their top pockets, like a pair of period philanderers – you expect them to be joined by Terry-Thomas, and Leslie Phillips in his heyday. I find the effect very charming, as I sit, slumped, pot-bellied, in my chair, wearing an open shirt over a half-open shirt, baggy trousers, espadrilles, cigarette hanging from my fingers, mouth half-open in a half-yawn, my proper companions Annabelle and Hyacinth, hanging about on a pavement outside Tesco's, is where I probably looked as if I should have been.

I've just remembered that Peter, Edward and I are all the same age, sixty-seven, Barbara Jefford is thereabouts or more so, Harold is more so – three actors, the writer and the director all between sixty-seven and seventy-five. The other two actors, Sally Dexter and Steven Pacey are three decades our junior. Is this desirable? And if so, to whom? And why?

These two, Sally Dexter and Steven Pacey, are young and therefore desirable – no, young and also desirable is what I intended to write. They are also talented actors, which makes them doubly desirable and are already playing their scenes together with great charm, and sexily – or, more interestingly, flirtatiously. What is lovely about Sally in the part is how versatile she is as a woman – girlish, maternal, sisterly, a mistress, a daughter, a wife, depending on the immediate needs of the men (and the woman) she's with, almost a perfect female in Goethe's accounting, plus the gift for deception and a weakness for jewellery, which make her in fact more perfect than Goethe's perfect woman – a woman without a weakness being too frightening to contemplate, a monster, inevitably – what would sex with such a woman be like, I wonder? How could you make love to a woman without a weakness? Probably she'd have to make love to you, perfectly? Would this mean, with infinite variety? But she'd have to desire you surely, and if she desired you she couldn't be perfect, you would be her weakness – well, that might work.

ON A HIGHER LEVEL

The German professor of German at Dalhousie University fifty years ago was Frau Doktor Richter, the widow of the original professor of German, who had been knocked down and killed while cycling towards his classes one spring morning some, oh, let's say sixty years ago – very few people bicycled in Halifax, Nova

Scotia, in those days, so I suppose the driver was taken by surprise, as was the good Doktor. Frau Doktor Richter was almost certainly the only person in the whole of Nova Scotia, possibly the whole of Canada, qualified to take over his position. She was in her late sixties when I attended her seminars, stout and serious and handsome, with twinkling blue eyes and a quick smile and no sense of humour – though this is probably unfair, as I only understood her when she spoke English, and her English, though accurate, was slow and pains-taking – pains-giving too, when returning one of my completely bogus essays composed in a language that was mainly guesswork – I used to put an *ich* and *er* at the end of English words, and sometimes I spoke English with a thick German accent taken from American movies about the Gestapo – the only written phrase in which I had any confidence, and so employed repeatedly, was '*Aber das kann ich nicht*' which means, or I hope it means, 'But that I do not know.' Her passion in life was for the literature of her country, and her passion in that literature was for Goethe, whose poetry and novels I found it difficult to understand, as my reading German wasn't much of an advance on my writing and speaking German, and Frau Doktor Richter insisted that we read everything in the original. Fortunately she conducted the most interesting parts – the biographical parts – of her seminars in translation, first a long paragraph in German, then a few short sentences of paraphrase in English, which is how I came to discover that Goethe at seventy had some kind of relationship with a girl of seventeen, whose name I can't remember but might come back to me. What kind of relationship? I asked Frau Doktor. 'It vos a ferry luffink relationship,' she said, twinkling at me solemnly through her glasses. 'Very loving?' 'Ferry luffink, yess.' Everyone in the seminar waited for the next question, which I felt obliged to ask. 'Was it a sexual relationship?' 'Yess,' she said, 'yess, it voss. But only on ze higher leffel!' At that age – I was eighteen – I had only had sex on one level, and it was a pretty low one, since it was with myself, but I knew instinctively that Frau Doktor Richter was making the best of a bad job, or a good job if you were Goethe, who was the first old man I ever envied. I wish I could remember the girl's name – it was oddly ugly, even when spoken by the soft-voiced Frau Doktor.

Her name was Vulpius. Kristina Vulpius. I'm pretty sure that was it, although probably not how it is spelt.

TOOTHACHE

If I'd been told then, at the end of the seminar, that one day I'd be sitting in rehearsals of my own play with a famous writer directing in it a clutch of highly regarded actors, would I have been envious? – well, that's absurd, how can one envy the self that is fifty years away, and that one's going to end up with or as anyway? What I really mean I suppose, is the other way round, how I envy that eighteen-year-old, and wish he hadn't ended up as me, sitting in rehearsals etc. in the afternoons of the spring of 2004 – or indeed sitting in my study, writing this. I'd like everything else to be the same, my context, my environment, my world – Victoria, George, Toto, Errol and Tom, Harold, Antonia, all my friends – but at the centre of it a different, kinder, more intelligent, more energetic – that above all – more energetic me, who had behind him a different lifetime, a lifetime of usefulness, of practical goodness – not that there's been much theoretical goodness either – and large-spiritedness, so much of me feels ungrown, so much of me unkind – but it's never too late, it is always said, never too late to change. Oh yes, it is. But that doesn't mean that it's too late to do good, find out where help is wanted and give it. No, it isn't, but given what I know of me, of my inertia and feebleness of will, any excuse will do, even my vices – yes, I would certainly go forth and do good in the world, if only my vices would let me. Alas, I am what I am, alas. Know what I mean?

I'm writing down these thoughts because they tend to intrude more and more often, and not in searingly painful stabs like flashes of guilt, but in a dull and aching, almost boring way, like an old toothache that has returned without your noticing it really – and then it is sapping away at you, you pat it and stroke it with your tongue, it subsides, but still throbbing, and suddenly there it is again – this is what goes on in me morally, if it is moral, during rehearsals, so that though I take in all the pleasant things, like the actors and the director going about their work, enjoy the jokes, the rides back in Harold's taxi when we discuss the text, for instance – through it all the moral toothache is throbbing away until it is all I really think about, why am I not a good man, why have I not done better, why am I sitting here chain-smoking in a rehearsal of my play, lazily surveying all the excuses for not having done good in my life – oh yes, because of my vices etc. I suppose the soft war between the entertainment of the rehearsals and the discomfort of the moral tooth settles into a truce, which is really indifference, when it comes down to it.

AND A GLIMPSE OF THE UNIQUE REAL THING

at least until Barbara Jefford has a scene, then I become riveted, even at this stage of rehearsals, I can't remember seeing anything like it in a rehearsal room – I don't mean that she's doing anything astounding, in fact I suspect that I'm the only one who sees it so clearly, not because I've any special gifts, or am more finely attuned to acting than the others, but because I wrote the part, I know Mary for what she is as a character, and Barbara Jefford isn't impersonating her, acting her – when she's fluffing her lines, fumbling for a word, she is emotionally so straight and direct that she already seems to be Mary Berenson, it's Mary Berenson that can't find the word, has lost the line –

So that's b) done with, on to a).

TRUE COMPLIMENTS?

It's hard to tell with books, because no curtain goes up, no lights go down, reviews start to appear before you're actually on the shelves (or shelf), and the publishing party, launch, launch it's called, can take place before or after the official publication date, which therefore seems quite arbitrary, and has to be remembered as a date, which I can never do – but there was a party, launch, and it took place this evening, in a room at the top of the Groucho Club. It wasn't a small room, but it seemed so because there were so many people in it, all of them friendly and shouting quite loudly. At a certain point, quite early on, my editor, Ian Jack, made a muttering speech in Scotty – it was very flattering, from what I could make out of it, too flattering to put down here, and he looked sincere – I suppose he had to, I mean it would have been a poor show to have one's editor speaking well of you in a manner that was noticeably insincere, of course the great thing about Scotty is that it's a language in which it appears impossible to tell lies, which is why so many of our most successful current politicians speak it, whether they're from Scotland or not – would

Blair be an interesting exception, I don't know whether he's Scotty in the sense that I am (in the blood but not the bones) but I do know that he was educated there, even so there isn't a trace of it in his speech, which is why he produces the opposite of the usual effect, his every sentence sounding like a lie even when he's telling the truth, although I don't know how we'd know he was telling the truth – how do you distinguish between sentences that are actual lies and sentences that merely sound like lies? – he has the liar's trick, too, of widening his eyes when delivering his real as well as his bogus lies, so you get no help in that direction, whereas if he'd taken advantage of his education to learn Scotty he'd probably also have learnt to shift his eyes about when speaking it, thus reinforcing the appearance of truth – Ian Jack, for instance, in his little speech about me, seemed to manage the almost impossible feat, in a room jam-packed with people, of not looking a single person in the eye, his eyes shifted about at stomach level, or perhaps a jot lower – of course I may have got it all wrong, perhaps almost nobody in the room believed what he was saying about me but me. Anyway when he finished he gestured to me, and I said a few words – very few. Enough to make up three short sentences, in which I complimented myself on having Granta for a publisher, Ian Jack for an editor and Victoria for a wife. I don't know whether my eyes shifted and my accent had a burr in it, but I was telling the truth on all counts. Nobody else spoke. The party went on. We came home. That's all I'm going to put down about *The Smoking Diaries*, for one thing there is a far more pressing matter to consider –

HIS CHARMS

Now in my view he is perfect – fat, round, black, long-haired, his eyes are little saucers and his walk a dainty waddle. He started life with us as a stray, his first appearance, via the dog flap in the kitchen door, was under the kitchen table, his next was on the kitchen table – he wasn't chased to either of these positions, in fact George, our only dog at this time, accepted his presence from the start, seeming almost to usher him in through the flap, and would often be sitting at his side when Victoria or I, or both together, came into the kitchen, and though Tom, our elderly but dapper – now very old, and still dapper – short-haired female cat with white splodges on her chin, and on her sides and her ankles, hated him, she kept out of his way, as if he were the landlord and she the sitting tenant. At first we shooed him out, thinking that such a portly, indeed pampered-looking, creature must have a substantial residence close by, and that he was merely slumming in our kitchen, or had taken a barrier-breaking fancy to George, but our shooings never flustered him, he seemed to be exiting through the flap by choice, as if remembering an appointment, and sometimes the flap would still be swinging from his departure when he re-entered, and settled comfortably under a chair. Eventually we found him in other rooms, the sitting room, the bedroom, nestled in one of George's beds, or if he was in the kitchen he would be polishing off one of Tom's meals, or eating with George from George's bowl. I knew from the very first encounter that he was here to stay, and I admit that I wanted him to stay. I admired him for his insouciance, his implacable will, his evident sweetness of disposition, and his good looks, and though I agreed with Victoria that his habit of spraying in the areas which he thought Tom had laid claim to was disgusting and unhygienic,

I persuaded her that with certain amendments of a surgical kind –. So it was settled. But before we took him to the vet, which we looked on as a sort of adoption process, we put up posters on trees and lamp-posts in the neighbourhood, describing him and advising where he could be found. They stayed up for two weeks, and when no one came forward, we took him across the road to the vet and made him ours. Now he sleeps on our bed with George and Toto, allows George to hump him before meal-times, allows Tom a fairly free passage and was among the first to welcome Toto into the house – when he's not lying nose to nose with George, he's likely to be lying nose to nose with Toto, or sitting at my feet in the study. He would like to sit on my lap, I know, but I'm allergic to his long hair – when I stroke him, which I can't resist doing, my hand comes up in welts, and my eyes run, but apart from that he is, as I say, perfect, and I adore him. Nevertheless, nevertheless – I am not going to say that I've stopped loving him, but I find his behaviour harder and harder to accept, it's beginning to affect my feelings, to tinge them with a certain amount of revulsion. He's just come into the room, has gone under the desk, is brushing against my ankles – so I can't possibly go on with this.

A STAR IS BORN

I'm currently – even as I write this – being filmed. There's a camera on me, being held and pointed by a tall, pleasant, smiling young man called Patrick. Crouched beside him Margy, the director, holds a metal box with a screen in it which shows her what Patrick the cameraman is filming. Behind Patrick stands Andy, a shortish young man, also generally smiling, who is recording the sounds of my typewriter, the keys of which are clogged from months of disuse. I am in my study, at my desk, at my typewriter, pretending to be me, doing something I always do, although I haven't actually done it for a while – I wonder how long they'll want me to go on doing it, I find it slightly umiliating – what does it mean to feel umiliated? – to umiliate yourself? – I'm writing umiliate because the 'h' on this machine, one of my old Olympia portables, is beginning to stick – now I'm getting te old rytm back, te singalong of te typewriter, the trut is tat it's suc a long time since I sat at one, aving mainly worked by long and on yellow pages for my recent plays and diaries, and so te abit, wic I tougt would be te abit of a lifetime as, it would appear, would it not, become lost to me, but ten again ere it is growing and saping sentences wit every downward stomp of my two fingers. O, I've certainly lost my old ligtness of touc, well, it wasn't particularly ligt, certainly not dainty, but a great deal less stompy tan tis – I ave the feeling, toug, that now the 'h' is beginning to sort itself out – my insistent beating down on it is getting it used to stamping its mark on the paper and then releasing itself, if slightly sluggishly, back into its slot – here we go, look at thathhhhhere we go, I'm off with a flouris of hhhhhhhhhs. Well, I'm off camera now, they've gone, Margy the director, and Andy the sound man, and Patrick, the cameraman, gone to their world of light, and I alone sit lingering here, a private man again, in sole possession of his study, his pad and pen, his 'h' and his life.

ERECT IN THE GARRICK CLUB

It all began in the Wolseley, when I joined Victoria and some friends for dinner – she'd come from the theatre, I forget what she'd seen, and I'd come from home where I'd been doing I forget what. I pushed through the doors, as they used to say in the sort of books I once loved, I pushed through the doors of the restaurant, stood gaping around, and had just spotted in a far corner the bushy hair above the beautiful and beloved face when Alan Yentob sprang in front of me, seized my hand and stroked it, saying that this very evening, a mere few hours ago, in fact, he'd finished reading *The Smoking Diaries*. 'I'm sure we can do something with it,' he said, speaking from under the hat of the Head of Culture – I forget his exact title at the BBC – 'What do you think, would you like us to do something with it?' I said yes, I'd love them to do something with it, as long as it didn't consist of my appearing on one of those panel discussions with the sort of people who use words like 'comfortable', 'uncomfortable' – 'I don't feel comfortable with this' – 'It makes me uncomfortable' – 'this' or 'it' not being a chair, or a hat or a thumb, but someone else's attitude, behaviour, piece of writing – 'I just', yes, there's usually a 'just', functionally strange but effective – it manages to intensify without in any way defining the moral power of not being 'comfortable', the implication being, I suppose, that these people possess a balance so delicately moral that it can only express itself in that softly self-centred way – a bit like Lady Bertram in *Mansfield Park* when talking about her physical well-being, but at least we know what it is (her sofa) Lady Bertram is making herself comfortable on, while these people, yes, let me call them 'these people!' are making themselves comfortable on their vanity and your good manners – we never say back to them, 'Well, if you're not comfortable with it, why don't you adjust your position?' because we know that in fact they're saying to us, 'I'm not comfortable with it, so kindly adjust your position' – of course, I didn't go on to Alan Yentob about 'these people' and 'comfortable' and so forth, I merely said I didn't want to be on a book panel, or have *The Smoking Diaries* touched in any way by a book panel. 'No, no,' he said, 'a proper programme. I know there's a programme in it somewhere.' He took down my telephone number on the sort of slip of paper you find in a corner of your jacket pocket three months later and put it in his jacket pocket. 'I'll call you,' he said, 'in the next few days.'

Victoria asked me what I'd been talking to Alan Yentob about. I said, oh, something about wanting to do a programme on *The Smoking Diaries*, he says he's going to phone again in the next few days to discuss it, but he won't – I was pretty sure of this, as I've dished out my telephone number to many people over the last few years, some of whom wrote it down in impressive-looking Filofaxes, others punched it impressively into their mobiles, both lots passing it straight on to various commercial enterprises, judging by the number of unsolicited phone calls I've received from double-glazing people, for instance, which I suppose is better than the sort of stuff I've started getting through the email – offers of penis-expanding drugs, vastly superior to Viagra, they claim, delivering an erection within minutes and sustaining it for four days. But how would one cope with a four-day erection? One would have to get a whole new wardrobe of loose garments, or stay in one's home, probably confine oneself to one's study, though perhaps I could go to the Garrick. Could they black-ball you for strutting about with an erection. But why strut? Why not saunter? – saunter about with an erection for four whole days at the Garrick Club, cut some ice at last, though not necessarily. On one of the few occasions I've had lunch there I sat at the long table next to a famously elegant, in clothes and prose, novelist, who got up in the middle of someone else's sentence, announced that he needed a piss, unzipped his fly as if he were going to take it there, over his, or possibly my, *crème brûlée*, then headed towards the door, half-cocked. He returned a few minutes later, zip still down, fly gaping, I noticed that both his shoes were wet, so I wondered, I wondered – well, we shall find out, as Larkin says in . . . 'The Old Fools' i'm pretty sure.

THE IMPORTANCE OF PEEING IN THE RIGHT PLACE, AT THE RIGHT TIME

Alan Yentob, who I knew wasn't going to phone me in the next day or so, phoned me in the next day or so, and we arranged to have dinner, plus wives, at an Italian restaurant above a pub somewhere off Notting Hill Gate. A good choice for food, a lousy one for conversation. It was crowded, and the acoustics, as is the fashion in London these days, were dreadful – you had to strain to hear a sentence from the person next to you, and had to shout to make yours heard it was nevertheless a relaxed and pleasant dinner, Alan's wife, Philippa, charming to look at, charming to try to hear – the play of her features etc. when she said how much she'd enjoyed *The Smoking Diaries*, if it was *The Smoking Diaries* she'd enjoyed. Alan outlined his idea for a programme, which would consist of conversations with me, intermingled with lots of readings aloud by me of passages by me, and perhaps visits to some of the locations – the book starts in Barbados, I pointed out, in one of the world's most charming hotels – no, he said, the BBC couldn't run to that, besides we didn't have the time, he already had the dates for the programme, it would be transmitted in the first week of June, so we'd have to start making it straight away, he'd introduce me to the director he had in mind, a talented and intelligent young woman he was sure I'd like, we'd work out a schedule, could I be free from next week on? I said I would clear my diary of its empty spaces immediately. From then on we bellowed and mimed our way through other matters, mutual friends, past experiences, among them a film he'd commissioned me to write, called *Unnatural Pursuits*, in which Alan Bates played me, right down to my chain-smoking, my pigeon-toed gait and my wheezy laugh, as I followed the fortunes of one of my plays from London to New York by way of Los Angeles and Dallas. There is a scene in a hotel in Dallas when I'm slumped in my bedroom at seven in the morning trying to drink away my hangover with a bottle of champagne. A piano strikes up, discordantly and as if in my skull. I totter out to the landing, stare down into the lobby. A group of Texans in stetsons, dinner jackets and long dresses are gathered around the piano, about to sing. I raise my glass to fling it down at them, open my mouth to shout an obscenity just as they launch into 'The Yellow Rose of Texas' and I find myself, to my astonishment, joining in – yes, Alan, hungover, bawling 'The Yellow Rose of Texas' down into the lobby of the Hyatt Hotel in Dallas at seven in the morning, is one of my favourite moments in both our careers, and it came about because Alan Yentob and I had happened to be standing in adjacent urinals at a BAFTA function, and as conversation is mandatory in these circumstances, he asked me if there was anything I'd like to write for the BBC. So if you want to see yourself on the television screen, either as yourself or as impersonated by an actor of great wit, charm and style, get a stall next to Alan Yentob in a BAFTA lavatory, or stand gaping in a restaurant until he springs in front of you.

I JUSTIFY MY DRIVING HABITS

It's a sunny afternoon, and I've just come back from the churchyard at the end of our street, where I sat on my favourite bench and answered questions put to me by Alan Yentob, who was very relaxed and gentle except for a small patch when he probed away at my driving arrangements – my arrangements being that Victoria drives me when I need to be driven. He pointed out how in my book I describe Victoria driving herself and all the animals down to our cottage in Suffolk, while I travelled down by train, first-class smoker. He seemed to find this in some way unfair on Victoria, a lot of people do, but should they bother to ask Victoria herself, she would explain that the last person she wants on a long car journey is me – well, perhaps not the last person, she wouldn't want a car-jacker, for example, but I'm the last person among the people she knows well. I'm impatient, irritable, and fill the car with my smoke, so obviously she prefers driving along listening to an opera and talking to her companions of choice, the animals. As for driving me about London, that's an entirely different matter, a source of pride to her, as if, really, I were a large dog, a bloodhound or a beagle, perhaps, apart of course from the cigarette, though, come to think of it, beagles have an infamous connection with the tobacco industry, involuntary chain-smokers used to establish a link between smoking and cancer. I'm against banning smoking, but I'm for banning scientists who force dogs to smoke, I'm for jailing them, actually.

I can't remember whether the interview/conversation with Alan Yentob followed the lines of the paragraph above, from Victoria's driving me, the rights and wrongs of it, to smoking beagles, but it was rhapsodic in that sort of way, but given – I hope – a sense of purpose by Alan Yentob's, well, rather bloodhoundy or beagly manner, tracking a scent of a thought or an argument even if it looped in haphazard circles and brought us back to the side of where we began.

HOIST BY MY OWN PETARD

The most difficult thing about my reading aloud to the camera is that I have to smoke, and to smoke all the time, a matter of continuity, as I always light a cigarette at the beginning of a passage – it's called *The Smoking Diaries*, after all, and as the publishers, Granta, have with great enterprise issued books of matches with the title and my name on it, I'm anxious to get them on camera as often as possible, striking the matches sideways for maximum exposure, then holding the match-book casually towards the camera as I lift the lighted match to the cigarette between my lips, a manoeuvre which, having used a lighter for the last thirty years, I'm not very expert at. I often blow the match flame out before I've lit the cigarette and have to do it over again – but once I've started to smoke, this is the point, I'm committed, I can't be seen to be smoking at the beginning of a sentence and then, when the filming stops suddenly because, for instance, I can't think of a way to end the sentence, be without a cigarette when the filming begins again we would have a brief but bewildering passage in which I'd be smoking, then not smoking, then smoking – viewers will wonder what is going on, then think the conversation is completely phoney, which it is, at least in the pretence of flowing seamlessly along – so, so, so having always to have a cigarette on the go is beginning to have the effect of aversion therapy, really, eyes smarting, throat dry and raw, head aching, stomach acidy – hoist by my own petard is one of the phrases that springs to mind – I had a cigarette between my lips even when I walked up the street to have my usual coffee at the Renaissance, Patrick the cameraman running backwards in front of me, Margy running backwards beside me out of frame. Normally I find it difficult to walk far without wheezing to a stop, but for some reason, when a slow, stately gait, with pauses, would have been the most convenient style, I found myself pattering along in my espadrilles at three times my normal speed, and all the time puff-puff on the cigarette – then back twenty yards because I'd zipped past the camera without realizing, so another cigarette, more puffing and pattering – during one of the botched attempts to keep the camera and Margy in front of me, a man who was standing by the bus stop, vaguely taking me in, then noticing the camera, then connecting me to the camera, spat at me – he was rather seedy-looking, it's true, with some wispy blond stuff on his chin that wasn't quite a beard and wearing battle fatigues, are they called? – khaki trousers with what looked like camouflage patches on them – a lumber-jacket sort of shirt, altogether seedy-looking, military-style aggressive and spitting at me. I felt that I had nothing in common with him at all, and yet understood completely why he wanted to spit at a figure who looked as louche as himself but went around with a camera trained on him, from the belief that not a minute of his life should go unrecorded for posterity, and furthermore must have had the funds to ensure that it wouldn't be, who did I think I was, who do I think I am? On top of which the waiters at the Renaissance didn't like the camera either, perhaps they thought I was an investigative reporter who had been undercover and was now emerging to expose them as – as what? I finally persuaded them that the camera was for me, not them, and was allowed to sit down. They then brought me the wrong coffee, the 'they' here being the indignant pronoun, because the waiter concerned who had brought me the right coffee – a small espresso in a large cup, a jug of hot water on the side – day after day for months, now brought me a revoltingly thick-foamed cappuccino. Instead of sipping my usual sophisticated coffee in my usual relaxed and sophisticated manner, I sat stirring what looked like a child's pudding while gazing in an appalled way at what would be for the audience nothing in particular. How would they know that in fact it was at Patrick the cameraman standing in the middle of the road with his camera aimed at me, and seemingly on the verge of taking a step forward under a bus coming down the avenue, or backward under a bus coming up the avenue. Let's hope they decide not to use that bit of film. And also the bit of film they shot of me in the study, when I thought they'd finished. I was slumped in the armchair, and patting my stomach, which felt and looked rather bloated, when from some instinct I turned my face and, yes, there he was, with his beard and his camera and his pleasant smile, filming. Tomorrow – something's happening tomorrow, fortunately I can't remember what it is. I'll take a sleeping pill and see if there's some cricket on television, there's bound to be cricket somewhere in the world where it's not three in the morning, our time.

EXKIEWS MY VUSE

A taxi arrived this afternoon to take me to rehearsals. I was surprised to see it, as I hadn't consciously ordered it, but I suppose I shouldn't have been further surprised to find Margy already in it, along with Andy the sound man and Patrick the cameraman and his camera. They had a newspaper for me to pretend to be reading – the *Guardian*, of course – and had got permission from the driver for me to smoke. I wanted only to pretend to read the *Guardian*, but inevitably found myself reading the sort of article that is precisely the reason I never read the *Guardian*. When we got to the rehearsal room, I had to wait in the taxi while they arranged themselves so that they could shoot me getting out, then they shot me going up the stairs, then pushing the door open, then they went away and I went in – there was Harold at the table, staring down at a script which he was tapping with his finger like a schoolmaster, and Peter Bowles and Edward Fox standing in front of him, like schoolboys who had been caught cheating. 'What have you been up to?' he asked, as he always does – an exciting formulation, I find, suggesting activities he couldn't conceivably expect me to confess to. 'Nothing much,' I said, 'just doing this BBC thing –' 'BBC thing? What BBC thing?' – he has an extraordinary memory, able to recall passages of poetry, Shakespeare, not passages, merely, but pages, I envy him the gift enormously, thinking how useful it would be if ever I were taken hostage – all I've got to keep me sane in captivity are fragments, most of which have only stuck because I hate them so much – 'Sir, no man's enemy forgiving all, but will his negative inversion be prodigal' – think of that running through your head time after time, as you struggle to recall the first line of a poem you love – and if at last you manage to get going with 'Busy old fool, unruly Sun,/Why dost thou thus' and you romp along to 'Nor hours, days, months, which are the rags of time' something sidles in, and you go – 'Which are the rags of time, that with this strange exkiews? Pardoned Kipling and his views/And will pardon Paul Caud-elle- uh/Pardons him for writing welle-uh' and you check yourself and go back, 'Time that with this strange ex-cuse –/Pardoned Kipling and his vuse –/And will pardon Paul Claudel/Pardons him for writing wel'. It's hopeless, you realize, you can't get it to rhyme properly without mangling the last words of each line, whichever way you go at it, but on at it you'll go and on, writhing in your captivity, struggling to make rhyme and reason – consider the meaning of those two lines, see a classical statue, TIME holding out a PARDON to three figures bending in supplication at her feet, Kipling, Yeats and Paul Claudel, each carrying a basket of VIEWS, peeping out like malformed babes – it's called personification, I think – EARTH, receive an honoured GUEST – best room, long stay – William YEATS laid to rest de dum de dum de dum de dah! The lines usurp all the lines by other poets you cherish, entangle you in frustration and ugly thoughts, better hope that you succumb quickly to Stockholm syndrome, come to share your captors' literary favourites, might be educational if they're Muslims, they'll pack your head with all those beautiful passages from the Koran that Mr Blair reads to himself every night, and then they'll saw it off in front of a camera. Perhaps Margy and Alan Yentob have something like that in mind for me, Alan says that the end of the programme is going to be unusual, and I've become very obedient, so if they ordered me, now Simon, time to kneel down, we'll put something over your eyes and around your wrists, now push your head forward a little, there's a good Simon, and Alan will –

AND SEATED AT THE END OF AN AISLE

Oh yes, Harold's extraordinary memory for lines – he has the gift, actor's gift, no, it's more than an actor's gift, it's no doubt not unique to Harold, but he's the only person I know who has it to the extent that he has it, and it may be a condition of his capacious, long-range memory that he has trouble remembering the answers you gave to questions he asked only yesterday – 'What BBC thing?' is a good example – I'd been into the BBC thing with him quite a few times, because I knew that at some point Alan Yentob and Margy will want to involve Harold himself or get his permission to involve the production – how could they not? After all, at the centre of the film of *The Smoking Diaries* is a wretch who's just put a turkey called *The Holy Terror*, on a West End stage and might shortly be putting on another West End stage another turkey, called *The Old Masters*, whose first night falls on the last day of filming – so for one thing they need to persuade Harold to let them into the theatre, to capture the audience's response at the curtain call, to follow us about beforehand and afterwards – It's unpleasant to write this, it brings the event nearer, the lights going down, the audience rustling and heaving like a small sea, and there are the reviewers, sitting on the aisles, like school prefects and rodents – I can't think of any rodents that sit on aisles, so let's leave it at school prefects.

DIFFERENT MOODS, DIFFERENT TENSES

Victoria's going to bed, and I'm doing this. Let's put it in the present tense, to help me remember.

So here we are, Victoria and Antonia and I, walking down Panton Street, having come into it from around the corner and down the street, whatever it's called, where there's a wine bar. It's a loathly wine bar, everyone seems to enter it shouting and already drunk and sitting solitary and dark in its unsavoury hurly-burly is Harold, at a table in a corner, with an opened bottle of white wine and some glasses, waiting for us. I went to the bar and ordered a Diet Coke, which they served from a tap into a tankard-sized glass, and then threw into it ice and plastic lemon-rind in order to kill off the effervescence without cooling the liquid, I suppose – it was warm and fetid and looked as if something frog-like might stick its head above the surface. I left it on the counter with an emphatic gesture of disgust and went to the table, where Harold spoke calmly through the din about the actors, he said that they were in 'excellent nick, really looking forward to the evening' etc., swallowed a few times as he always does when he's nervous – you actually see his Adam's apple bob up and down – drained off his glass, and said that we'd better go. Yes, we agreed, we'd better go. So up the road we went, around the corner into Panton Street. Suddenly, in Panton Street, running backwards in front of us were the now, to me, familiar figures of Margy the director, Patrick the cameraman and Andy the sound man – I wore on my face, for the camera's sake, the most unlikely first-night smile of my life, my mouth stretching, it would have been from ear to ear, in the old phrase, if my ears weren't so far from my lips. Waiting outside the theatre was a pack of newspaper photographers etc. They spotted the playwright, and therefore star of the evening, Simon Gray with his lady-wife, Victoria, on his arm, ran towards them, then accelerated past them to the Pinters, who obliged in their respective styles, Harold by turning his head away, Antonia by smiling absent-mindedly. The autograph hounds followed the photographers to the Pinters, not so much pushing past the playwright and his lady-wife as shoving them sideways, into the gutter.

Margy and Patrick the cameraman stuck to their drab task, which was to follow us into the lobby, and then down the little hall into a private room, where they left us. Harold and Antonia arrived a few minutes later, most of their clothes intact. We sat not saying very much, although there was some coughing, because I filled the room with smoke at astonishing speed, almost as soon as I lit up, in fact. The stage manageress, whose name is Pea – 'What's your real name?' I asked her once. 'I'm not telling you,' she said. 'Why do you think I changed it?' – so in her past is a name to which she prefers the name Pea – came in to announce that the show was about to begin. Harold had secured the box that was directly off the private room, so he and Antonia had only to move a few steps. I had secured a couple of seats at the back of the dress circle, rodents', no, prefects' seats on an aisle, close to an exit, which took some getting to, we just made it as the house lights were going down. I picked out Barbara Jefford making her way to her on-stage chair, sitting down, stage lights up, and there she was, in the sunshine in the garden of I Tatti, as settled as if she'd been there for at least an hour. She clutched at her stomach, she groaned, and we were off.

In the interval we sat in the private room with our drinks and told each other that it seemed to be going OK, that the actors were on song but Edward not actually singing, as is his tendency when tired or under stress, that the lights were on cue, etc., and so forth. Realizing that the room was entirely without any form of ventilation, which explained the speed at which I was filling it with smoke again, I went outside, pushing my way deafly through the crowd in the lobby onto the pavement, and then along to a pub nearby where I discovered a television set showing a European Cup match, a small set on a high shelf – one had to stand with one's head at an awkward angle to see the screen. I can't remember which sides were playing, but one was dashing, the other stubborn, which suggests that it might have been the Czechs (dashing) against almost any other team. I made it back just after the second act had started. It was beginning to rain lightly but with purpose as I went into the theatre –

LIGHTS DOWN

We folded the actors into our arms, thanking, congratulating, kissing, fondling, fawning – these little ceremonies of mutual devotion are often sneered at – luvvies at their luvvying – but really if you observe them with an anthropological or zoological eye, they would be seen to be no different in kind from the rituals practised by George and Toto and Errol when they're gathered together in the kitchen for their dinner, for instance – they rub noses and dance under the table and at a certain point, as tins are being opened and packages shaken, George (spayed bitch) will mount Errol (neutered tom) and simulate fornication – they both simulate it, actually – Errol throbbing, heaving and squealing under George bucking, heaving, eyes rolling – well, I don't mean anything like this actually happens backstage, after a first night, at least not that I've witnessed, nor even its equivalent, my point is only that there are moments in the lives of humans, as in the lives of animals, when something of consequence – the arrival or non-arrival of bowls of food for the latter, bad or glowing reviews for the former – is nervously but keenly anticipated, and physical contact with one's colleagues is needed – George fucking Errol, Harold hugging Barbara Jefford, Toto nuzzling George, Edward Fox rocking in Sally Dexter's arms, I taking Peter Bowles by the shoulders – the instincts of the herd, really, however gruesome. I wonder if we could make gruesome into a collective noun, a gruesome of producers, for instance, was fondling a coven of critics –

WHAT BECAME OF A TRANSITUS 'C' SCHOOLBOY

Most of the audience were gone, but Stephen Lushington, my old housemaster, not in the true sense 'old' – though well over eighty, he's many steps to take before getting anywhere near his chronological age – stood with his wife, Beatrice, who is blind, sheltering in the doorway, wondering how to get to the party, to which, not having foreseen rain, they'd intended to walk – as they were my guests, and I'd already put them through two hours of my writing, I urged them to have first use of our car, which would come back and collect Victoria and me when it had dropped them. Now there's a period of confusion here I can't work out how we finally made it to the party, but we went with Harold and Antonia, so I imagine they must have seen us sheltering in the doorway, picked us up, and taken us with them to the church of St Martin-in-the-Field, in St Martin's Lane, to the crypt of the church, an odd venue for a theatrical party, which seemed even odder when we stepped out of the car, and Antonia led the way through the drizzle down a short path that was littered with winos, beggars, the defeated – cheerfully defeated inasmuch as they raised themselves up, in biblical fashion, and advised Antonia not to go in there – 'No, don't go in there, me darlin'' – what used to be called a crone cried out – much laughter and raisings of bottles, cans, skirts and trouser legs – it could have been from a Buñuel film, *The Discreet Charm of the Bourgeoisie* – except the merriment wasn't sinister or even satirical, it was affectionate, as if we were four rather endearing outcasts, simple-minded, to be protected from a world of which we knew nothing, and sent back to our own world, of chandeliers and champagne –– we retreated to the car, and were driven seven yards or so to the next path, then passed through a door that looked exactly like the door we'd been warned against. We had some difficulty making the entrance that we would have liked, playwright and director and wives, come in out of the rain to celebrate much-deserved whatever it was going to be, because we were blocked by a powerful young West Indian – possibly, from his accent, Barbadian – who demanded to see our invitations. We didn't have invitations – why would we require invitations, we were the author, we were the director, Harold explained in short, stabbing sentences. 'Be that as it may,' the young man said, he had been ordered not to let anyone in without an invitation, he was perfectly polite and perfectly adamant, but he was beginning to fall into a bouncer's posture, hunched, arms swinging free – 'To hell with that!' Harold said, and with an unbounceable strut went past him, the rest of us sidling quickly after him before he vanished into the shadows of this low-ceilinged, ill-lit vault where once, from the feel of it, they must have stored bodies before burial – Alan Yentob and Margy and the cameraman and the sound man were already there, and followed me as I shook hands, kissed proffered cheeks, proffered my own – the ones on my face – for kisses, generally luvvied about, in other words. There was a nice moment when Stephen Lushington and I were arranged with our arms around each other's shoulders, smiling into each other's faces, like a couple in a newspaper article – 'Found after a fifty-year search, missing housemaster' or 'Found after fifty years' search, missing Transitus C schoolboy'.

THREE OUT OF SEVEN

I had a few sharp words, unfilmed, I hope, with a producer figure who jumped straight, without a word about *The Old Masters*, into an account of a production he hoped to launch of one of my old plays, *Otherwise Engaged*, with Kelsey Grammer in the lead. I'd directed Kelsey Grammer in a play of mine in New York long before he turned into Frasier, of the world-famous television series, in fact in the days when I'd known him I'd occasionally had to lecture him on his unpunctuality and, well, some other problems, which were almost as serious as mine, along with his habit of falling asleep when I gave notes, all of which, I told him, pointed to a lack of a future. The producer-figure said that Kelsey Grammer had told him that the main character in *Otherwise Engaged* was the only part in the whole world that might lure him back to the stage. 'He did Macbeth last year in New York,' I said, 'so he's already been back on stage.' 'That's Shakespeare,' he said rather foamingly. 'You're the only living writer –' 'What did you think of *The Old Masters*?' 'Oh, very good, very good, but if we can get Kelsey Grammer we can go ahead with *Otherwise Engaged*. Subject to dates, of course.' I felt an odd, blurring sensation. In the original production of *Otherwise Engaged*, which Harold had directed, Alan Bates had played the lead, Nigel Hawthorne had played his brother, Ian Charleson had played his lodger – it had opened at the Queen's Theatre, then, after six months, moved to the Comedy, where *The Old Masters* is now playing. Of the original cast of seven, Alan was dead, Ian Charleson was dead, Nigel Hawthorne was dead, and here were Harold and I, back at the Comedy in the same capacities, though with different wives, both of us now older than the three when they'd died, Ian Charleson hadn't got much beyond thirty, an early victim of Aids. 'Really,' I said, 'this is a first-night party for *The Old Masters*, it's here and now. *Otherwise Engaged* was in the long-ago on the one hand – and in the might-be, subject-to-dates-of-course on the other' – actually I rather snarled it at him, quite unreasonably, I imagine, from his point of view, turned on my heel, Harold-style, and left him there – Well, I mean! And Really! I found Victoria. She was talking to Lucy, who was looking both glamorous and kindly, an unbeatable combination in a young woman. She gave me a kiss and a cuddle, and told me the evening had gone well, thus completely fulfilling her daughterly duties. Victoria said that Harold and Antonia had just left for Sheekey's, in the bar of which only a few weeks ago we'd seen the man slam down his programme of *The Holy Terror* in a pantomime of rage and disgust – 'Let's go,' I said, and explained to Alan Yentob and Margy that we were off, and where to – I could see flares of interest in their eyes, so I said I didn't think we wanted the camera on us as we ate and talked about the evening, it really was a private business, old tradition, the four of us reliving the immediate past, and pasts beyond that.

THE TURKEY QUESTION

We could see Harold and Antonia moving slowly ahead of us, picking their way past the Duke of York's, which only a few weeks ago had housed *The Holy Terror* and was now lying in wait for the next show, *Dirty Blonde* about the life and times of Mae West, which a close friend of ours, Dena Hammerstein, was producing – not a lucky theatre, I'd warned her grimly, as the show before *The Holy Terror* – it was called *Calico* – about Joyce's relationship with his daughter, had closed in a couple of weeks. On the first night of *The Holy Terror* a man who looked as if he'd run all the way from Heathrow or even Gatwick to the box office, his chest was heaving, his face was sweaty, urgently demanded three tickets for *Calico*. He refused at first to believe that it wasn't there to be seen – 'But it's only just opened! I read about it in the plane, just a few hours ago, in the plane! – how can it have closed?' Overhearing this in the lobby, I had one of those feelings, shameful and smirky, that I suspect the gods take note of. 'There's *The Holy Terror*,' the man in the box office said valiantly, 'it opens tonight. There are still a few tickets left –' '*The Holy Terror*! *The Holy Terror*! Why should I want to see *The Holy Terror* when I've come to see *Calico*?' I wondered if there might be a similar exchange on the first night of *Dirty Blonde*, some desperate creature exhausted from the airport, demanding tickets for *The Holy Terror* and being offered tickets instead for *Dirty Blonde*.

I pointed out a tattered poster for *The Holy Terror* – it must have gone up tattered, I said, it hadn't been there long enough to have been tattered by the elements – and look! Victoria said, gazing up from the edge of the pavement, and yes, there it was, announced not only in the down-at-heel poster but actually in lights, like a tawdry tombstone – Simon Callow in *The Holy Terror*, by me.

Harold and Antonia turned down the lane that Sheekey's is in and we trailed behind them, contemplating the swings of fate, at least we hoped they were swings, from *The Holy Terror* to *The Old Masters*, there may well be no swing at all, *The Old Masters* may turn out to be another turkey – but why 'turkey' by the way, why do we also call a flop a 'turkey'?

END OF AN EVENING

Over dinner the director and his wife assured the author and his wife, and vice versa, that the evening had gone as well as can be expected on a first night with a new play, the cast had hit their stride early and never faltered, the audience had been benevolently disposed, and as for the critics, one of the nice things about the evening, we all agreed, is that we hadn't seen a single one, not that we could identify anyway, although we were assured by the management that they had all been there, on their aisle seats, pads in hand, opinions at the ready. One of us recalled the life of the composer Warlock – I forget his first name, if he had one – who was also a music critic, writing under a name I must also look up – and although he was well-known in each capacity, nobody knew he was the same man – in fact he reviewed himself increasingly viciously, and was eventually found dead with his head in a gas oven, suicide therefore, or perhaps self-murder would be the more accurate term – the question of course is, which murdered which, the critic the composer, or the composer the critic? Each clearly had a strong motive – although it might conceivably have been death by misadventure, the composer turning on the gas, the critic putting his head in the oven to see what was up – and then we enjoyed the memory of a recent production of a play generally and rightly regarded as a modern classic, in which the leading actor had mangled virtually every single line, causing all the other actors to come in at the wrong places with lines they had to get wrong so that they connected to the leading actor's wrong lines – it was a textual slaughterhouse, the night we saw it. Outside the theatre, on a placard jammed with quotes, there was one that proclaimed, with Olympian authority, 'Every line spot on' – 'Every fucking line spot off,' said the defeated director, who'd been in love with the text since his schooldays. One evening an elderly lady, perhaps mother to the playwright, or the director, or one of the actors, sat in the stalls reciting the correct lines of the play, quite loudly, as if she were doing a simultaneous translation –

So the talk went, vindictive, malignant, vengeful, agreeable, until a selectively shaven chap, one cheek and half his chin gleaming, the other cheek and other half of his chin stubbled, got up from a nearby table and came over. 'How's it going?' he asked. 'How's what going?' Harold growled, jaw jutting. The chap, youngish and a director of some distinction, looked yearningly towards the chair he'd just left – he'd had experience of Harold in this mode, obviously, and was now recalling it – 'The play,' he said. 'What play?' Harold asked him. 'Well, your play. His play,' nodding at me. '*The Old Masters*,' I said, quite anxious to avoid what was already happening. 'That's the one. *The Old Masters*.' 'What about it?' Harold was staring straight up at him, his eyes had turned milky with a dark glitter in them. 'What about it?' he said. 'Well, it's in previews, isn't it? How are they going, the previews?' 'We've just,' Harold said crisply, 'had a first night.' 'Oh,' said the youngish director, 'I hope it went well.' 'What do you mean, went well! Went well!' 'Anyway, good luck,' said the youngish director, as he backed away, not to his table, but into the next room, and from there doubtless to the street, and away, away. 'Went well,' Harold repeated several times. 'Went well! What did he think he meant?' We tried to explain to him what we thought he thought he meant, but were really too tired to do a proper job of it – probably the half-shaven director had inadvertently reminded Harold that however much he believed in the play, however fine he knew his production to be, *The Old Masters* would only survive if other people allowed it to – oddly, Harold looked the least tired of the four of us, though in fact he was probably the most tired, certainly far more tired than me. He'd had a month of intense rehearsals, three weeks in Birmingham, then putting the play into the Comedy for previews and now a first night, and he'd had almost a year's illness behind him, was in fact still frail from it when he'd taken the play on back there in Barbados, whereas I had gone in to rehearsals at my convenience, and I'd only stayed long enough in Birmingham to see what a terrific job he'd done and to make a few small cuts. Why stay longer when you were staying at the Hilton and couldn't open the window, the air-conditioning not working, during a heat wave? Most of the time, right up to and including the first night, I'd been cavorting for the camera with Alan Yentob, Margy the director, Patrick the cameraman and sometimes Andy the sound man, a business I'd only found tiring because of the non-stop smoking. I looked at Harold, alert in his exhaustion, and suddenly realized that our long professional association was now ending as one would have prayed for it to end when we'd begun it. It had survived some blizzardy spells, rows, froideurs, etc., but still, here we were, in Sheekey's, half our lifetimes on from our first first night together, celebrating what would certainly be our last.

We went back in the hired car, I sitting in the front, Harold between Antonia and Victoria in the back – they got out first, in their bit of Holland Park, we drove on the few minutes to our bit, took George and Toto for a walk, they saw off the usual foxes and other shadows under a bright moon, Victoria went to bed, I came in here, and here I am, doing this, and Brendel doing Mozart behind me. Now I shall sit for a while, and listen to him properly, while I smoke.

THE TURKEY QUESTION ANSWERED

All the main reviews are now in. Judy says they're OK – the advance is high and rising, we look set for a decent run, there's been foreign interest – in fact it looks as if it might be a success. I must be careful. The last time I told myself I had a successful play in the West End was on the evening before one of the two stars, and therefore half the reason for the success, departed for foreign parts, the resulting headlines closed it in three weeks. Oh, I see why 'turkey'! – because a turkey can be said to have no future, you look at a turkey gobbling its way across the farmyard, and you're looking at a dinner, Christmas or Thanksgiving, though in fact you're unlikely to find a turkey to look at in a farmyard these days, you're most likely to find him in a factory, in a coop just slightly larger than himself, immobile therefore and stuffed with chemicals, a creature not only without a future but without a present, thus making it an even closer analogy to a stage turkey, in that the cast, if it has any sense, will also be stuffed with chemicals. But let us say for the purposes of this discussion and for sanity's sake that my new play is not going to be a turkey but a golden, well, silver goose – well, then what? What then? So what? Some money perhaps.

And now to bed. Oh, Christ! Before I go there's something I must do – I've written and written about *The Old Masters* and haven't once mentioned the two men without whom I'd never have written it, Roger Jenkins and Simon Langton, to whom therefore I must pay

AN OVERDUE TRIBUTE

Very different in demeanour, personality and physique – Roger Jenkins is small and scampering, Simon Langton tall and relaxed, but I always see them as a unit, like a couple on a bicycle, sometimes Langton on the handlebars, Jenkins pedalling, sometimes the other way around – I think it was Jenkins who approached me with the idea of doing a filmscript about Berenson and Duveen, and when I found myself unable to do it, it was Langton who phoned to ask whether I might consider trying it again as a stage play – and when I'd done it as a stage play together they purchased the rights forthwith, then refused the control over the play that the rights gave them, asking only that they should be colleagues, fellow adventurers, fellow sufferers in the process of getting it on. Over a number of years – years! – we had regular dinners to discuss casting, directors, ways of finding other producers who could raise money – and if there was an undercurrent of hopelessness as dinner followed dinner, with only rejections and humiliations to report or conceal – for example, they sent the play to the artistic director of an Irish theatre, I bumped into him at a party, he was drunk and disorderly, with wandering hands, not sexually wandering, but Irishly wandering, he liked to place them on your shoulders or around your waist – he'd read the first act on the plane over from Dublin, he said, he'd enjoyed it, yes, yes, honestly enjoyed it, looked forward to reading the second act on the way back, was shore he'd enjoy tat too – no, no, don't bother, I said, please don't bother – the disgusting truth, and he knew it, was that really I was beseeching him to put the play on his stage – how could such a man, I nevertheless thought, or rather how could I stand there having my shoulders groped by such a man! but no, I said, no, no, don't bother – take your time, read it when you can, there could be no better place to start the play than in a theatre under your management, but really don't feel you have to read it. He twinkled at me in a fiery sort of way, patted my elbows, then lurched off to fondle other writers, who, I hoped, treated him with more – more – dignity. In due course I heard that the Irish rascal wouldn't dream of having my play on his stage at all, at all – no doubt Roger Jenkins and Simon Langton had similar encounters too shameful to pass on to me, but it was understood between us that we'd been through things, not to be talked about – as if there were priests, choirmasters, scout masters in our backgrounds. The only problem with people who behave as well as Langton and Jenkins is that they tend to get treated badly, if only by neglect – naturally modest men who didn't like to intrude even in matters that affected them directly, they were frequently forgotten when it came to making decisions – the casting, for instance, went ahead without their being consulted, though I think, I hope, I kept them abreast *post facto*, when it was too late for them to object or to register reservations – they dealt with this by being, or pretending to be, delighted with each decision, although conversations with Roger Jenkins can be slightly confusing, as he has the kind of deafness that sometimes allows him to hear exactly the opposite of what you've said, it either obliterates a negative or supplies one, so that he exclaims joyfully when grief is in order, and vice versa.

THE PROSPECT OF AN EVENING WATCHING THE TELLY

In about half an hour we're going around to Margy's flat to watch ourselves as we will be seen in approximately two million homes. I would like to say, in a dignified sort of way, that thus our privacy is being invaded, but in fact you could look at it the other way around, and consider that Victoria and I are about to invade the privacy of a couple of a million homes, or perhaps more accurately are about to inflict our privacy on a couple of a million homes. I may also, of course, have got the numbers wrong – it may, when it comes to it, be a couple of hundred homes, or even a couple of homes, one of which will be Margy's, whose home we will thus be invading twice, simultaneously. When I come back I shall almost certainly avoid writing about the experience, and try to return to a subject still much on my mind, which is of course

ERROL, HIS DEFECT

I've never attempted to conceal from myself that he is very greedy, the consequences of his greed are immediately apparent in his bulk, but his bulk has always, for me, been part of his charm – he carries it on short, skipping legs not exactly lightly but easily, in comfort and with style – 'a dainty waddle' I believe I've described his walk as, but that only captures his routine, unhurried movement from a) (sofa) to b) (armchair) – it doesn't encompass his movement towards the kitchen when he hears me in it, or sees me going towards it – then the short legs move so rapidly they're almost invisible, he looks like a large black fur hat skimming across the floor, although you can hear the pitter-patter of his feet as he comes along the hall, or quite loud thumps, so close together it's almost a continuous noise, if he's coming down the stairs – once in the kitchen he stalks me, treading on my heels as I move from table to sink to fridge to cupboard to table, generally silently and therefore at risk to himself – if I were to step back suddenly I'd hurt his head – no, more likely I'd trip over him and hurt myself – badly, too, given my weight, size and age. At first I tried to ignore him, thinking that rules are rules and mealtimes are mealtimes, but as soon as I'd sit down to eat he'd stand on his hind legs and, using his paws like clubs, batter away at my calves and knees – if I ignored him or knocked him away he'd get onto one of the chairs, clamber onto the table and advance on my plate, head lowered, butting at it. My solitary lunches, which I've always enjoyed so much, calmly eating while calmly reading, degenerated into dreadful scuffles, punctuated by shouts, swearwords, until I gave up and popped some food into his mouth, but it was

NEVER ENOUGH!

He'd be back at my plate while he was still swallowing and the thing about Errol, who is a stray, don't forget, and took over the house in methodical stages, is that he doesn't take no for an answer, and never takes offence – if you sweep him onto the floor he gets straight back onto the chair and sprawls his way onto the table and butts his way to your plate, which he also reaches for with outstretched paws. This situation is entirely my own fault, as Victoria explains to me, for having fed him scraps in the days when he merely stood on his hind legs and pummelled my legs. If I'd refused him then he would have accepted the situation in the end and left me alone, as no cat likes to stand bolt upright whirring his paws for no gain – after all, it's an unnatural act that drains the energy, and probably strains the back – but once he grasped that I was weak, a giver, he decided to become strong, a taker – yes, he's turned himself from a beggar into a mugger, and I'm his permanent victim. I would like to say that we've reached accommodation, but it's the kind of accommodation that Brits of yore achieved with the Vikings – before I sit down to eat, I put some of my food onto a saucer, which I place outside the kitchen and as soon as he's bent over it I shut the door. What depresses me most about this is that he is massively overweight, more so and more so, you can tell by the way his head seems to have grown smaller every time you look at him, and though I acknowledge that gluttony is part of his character, part of the charm of his character, it is inexcusable of me to gratify it and so hasten him to an early grave, simply because I lack the strength of will to refuse him. I wish the dogs would do the job for me, and chase him off every time he comes mugging, but really they're just as weak, just as devoted, allowing him access to their own dishes, and cleaning him up when he's too indolent to do it for himself. At least I don't have to do that, go down on my hands and knees and lick away at him, I hope it never occurs to him –

FRIENDS AND BROKEN PROMISES

A friend phoned this afternoon to say that there was a piece in the *Guardian* about the television programme, had I seen it? I said I hadn't, and didn't want to, I no longer read reviews. She said I really ought to make an exception of this one, which anyway wasn't really a review, was more a meditation, and was quite delightful, was the word she used, delightful. On my way up to the Renaissance I bought the *Guardian*, and when I got there, having signalled for my coffee and settled into my chair on the pavement, I opened it and found the piece – the words that immediately caught my eye were 'obese' and 'slob' – there was a photograph in illustration – so I closed the *Guardian*, thinking that perhaps in context the words meant something different, but better not find out, and then indulged in a little meditation of my own, on the contradictory nature of friendship, and on the inevitable and deserved consequences of breaking promises one has made to oneself –

Well, tomorrow we go to Suffolk, where we'll stay for most of the summer. Let's hope this chaotic spirit finds some peace, or at least placidity. And why not? There will be long walks around the fields with the dogs, the pigs to feed, and the black swans, serene in their pomp –

PART FOUR

PART FOUR

TROUBLE WITH THE BLACK SWANS

There are three of them this summer, old Mum and old Dad, and one offspring, as black as they are, but slighter, almost but not quite grown up. They make a magnificent trio, gliding in a compact triangle through the murky water, sweeping around the moat's bends, sometimes drifting lazily and nobly around each other – we love watching them, and love their grateful honks when they see the bread, their ceremonial dips of the head before they surge towards it – and then the comedy of their scuffles with each other, the brutality with which Mum and Dad barge their only child off the crusts, and then when it's over off they swan around again, a tight-knit and royal little family – so it was when we got down here last week, but in the last few days they've taken to not being on the water, at least when we arrive to feed them – they're generally out of sight, behind a tree on the bank, or a tree in the field quite some way from the moat, and when they see us, and always before we've seen them, they lumber out, as if they've been waiting in ambush. Victoria retreats with George and Toto. I briefly stand my ground, casting my bread towards them. Mother and child stop to feed, but not Dad, he keeps on coming, trampling on the lumps of bread, crashing through the long grass, towards me – he has a strange gleam in his eye, not hostile, in fact eager and friendly but greedy too, as if he's anxious to get to the source, or perhaps he harbours dreams of taking it from my hand, the whole family gathered around the great provider – well, whatever his intentions I lose my nerve, tear the remaining bread into lumps as I back-pedal, hurl them at him, and then turn and run, slowly, ponderously, wheezingly, and only fractionally faster than Dad, whose implacable waddle has staying power, which I haven't – as long as he doesn't use his wings, I keep thinking, dreading the sound of his great wings beating, the rush through the air, and I a wrinkled male Leda, taken from behind –

So far he's stopped in his pursuit, as if realizing that he's missed the point, which is to get himself fed – when I turn to look he's swaying his great, black, feathery body towards wife and child, who are getting the bread down as fast as they can while they have the chance. This has happened three afternoons in a row, and I'm sitting here now, in my study in the garden, noting that the hour is approaching, and yes, Victoria and the dogs are getting ready for a walk, she's putting them on their leads, and I should be heading for the kitchen, to get the bread which we buy especially for them – they're very fussy, they don't like brown bread, or organic or home-baked crusty expensive breads, they like doughy white bread, the sort that comes factory-sliced and factory-wrapped, looks and smells as if it's made out of chemicals, at twice the size and half the price of edible bread – well, *chacun à son gout*, but I don't think I can give them their *gout* this afternoon, what I'll do is – we'll walk to a safe distance from the moat, I'll command Victoria and the dogs to stay – 'Stay, ladies!' I'll say – then I'll take a few steps forward, honking, and if they return my honks from the water, which they always do if they're in the water, we'll all go forward and I'll feed them, but if they meet my honks with silence, I'll know they're lurking on dry ground, out of sight, and we'll hurry on.

I'm back. They were on the water, so that was OK. What wasn't OK was

THE PIGS!

I went to say hello to them and give them their scraps, while Victoria went on with the dogs. There are five of them, just as there were last year, but they're not the same ones, they're new, replacements, so to speak, for reasons I don't want to go into but could be guessed at from the contents of our fridge a few months ago, packages of pork sausages etc. – gifts reluctantly accepted and mournfully consumed. These five are smaller and leaner than their five predecessors, with a quick, scuttling run that turns into a gallop when they get into their stride – they appear from different parts of their vast sty, a couple of them bursting through the undergrowth to your right, another out of the ditch to your left, and the third from out of the nettles right in front of you – they stand in a line and look up at you pleadingly, and with almost dog-like devotion – you think they're going to beg prettily, like George and Toto – well, this is all quite charming, their little ways are usually quite seductive, and indeed were just now, until I'd emptied the carrier bag of its swinish titbits and turned to catch Victoria up. There was a hideous noise behind me, of snouts smashing against wire fencing – they were hurling themselves at it, their tiny eyes gleaming with what looked suspiciously like lust, but was probably just rage. Either way they really did look as if they were out to get me, and when I hurried off, walking along the road that runs beside the sty to catch Victoria up, they continued to hurl themselves at the fence, butting and kicking at it and then, realizing that I was almost gone, raced after me with a thunder of hooves, passed me and began their assault on the fence further up, obviously planning to cut me off. Then what? Gobble me down as a prime titbit, or maul me to death in revenge for what? I give them tasty scraps, after all, I am a patron, trustworthy and punctual – perhaps they picture me going to the fridge a year from now, reaching in for a package of fresh sausages – anyway, instead of trusting to the fence to hold, I swung away briskly into the orchard, and caught up with Victoria on the edge of a cornfield, very high corn, into which Toto vanished, so we spent an hour calling 'Toto, Toto, come on, come, Toto' – once we saw her about twenty yards away, her head and her front paws showing briefly and desperately above the stalks, but looking the wrong way, and that was it, she'd obviously lost her bearings, too many bewildering scents of mice, rat, rabbit and hare to find her own scent and get back to us. She'd be sniffing and running in circles, getting more and more exhausted, frightened, finally collapsing, tongue lolling, eyes staring hopelessly – or so we imagined as we went back to get the car, drove to the field, up and down the side of it, at least Victoria did, while I hung out of the window, watching out for her, willing her to hear the familiar motor. We stopped at last and got out. The sun was going down, the endless East Anglian sky darkening, the cornfield darkening, our hearts doing much the same, and George standing with a melancholy stoop, her favourite posture when Toto's gone awry, and then we all heard it, a heavy breathing at our feet, and there was Toto, her golden muzzle pitch black from burrowing into the earth, burrs and twigs and clots of dirt in her fur. We might have suspected her of not having been lost at all, but simply of having had a high old time down there among the stalks, if she hadn't keeled over on her side, from what was evidently a combination of fatigue and relief.

So what's going on down here in Suffolk? Not with Toto, that's routine behaviour, made exceptional by the corn, but with the swans and the pigs – their behaviour has been bizarre, though I don't know whether out of character – species character, that is – because the only pigs and swans I've been close to are the ones down here in Suffolk, in this little piece of Suffolk, where the swans used to take their food on water and the pigs battered and buffeted only each other for theirs, and my role was to stand on moat bank and at sty fence and cast bread to one and vegetable matter to the other – obedient, not to say obsequious, swans and pigs who once knew their place and mine, but who now pursue and harass me, forcing me into unseemly jogs and ponderous, cowardly sprints –

I think I know what's going on, actually, actually I think it's because the surrounding farm has turned organic, everything grown here is now organic, the corn, the wheat, the apples, the pears, the potatoes, and with them come more wasps and hornets than have ever been seen before, invasive, aggressive wasps and hornets as big as my thumb. How can the pigs and swans not be affected? They're becoming, perhaps have already become, organic too, and so are behaving organically. Eventually, I suppose, the people will become organic, Victoria and I will start to behave organically, as will George, Toto, Errol and Tom – this is what happens when you stop interfering with nature, nature starts to interfere with you. God knows where we'll end up, especially if He's turning organic too.

A CORPSE IN THE MOONLIGHT

It's late, but that's not it. I'm not tired. I'm anxious. I'll write about what Errol's just done because I don't want to think about what I'm anxious about, there being no point to it, the thinking leads to no solutions, in fact only intensifies the anxiety, but once it starts there's no stopping it, except chemically, so I'll take a couple of sleeping pills and – the thing about Errol being a cat, in spite of his extraordinary gift for relationships, his kindness, his warmth, and indeed his sloth and love of good living –

Tomorrow.

It is tomorrow, and here's what he did yesterday. I was sitting in my study in the garden at about two in the morning, the window wide open for the breeze – generally all you get at that hour are moths and mosquitoes – the black beetles and spiders that are quite active on my desk (the spiders) and the floor (the beetles) don't come through the window, they're residents, and I'm so used to them that I scarcely notice them – but anyway there I was, at my desk, not writing, inert really, with Errol slumbering in the armchair beside me, when something quite large hurtled through the window almost into my face, banged into the wall behind, slid to the ground, then flapped up to the ceiling and fell onto the top bookshelf. It was the size of a small crow, but not a crow because it had a grey chest. It began to stir on the bookshelf, then to flutter, then to flap, rising to the ceiling, falling to the bookshelf, then rising again to the ceiling. I did the only thing I could think to do, which was to open the door and hope that it would make for the garden. Errol meanwhile had woken, stretched, and was taking up a thoughtful position under the bookcase. I went across to pick him up and carry him out, just as the bird launched itself across the room, bounced off the wall and dropped behind the television set. I can't say that Errol sprang, it was more a rapid mince between my bent legs and my down-reaching hands, and then he too was behind the television set where I couldn't get to him, so I left the room, trying to make myself deaf to the scuffling noises.

I stood outside, waiting. Beautiful night, moonlit, soundless – wherever you are in London, at whatever the hour, there is always the sound of the city, but in Suffolk there is, or appears to be, complete stillness and silence, at least in the hours after midnight, when you feel you can hear it, palpable – and there was old Errol coming out into the garden, his jaws stretched, something dark throbbing between them.

Well, what then? I went into the kitchen and sat with a Diet Coke, smoking. George came from the bedroom, licked my hand – in London she does this almost every night, a little ritual of affection, before she goes on down into the garden for a pee. Here, as my study isn't on her route, she only does it if we coincide, as we did now, in the kitchen. She went out through the flap. A few minutes later she came back in, nodded at me, went through to the bedroom. I could hear her hind legs scraping on the floor, and her grunts, as she heaved herself onto the bed, no doubt stretched herself out between Victoria and Toto. Then the assassin Errol came in, brushed against my leg, purring, then minced off to the bedroom, no doubt to squeeze himself between Toto and Victoria or George and Victoria. I looked in the sitting room – Tom asleep in an armchair. So everyone safely to bed, I thought. I went into the garden to check on the little red and black heap, its feathers shining in the moonlight. I decided it could wait until tomorrow, and then, deciding it couldn't, got some kitchen roll for a glove, picked the heap up, carried it to the end of the garden and lobbed it over the fence, into the field of organic corn.

THREE ANECDOTES, WITH AN IMMORAL FLAVOUR

A man, young, from the sound of him, has just phoned on behalf of BBC 3 or 4, to ask if I would contribute to a debate on smoking, whether it should be banned in restaurants, bars, etc. I said thank you for thinking of me, but I'm in Suffolk, furthermore, etc. – as I talked to him I realized I was wheezing. I also coughed once or twice – not a voice you would want to hear defending smoking, unless you were against it. What you want is a firm, clear voice, rather like his, in which to tell point-making anecdotes – that time in Athens, for instance, springs to mind, when the old American guy and the receptionist – no, try for a dignified tone, worthy of the subject matter –

Well then:

1)

At the front desk of one of Athens's most distinguished hotels – grand, seedy and unaccommodating – a little old American chap with a feeble voice but excellent manners was presenting his case to the receptionist, who was like his hotel in its seedy and unaccommodating aspects, while lacking its grandeur –

'Well, sir,' the old American said, 'you see, we in the United States prefer to eat in restaurants where there's no smoking. We feel that smoking is an unhealthy and unpleasant habit, you see, so my wife and I were wondering, would it be possible for you to make part of the restaurant suitable for non-smokers?'

The receptionist looked at him with puzzled contempt.

'It would be a great help to us Americans –'

'In our restaurants there is smoking.'

'Yes, sir, but couldn't you oblige us Americans who don't like to sit in a smoky atmosphere?'

'No,' said the receptionist, and turned his back on him to answer an unringing phone.

The old American waited a few minutes, then trudged back to

his wife, who looked like his twin, in a skirt and a blue rinse.

'What did he say, dear?'

'They said – they said they would see what they could do, dear.'

'Oh, that's good,' she said. 'That's really good.'

The receptionist was now talking to a colleague, both laughing in the direction of the ancient Yankee-Doodles, who were tottering arm in arm towards the heat, grime and nastiness of outdoor Athens, a heart-wrenching sight.

I imagine they're dead now, possibly the receptionist and his colleague are dead too, why not? Or retired on their tips and credit-card scams. The thing is, though, I can't recall my attitude at the time, or even work out my attitude now. On the one hand it was a neo-colonialist impertinence of the Americans to make the request, which, on the other hand, I saw, and can still see, was perfectly reasonable. The receptionist was a shit, whose main pleasure in his work was in expressing his contempt for the guests – furthermore I believe that he stole one of my credit cards – I'd put two or three on the counter while searching for a third or a fourth, and I'd only put two or one back into my shirt pocket and didn't discover a card was missing until I answered the phone that usually didn't work in the small house in the middle of the island of Spetses, at an address which was unknown, so we thought, to everybody in the world except, as it turned out, to the lady from the Diner's Club, who reached us from where? – somewhere in Cincinnati, possibly. She wanted to ask me whether I'd recently bought half a dozen shirts, many gallons of gas, a television set, etc., etc., in Athens. When I said I hadn't, she said, 'Then your card's been stolen, sir.' My mind went straight to the receptionist, I saw him quite vividly, settled in front of his new television set in one of his new shirts, a silk affair with orange and black dots – and yet, such are the paradoxes of the human heart, I find my sympathies mostly with the thieving, ill-mannered receptionist rather than with the enfeebled, dignified old Yankee-Doodles. Is this really a point-making anecdote? If it is, what's its point, because I clearly haven't found it, but then the moral of any story involving Greeks is likely to be obscure.

2)

Consider the catamaran that takes you from Athens to Spetses, a marvellous outfit in blue and white, with a luxurious upper compartment in which you could buy a seat for a small supplement. The counter used to be covered by plates of caviare, bottles of champagne, cheeses, cakes, and you were invited to help yourselves – the seats were armchairs, most of them unoccupied, and ashtrays were everywhere. But the last time we were on it, the line had a new owner, the caviare, champagnes, wines, cheeses, cakes all replaced by saucers of crisps and pretzels, the only drinks were soft drinks and beer, locked in a large glass safe, to which the steward, who used to be jovial, had a key – a key! – and of course the ashtrays had gone, smoking wasn't permitted anywhere in the boat except by the crew, all of whom appeared to chain-smoke, including the one-time jovial steward, who had a cigarette between his lips when he told me to put mine out – but I suppose he was Greek and unionized, and I wasn't – I remember noticing the supplement had gone up too – but to extrapolate from the xenophobic particular a universal moral law, as Kant advises us to do, it would be this, or something like it: most campaigning non-smokers are at heart criminals and bullies –

3)

for example, at an airport check-in, I remember it as being in Holland, possibly Amsterdam, which is confusing because I haven't been to Amsterdam, or anywhere else in Holland in the last forty years – anyway, to revert to the xenophobic particular, she was American of course, and she'd just joined the queue – inserted herself into it, and not in the middle, at the head, pushing in front of me just as it became my turn to step up to the desk. I rose to my full height, about six foot by the old reckoning, 'Excuse me,' I said, 'excuse me but actually I believe that I –' 'Hey, you! Hey, get that thing out of my face, you wanna kill me or what?' So instead of arguing about her right to jump ahead of me in the queue, we argued about my right to smoke in a place where the right to smoke had never yet, in my experience, been questioned, and were still arguing as she received her boarding card. No, this didn't happen to me, it happened to my brother Piers, so it might well have happened to him at Amsterdam airport, at the time in his life when he was a great traveller and a heavy smoker – later he gave up travelling because he was frightened of going in an aeroplane, and smoking because he thought it was killing him, though there he was wrong, it was drink that was killing him, just as it was drink that made him frightened of flying, induced his claustrophobia, convinced him that Hell was a geographical as well as a theological fact and that he was predestined to a place in it, and it was drink that destroyed his career, endangered his friendships. In my own case I gave up drink because it was threatening to do to me what it had done to Piers, although there were variations – I wasn't afraid of flying though I had difficulties getting to the airport, I didn't believe in Hell except as a metaphor, most of my friendships were perfectly safe as I was too inert to do them serious damage – but I can't give up cigarettes, which are helping to kill me, that's the phrase that's most commonly used – 'If they're not actually killing you, they're certainly helping' – but helping what, helping whom?

DOES IT MATTER?

Ironically, now I'm writing about smoking – no, I mustn't go on with a sentence that begins with 'ironically' – there was that very nice young man at Alan's funeral who spoke of how he'd been present in the same church for the funeral of Alan's son Tristan, then for the funeral of Alan's wife, Victoria, and now, 'ironically', for the funeral of Alan himself. Not only, what did he mean? What did he think he meant? Or think the word meant? Surely he must have realized that when Alan died his funeral would, as a matter of course, be held in the same church as his wife's, his son's and both his parents', so he can't have meant coincidentally, a common and slovenly modern usage, as it was quite the reverse of a coincidence, and he can't have meant an utterance that said something different from what it seemed to be saying, which is the old usage – in fact, the natural adverb in the context would have been 'naturally' – though I suppose he might have begun, 'So here we are again!' which could have had a touch of irony in it, as it certainly had when another young man said it at the beginning of his speech at his father's fourth wedding.

CONVICTED

I visualize it often, this mute, passive, helpless creature pushed and prodded by creatures rendered semi-human by their uniforms and power – and my fellow inmates, some of them at least semi-human in their attitude to violence, myself gradually assimilated into their world, a freak because of my age, my accent, my feebleness, my lack of survival knowledge – I see no hope for myself at all, not even in my passivity, and then the noise, the noise of clashing stereos, of voices shouting above them, the foul language, every noun and verb preceded and followed by an obscenity, no, by the same dreary obscenity, more a verbal tic than a word that has meaning. And then there'd be the food, of course, and then meeting my visitors. But would anybody come, would I want them to come, because this is what visiting me would entail – demeaning and lengthy ceremonies – searches, palm-stamping, etc., on arrival; demeaning and lengthy ceremonies – searches, palm-unstamping, etc., on departure, both ceremonies designed as deliberate side-effects to the punishment, really. You know this prisoner you're visiting, do you? In what capacity? Write it down. Empty your pockets. This is for him, is it? Put it there. Give me your hand. Put it there. What's that behind your eyes? Humiliation? Whose fault is that? His fault for being in here. Your fault for visiting him. Most of the packages they'd bring for me, books, cigarettes, money, would be forbidden on different grounds, although there would be free and easy access for drugs, alcohol and pornography – would that thought cheer me up as I sat in a chair in a costume with the name of the prison on it, an orange, or a yellow, or a green costume, sharing a joke with my visitors?

But why should I have to go to jail? I haven't done anything illegal, to my knowledge, nor immoral – at least not for years. I haven't lived, am still not living, a good life, a life of active virtue, I concede that, but whatever harm I do is unintentional, the consequence of humdrum selfishness or thoughtlessness, all my malice I keep penned in, except in the occasional remark to Victoria or a close friend, someone I can trust – but really my fear has nothing to do with what I've done, or even haven't done, it's to do with who and what I am, the world of this who and what is filled with – no, that's not true, not filled with, infiltrated by, my world has been infiltrated by police people, social workers, judges, recorders, prison wardens and jailbirds – I carry them with me through life, my just deserts. And they like to walk about in my skull at all the dead hours, the alternative to death, and which, I must say, never strikes me as a favourable alternative.

Of course I'll never end up in prison, why should I? Well, why did he and he and he and she? And don't forget those like poor

BUGALL

I don't. In fact, I think about him ridiculously often, really, considering how inconsequential in the large scheme of injustice his story is, and how long ago it was, back there in the 1980s or 1990s. He was a barrister in Edinburgh who loved his work, was highly sociable in his instincts and clearly fancied himself a lady's man, something of a goer, an optimistic goer, though friends and colleagues, who chattered happily about him to the newspapers after the trial, suggested that he cut a slightly preposterous figure – foolishly self-regarding and off-kilter, a bit of a nincompoop, really –

There was a legal ball, an end-of-the-sessions sort of thing, with kilts and bagpipes and Highland flings – in the thick of it Bugall, having the time of his life with the young lady of his choice – though she said afterwards she found him a bit of an embarrassment, didn't really know him, just enough to accept his invitation –

They'd arranged to spend the night at the flat of friends of the young lady, because the ball ended late, and they had no transport. She retired to one bedroom, he to another. He undressed down to his shirt-cuffs, which were elaborate and separate from the shirt, then bounded into the young lady's bedroom, making a loud whooping noise, and flung himself onto the young lady, who tipped him straight onto the floor, where he fell asleep, or into a stupor, and was still in one or the other when the police arrived to carry him off to the cells. He chose to conduct his own defence – and why not? He was a practising barrister, after all, and this was a marvellous chance to hone and display his skills – that's why not.

His defence was this: if a young man took a young lady to an expensive ball, he was entitled to hope for a sexual reward. Of course he would never force himself on her, a rejection was a rejection, he was not a rapist, no, he was merely a normal man – come on, chaps! I mean! was his defence. Before he was sentenced he wrote a letter to the Recorder, begging him not to send him to prison. He got three years. The young lady, who'd been anonymous throughout the case, told the newspapers afterwards that she'd never wanted him to go to prison, had never wanted to ruin his life, she didn't quite know how it had happened. The newspapers had great fun with the story – particularly with the detail of the detachable but undetached cuffs, and the absurdity of his name, which wasn't actually Bugall, but something like that. One or two columnists took a more serious view, however, and congratulated the Recorder for sending out the right message, which oddly enough failed to reach Bugall, whose application for early release was turned down on the grounds that he was still transmitting the wrong social and sexual signals.

Well, if Bugall, why not you? I've certainly behaved as badly, if not worse, when drunk. On the other hand I no longer drink and anyway don't have the energy, on top of which I don't live in Edinburgh – my Scottish side comes from Glasgow, which must be a very different sort of place, at least if my grandmother was anything to go by – in fact, now I think about her, I realize that she had certain Bugall tendencies, in that she drank and she loved to romp on the bed – with me, actually – perhaps she's responsible for my lax moral attitudes, perhaps Bugall too had a grandma from Glasgow – could he have pleaded that in mitigation?

I hope he's all right, Bugall, and has good health and a good woman – and hope that his anonymous ladyfriend, and the friends who persuaded her to phone the police, and the police, and the jury, and the journalists who had such fun and copy at his expense, and above all the Recorder, are all in the place that they deserve to be in. Now that's the sort of thought which could lead to an orange uniform – pushed and prodded –

AT THE OVAL

The television is on, we're playing the West Indies at the Oval – so far we've beaten them six times in a row, three times in the West Indies, three times here, and we have at the crease now the England captain, Michael Vaughan, and a young Warwickshire batsman I've read and heard about, but not seen before – his name is Ian Bell, this is his first test match, and he has so far scored seventy. He looks very good. Michael Vaughan also looks very good, but then he usually does. I'm glad to see England playing well, of course, and with style, but I wish it weren't at the expense of the West Indies – oh, Bell is just out, caught behind, still on seventy – not long ago, not long ago in terms of my lifetime, anyway, the West Indians were the best in the world, brutally efficient fast bowlers, the best batsmen in the world and probably one of the two or three best ever in Viv Richards – they were relentless and dominating, not to say domineering, and one saw no end to their triumphs, especially over England, who often looked like schoolboys against them. But cricket teams, empires, theatre companies have their seasons, and in no time it seems their time has gone, their triumphs bewildering memories – well, that's OK for South Africans, New Zealanders, Indians, Pakistanis, and especially Australians, but it's not really OK when it comes to the West Indies – I hate to see the arrogant saunter of yesterday's teams parodied in the lazy and demoralized slouch of the present lot – I hate to see them losing, I hate to see us losing as well, what I would really like is for us to beat them by one close-fought and exciting match at the end of the series, a clincher that leaves everyone full of hope, looking forward to the next – Vaughan has just gone for sixty-six, driving when he shouldn't have and nicking to slip, and here comes Flintoff, who always reminds me of the cheerful half of a Housman poem, hale and hearty, a peerless youth, before Housman snuffs him out at the end of a rope. The camera's doing a pan around the ground, the Oval in the early evening, shadows and sunshine, ground pretty full, England, yes, England – still recognizably the same ground that Mummy brought us to, Nigel and me, when we were eleven and ten. She wanted to show us, to make us understand and feel –

I took a break, walked around the garden, sat smoking – here there hasn't been sunshine, here there's been rain, thunder, lightning and sunshine all mixed up, get a patch of sunshine while you can, so I sat smoking in a sudden patch of sunshine, George and Toto and Errol settled around me, Victoria in her study, I was gone for not much more than half an hour, I should think, with the video working to record Flintoff's innings, and came back in as he was saluting the crowd who were saluting his half-century. He stood with his bat raised, massive and young, blond hair curling out from under his helmet, his eyes clear and joyful – fodder for the slaughter in 1917, in Ypres or the Somme, body deep in the mud and entangled in barbed wire, hand outstretched, palm mysteriously clean, turned upward, doomed youth from the anthem, but here he is instead, the glorious young man of the moment, this moment in the evening of 19 August, in the year 2004, standing in the London sunlight in the centre of the television screen, his bat held up as if he'll be there for ever –

MORAL GEOGRAPHY

I'd thought I'd got rid of Bugall, at least temporarily, by writing it all down a few days ago, but he's obviously still much on my mind, in fact I found myself talking about him this afternoon, on the telephone with Ian Jack, editor of *Granta* and of *The Smoking Diaries*. He seemed to know rather more about the case than I did, probably because he'd thought of doing an article about it in the days when he was still a journalist. He said I was quite right, Bugall wasn't Bugall's real name, then told me what Bugall's real name was – is, I hope – but I've already forgotten it, infuriating because it's so like Bugall that it almost rhymes. He also said that I'd got a few of the details wrong – that the ball didn't take place in Edinburgh, for instance, but in London, that the sexual assault manqué also took place in London, for instance, and that the trial, for instance, also took place in London. I asked him to consider the possibility that Edinburgh might have had him extradited on the grounds that they could guarantee him an unfair and prejudiced trial, with a vicious sentence at the end of it, but he said that as far as he knew there was, as yet (as yet!), no extradition treaty between London and Edinburgh. Well then, I said, well then, the Recorder must have come from Edinburgh, because that's where everyone who has any power to do harm in England seems to come from, so it was in its moral essence an Edinburgh affair, whatever the geographical incidentals. He said he'd check the Recorder's biography for me, find out where he was born and educated, I said no need, facts were merely facts, mistakes merely mistakes, we didn't want either of them getting in the way of my long-held convictions, besides we might conceivably have been thinking of two completely different but coincidental cases, involving men whose names almost rhymed. Convictions, now there's a word – the Recorder was, like me, a man with convictions, and when he'd finished with a.k.a. Bugall, a.k.a. Bugall was also a man with convictions, or with at least one conviction, a man convicted, a convict in an orange uniform, poked and prodded –

Enough, enough, I want a Bugall-free, a prison-free evening, here in Suffolk. But I must remember to think carefully before speaking to Ian Jack about issues that have left scars on my soul, take into account that he himself is from Scottyland, has a retentive and accurate memory, and is generally in the right – on the other hand he smokes, and is from Glasgow, I believe, which makes him what Harold would call 'a completely different kettle of fish'. A sympathetic kettle of fish.

HOME

Well, we came back from Montreal with our jug ears and our crew-cuts, our Canadian accents and absolutely no manners, and she saw at once that something had to be done, and quickly – first, then, to the girls' school in Hayling Island, where Nigel and I and two others, the Puke twins, one of whom actually did verb his name all over my father, at Nigel's tenth birthday party, were the only boys. We were sent to it partly because it was the only school on the island, and partly because the mother hoped we would be introduced to more delicate ways of behaving and speaking, a course of feminization, really, of the sort now popular, I understand, with the police force, large businesses, etc. I suspect that Mr Blair put himself through something like it when training to be Prime Minister, which would explain why he speaks and gesticulates as he does, and why women don't like him –

A couple of terms at the girls' school was followed by two years as boarders at Portsmouth Grammar School, where we were reprocessed from Canadian louts with a few girlish manners into basic English males – we added 'sir' and 'miss' to our vocabulary in short order, were very well taught at the school in Portsmouth, and rigorously overseen in the boarding house – I remember having to stand in the corridor outside my dorm, holding up my wet pyjama bottoms for the interest and amusement of passing boys. Mr Poole, the headmaster of the boarding school, was of medium height with spectacles and thinning grey hair pasted to his scalp – his particular gift was for dressings-down. He would have you stand in front of him, with your head lowered and your hands behind your back, and tell you about yourself in a thin, staccato voice for what seemed like hours, and he enjoyed an audience, summoning other boys to gather around and listen to what he had to say to Gray Minor, some of it might apply to them too, etc. He would finish abruptly, wheeling off and out of the room, leaving you standing, head still lowered, before a semicircle of your peers – lifting your eyes to them, trying not to see their expressions, was the worst moment of the experience, and made you wish that Mr Poole was still in front of you, protecting you from them by telling you how disgusting you were – 'disgusting' was one of his favourite words, also one of my mother's, and is now one of mine, by the way. At the school itself there was Miss Foster, a pretty young woman, soft and round – I fell in love with her because she reminded me of Grandma, and furthermore took trouble over me, helping me to catch up to where I would have been if I'd started my education there – and Mr Watson, a cockney with a foul temper who must have been on the verge of retirement, or even beyond it – he read *Great Expectations* to us with gestures, growls, a vast range of facial expressions. I remember particularly how he turned the whole class upside down in the graveyard and dangled us by our ankles, every one of us, by the sheer power of his reading personality – he was a magnificent Magwitch, of course, but he was also Miss Havisham, Estella, Joe and Jaggers – for all his sudden and inexplicable savageries – a thump across the back of the head, the blackboard duster hurled at your face – he was a great teacher, of the sort now jailable, or would be if he weren't extinct.

FROM 0 TO 12

Three years jouncing in a pram or toddling in Hayling Island, five years smoking on the streets of Montreal or romping on the bed with Grandma, two terms in a girls' school on Hayling Island, and two years with Mr Poole in a boarding school in Southsea, the same two years with Mr Watson and Miss Foster in Portsmouth, and then another two years in London at a prep school in Putney, where my life was controlled by the perfumed, prowling Mr Burn and the gym-shoe-wielding, bottom-beating Mr Brown, is how I went from nought to twelve – the early years, neatly accounted for in the terms that mattered most, or matter most now, when I remember them – our Canadian accents didn't last long, not only were they feminized and nuanced out at the girls' school, but at home Mummy made us repeat after her 'the brown cow went round the white house' – can that be right, white house? – and 'how now, brown cow?' and so forth, until we were on our way to being plummy, our ears grew smaller as our hair grew out to a length where Brylcreem could be applied – no, the Brylcreem came later, in adolescence, but there was a sort of oil, paraffin oil – can it really have been paraffin oil? – for special occasions. But some of our Canadian attitudes were difficult to reform – in England boys of our class and age had had food rationing and proper teaching, in Montreal we'd had cream, butter, eggs, meat, poultry, fish, cakes, biscuits, chocolates, candy and cigarettes – and for education Captain Marvel, Batman (and Robin, the Boy Wonder), Superman, Superboy, Supergirl, Spiderman, the Green Hornet, and it was from American comics that we learnt that America had won the war, both wars, all wars – so we had a sturdy contempt for the perceived namby-pambiness of English life, at least in its social aspects –

JOHNNY, FROM THE CLOUDS

But then there was cricket. Mummy believed in cricket, her father had loved it, she herself had played it, it was at the heart of England, of being English, it was through cricket we would learn how to be gentlemen and, best of all, we would learn it out of doors. One afternoon she took us on the ferry from Hayling Island to Gosport, and then on the train to Waterloo, and then on the bus to the Oval – it was a weekday, sunny, and the ground was full – for a few years after the war the cricket grounds of England were almost always full, whatever the day of the week, whatever the weather. Surrey were playing Glamorgan – I'm sure it was Glamorgan because this was the first I'd heard of it, Glamorgan – and Mummy explained, or tried to, the rudiments of the game, i.e. that the jerk who couldn't seem to throw the ball properly, in fact didn't seem to know how to bend his arm, was called the bowler, and what he was doing he was doing on purpose, in conformity with regulations, and the two men who kept running past each other with lumps of wood, long handles attached, were the batsmen, who seemed feebly incapable of doing what any American would do – smash, thrash, belt and beat every ball out of sight – instead they sometimes actually missed it completely, at other times patted it along the ground, even when it was thrown up so slowly that a blind man could have had enough swipes at it to make contact, and then there were the cowardly protections around the legs, the comical little man with enormous gloves behind the three sticks of wood with tops on, and also there was the lack of noise, excitement, adventure – all those people, and all they did was clap, for reasons incomprehensible, though it's true that there were occasional exclamations, 'Good shot, sir!' 'Oh, well caught, well caught!' and 'Bowled, sir!' and 'Well played, jolly well played!' from Mummy, sitting on the grass behind the boundary, near the pavilion, dressed for the occasion in a floral summer frock, a large summer hat on her head, legs tucked athletically under her, a hamper containing boiled eggs, unwieldy chunks of bread and marge, and a thermos of sweet tea at her side, a perfect picture of an English mother at the Oval on a summer's day, but in memory with a whiff of something else about her, perhaps it was her cigarette smoke, and the red lips, that suggested another life, another history, of the wartime air base and waiting at dusk for Johnny or Jim or Jack to come plunging down through the darkening clouds, or limping back low over the trees, over the hedgerows, the fuselage leaking a black plume or billow – Jack or Jimmy or John – Johnny, it was Johnny, the lover I gave her in my play *The Late Middle Classes*, written when I was older than she was when she died – it was almost a paternal gift, you might say, from her ageing son to the ghost of his still-young mother. Anyway, back or rather forward to the Oval in the summer of, probably, 1945, Mummy clapping, smoking, crying out, 'Oh, well played, sir' – but it was no use, it didn't take, the game was obviously for very old people – and actually they were quite old, most of them, older than they should have been, because of the war – some of them balding, and some with spectacles, and some quite slow and fat, how could this be a game for boys who lived their internal lives as Superman, Captain Marvel, and in my case above all as the Boy Robin? – so we scuffled off and messed about in some corner of the ground, fought too, I expect, as we couldn't get through twenty minutes alone together without fighting, and viciously, thumbs in eyes, knuckles in nostrils, elbows, heels and toes, giving and receiving, then back to Mummy and the hamper for our picnic lunch, Mummy pouring out the tea from the thermos, taking the lumps of bread and margarine from the hamper, cracking an egg with a flourish, and out ran the yolk and the white, into her lap and over her frock, because she'd forgotten to boil it.

WHERE I WAS WHEN –

Now this was before I'd seen Denis Compton, I know precisely when this was, well, not to the day, the week or even the month, but to the year – I'm rotten at calendar chronology, I can never remember where I was or what I was doing in any given decade, I can't retain the numbers, can't see them in my mind, I'm only confident of the date of my birthday because I can recite it, and I have to say it to myself out loud before I write it down on forms etc. – so to myself my chronology is really a sequence of 'and then's – and then I went to Canada, then to Hayling Island, then – then-then – right up to where I am now, now I am in our garden in Suffolk, writing this – in the same way I couldn't tell you the date of J. F. Kennedy's assassination, even if you pointed a gun at me. Like everybody else, I can tell you where I was when I heard the news – in the University of British Columbia, getting out of the lift as a North Country Englishman, an expert on D. H. Lawrence, was getting into it. 'Kennedy's been shot,' he said, glowing. 'Good thing. Johnson will do much more for the poor.' I remember trying to get back into the lift for more information, but the doors slid between us. He might even have said, or tried to say "ta poor,' because regional English took you a long way in the English Department of British Columbia – so did a Canadian accent, but I'd given mine up before I was nine and it was too late to get it back, even with tenure and a rise in salary at stake – so I can remember that, and his accent, and his expression, but I couldn't tell you the day, the month, the year of John F. Kennedy's assassination, and here is the ghastly truth, I couldn't even tell you the decade without working it out, like this: lecturing at the University of British Columbia when I was twenty-six, born in 1936, 26 plus 36 equals 62, Kennedy shot in 1962. Or in 1963 if it was after my birthday on 21 October (Trafalgar Day). Of course I could find out by looking it up on Google, but why bother, as I don't really want to know, and will forget it immediately after I've written it down. By the way, it was raining in Vancouver that day. I think I remember that. But then it was always raining in Vancouver every day of the eight or so months I was there, or so it seems to me now. But here is the point – the one year I remember, that I shall always remember, is 1948, because it was in the summer of that year that I first saw Denis Compton, and it was at the Oval, and I was eleven, and within minutes of watching him I understood everything about the game that I needed to know – and also what it was to be in love – Boy Robin had transferred his affections from Batman to batsman, did I really write that? Christ! Hello, batsman, goodbye, Batman – well, I don't think I can take it any further, although I admit that I find it difficult to imagine how Boy Robin would fit into Denis's life, Denis liked the good things, most especially women, so that would cut that aspect out from both our points of view, inasmuch as I like women too.

WELL, AM I GAY OR NOT?

Although a woman who interviewed me recently concluded, or pretended to conclude the interview – she was putting various things that were on the table, most of them belonging to her, I assumed, into a capacious handbag, was in fact bending down into it, as a preliminary to picking it up and departing with it from the premises – with a last question: 'Are you by any chance,' she asked into the capacious handbag, 'gay?' These days perhaps one is obliged to take it as a compliment – 'How kind, how very kind, I am flattered, but actually I'm afraid I'm actually quite the opposite, sorry to say –' But what is exactly the opposite of gay? And what is gay anyway? All my gay friends are quite different from each other, with quite different sexual tastes, and I can't imagine what exactly the opposite of any of them would be, except perhaps in one case, his exact opposite would be Virginia Mayo, or close enough for me not to know the difference. They say that everybody in the world has a doppelgänger –

AN OUTLINE FOR THE FUTURE

If so, isn't it equally possible that everyone in the world has an exact opposite, that to meet up with him or her would result in a double death, as a single death is said to be the case when doppelgängers meet? But what I actually said to this woman, who asked me via her capacious handbag whether I was gay, was 'Why do you ask?' to which she replied that I seemed to have close relationships with my men friends, which is certainly true, yes, but where does sex come into it? The thought of having sex with any of my men friends is actually revolting – to me, anyway, and I'm pretty sure to them too, even, perhaps especially, the gay ones – the confusion was really hers, not mine – or are many of what seem to us the most natural and easy of relationships really a subject of baffled speculation to others, even to our other friends? Well, how can I say, all I can say is that there is nothing about sex that is comprehensible except the primordial purpose of orgasm, which will surely be removed when genetic engineering gets into its stride – babies produced without sex, so a procreative drive with no creation needed, soon to become a vestigial instinct, but there nevertheless, poignantly – why is it such a poignant thought? No couples ever fucking for a purpose, although no doubt they'll all have a sense of purpose, from simple pleasure through the range we read and hear about, revenge fucks, grudge fucks, vanity fucks, comfort fucks, equality fucks, but no life fucks, new life fucks –

well, if they find out how to prolong and prolong life, perhaps they'll eliminate the birth element altogether, no new life, just the old lives renewed, the process of rejuvenation starting at an officially designated age – when you get to forty you go back physically to twenty, but go on emotionally and intellectually towards sixty, eighty, a hundred, a thousand, for ever. Why should it be assumed that death is inevitable? There may be men and women now who don't assume it, who are starting their work in chemistry, biophysics, mathematics, from the premise that death is not inevitable, merely another natural process that can be circumvented as so many already have been – you can't put your foot in the same river twice. No, said the clever student, you can't put the same foot in the same river twice, and no, said the one sitting at the back, you can't put the same foot in the river even once, because there never is a same foot – so imagine molecular change being looped into a circle, and instead of growth or decay you get a foot that endlessly repeats itself – could the brain be made to repeat itself endlessly? If so, it would have one of the main characteristics of Alzheimer's – there's already more than a premonition, expressed in the government's increasing desire to eliminate our past. The quickest and most successful way of eliminating the past is to eliminate the memory, which gives us the perfected citizen of the future, a zombie.

A LOVE STORY: PART ONE

Errol got another one this morning. Don't know what it was except that it had a tail and it was twitching – when I rose to my feet with an oath, he hurried into the shrubbery and stayed there a while, then came mincing out, portly and abstracted – which brings me back to whether or not I'm gay. The reason I'm coming back to that is this – that it's been on my mind that I didn't quite tell the truth when I told the woman interviewer that I wasn't gay. I believe I went on to write a few more sentences about the implausibility of my being thought gay, even by myself – but the truth is that I'd forgotten that for a brief period of my life, well, two years – how brief is that in the romantic chronology of a man coming up to sixty-eight in a month's time? – I was in love with someone of my own sex – what an odd phrase, my own sex – his name was Robert Symonds. Queen's Scholar at Westminster School. We were in the History Sixth together. He was as tall as me, with a deep voice, deeper than most boys of sixteen anyway, and he could make it boom when he wanted, boom quietly in a normal conversation for comic effect, and he had a deep laugh, deep and frenzied, his eyes would roll and he would throw his arms up and make shapes with his hands and it would almost seem that his hair stood up with laughter – it was a complete cartoon of a laughing boy, it wasn't exactly false, but it was deliberate, stagy, and intended to convey more than you could understand by the laugh itself – he was amused, but he was complicatedly amused, there were references that were entirely his that this performance hinted at. He was much cleverer than me, I think, and introduced me to all kinds of mysterious names – Man Ray, Manolete, Modigliani, just to choose one letter out of the alphabet, Charlie Parker, Cervantes, Camus, to choose another, and the Surrealists. He admired Jean Cocteau, his poetry and the photographs of him as well as *Les Enfants Terribles*, he could quote patches of the dialogue, in French, and he was very good at Latin, Greek, and English, of course. He was also a very good actor, a hypnotic Antonio in *The Merchant* – at least I couldn't take my eyes off him, and can see him now, standing alone in a self-created space on the stage – the other actors around him only there to make him the centre – dark, melancholy, brooding, opaque, lots of words like that, lots of stuff like that. Actually I don't really know if that's how he was in *The Merchant*, I think I'm really describing the effect he had on me as he stood in Little Dean's Yard in the mornings, in the place he used to stand when he was waiting for me – my eyes went straight to him, I could see no one else as I came through the arch from Dean's Yard into Little Dean's Yard, the end of my journey from 47 Oakley Gardens, the beginning of my day – and those things happened – my heart jumped, the back of my neck tingled, there was a dizziness in the brain – those things happened as they were never to happen again, at least not with that intensity –

A LOVE STORY: PART TWO

and sometimes I couldn't see him, I would step through the arch, my eyes going to where he wasn't, and the lurch of disappointment, close to despair. I would check the faces, knowing that the one I hadn't seen immediately couldn't possibly be there, and then he'd be suddenly revealed in a group of other boys, or talking side-on to a master, looking indeed like a master himself, and he was so easy and adult in his manner with adults, as well as charming and intense and singular in his manner with other boys, that seeing him with one or the other instead of with me – I could scarcely bear to look at him as I lurched from disappointment through despair to an almost suicidal desperation, now identifiable, in my late maturity, here in my Suffolk study, at the tail end of a glorious August afternoon, as jealousy – easily identifiable, actually, because frequently experienced subsequently, but never experienced so bewilderingly – subsequently, I knew it for what it was, and behaved accordingly, in two ways simultaneously: internally, I was down on my hands and knees, 'Oh, you do love me, please, you must love me, look what you're doing to me, help me, deliver me with vows of undying love and comforting cuddles and before that sex – yes, yes, why don't we talk about my sexual jealousy after we've had some sex, when it won't matter so much because our minds will be clear and our hearts pure?' etc., but externally, to the naked eye, I was up on two feet and proud with it, indeed blustering and self-righteous – 'Jealous! Jealous of what? Him? Hah! I was fed up, slightly, slightly fed up because you two went off without any explanation, leaving the rest of us, including your aunt – who's come all the way down from Dorset – all the way down from Dorset!' etc. – just like Fanny Price in *Mansfield Park*, really, when she sees Edmund giving Mary Crawford the riding lesson that she's expecting for herself, and declares that her emotional tumult is out of concern for the horse – 'She thought it rather hard on the poor horse to have to do such double duty' is, I think, Jane Austen's sentence, and if it's not, hers will be better – actually, the horse doesn't get to do double duty, Edmund finding his own moral justification for weaselling after Mary instead of plonking away with Fanny – well, that's Edmund for you. And that's Fanny for you. And that's me for you. No, it isn't. At least it wasn't with Robert, fifty years ago. There was no blustering and self-righteousness, there was just –

I'll come back to this if I want to, at some other time. No, what I'll do is look up my novel *Little Portia*, where I give a version of those events, as one might say in an old-fashioned detective novel, a version of the events leading up to the death of Robert Symonds, my first true love – perhaps it was spelt with two 'm's – Robert Symmonds, yes, that looks right – a version of the events leading up to the death of my first true love, Robert Symmonds – I haven't got a copy of *Little Portia* here in Suffolk, so it'll have to wait until I'm back in London – I have a suspicion, though, that I was too careful, kept myself as a writer too fastidiously at a distance from what had actually gone on, by which I mean what I'd actually felt, to have been quite honest in the version – version of the events – and how can I hope to do it now, half a century on? – at least the novel was only a decade on. But a decade on I wanted to keep it under control, in perspective, somehow not too personal, while half a century on I'd love to go half a century back, back to when Robert Symmonds and I sat hand in hand in some obscure nook in the Abbey cloisters.

A LOVE STORY: PART THREE

Hand in hand? Yes. How quaint it seems when I write it down, how quaint the image, two full-grown boys, tall and well built, in their school suits that weren't quite uniforms, a liberal school prescribing only the colours but not the shades or the textures of the trousers and jackets, and allowing some slight varieties in the cut, but then there were the stiff white collars, big black shoes – so if not uniforms then a general sense of uniformity, and of uniform clumsiness, yes, that was it, so clumsily dressed we were, or dressed to make us seem clumsy, as we sat on a stone bench or the lid of a tomb, generally in the late afternoon, our hands intertwined as we spoke of our feelings not for but about each other – now what is this distinction? I suppose I mean that our conversation, sometimes tremulous, sometimes savage, nevertheless moved in speculations and observations, 'The thing about you, Simon,' and 'I often wonder, Robert, why you –', rather than 'When I see you in the yard, waiting for me, my heart dips with apprehension and

longing – it's because I love you.' 'Love me, what do you love about
me?' 'I love – I love –' What did I love about him? That he was
mysterious, unpredictable, would suddenly snatch his hand from
mine, get up and walk away, standing with his head bowed, as if in
despair at the company he was keeping, while I would sit staring
at him hopelessly. I could never go to him and touch him and say,
'What's the matter?' or the question asked truthfully, 'What have
I done? How can I put it right? Please forgive me.' It would have
been a breach of something I couldn't formulate then and still can't
quite understand, so let me think – well, perhaps going to him and
touching him would have had too many possible meanings – and
to touch him where? On the shoulder, like a policeman – or made
everything too explicit, and above all it would have been a trespass,
in the sense of entering dangerous and forbidden ground – on the
other hand it might have been cowardice, a fear that any gesture I
made would be met with contempt, or a complete departure –
perhaps he wanted me to go to him and touch him, the more
meanings in the touch the better – at least he was still there, averted
but present, and would return, I prayed that he would return.
Usually he did, would come back and sit down and say in his loud
offhand voice something that amused him, and he would follow it
with his loud, forced laugh, and our hands would touch, enfold,
fingers intertwining – how odd it seems now, the intensity of those
meetings, how odd that I remember the feelings so strongly but
can't recall a single conversation, a single sentence from any of our
conversations, although I remember the content, which he mainly
provided – Sartre, Man Ray, Cocteau, etc. – and of course my
sporting life, how incomprehensible he found it that I should spend
afternoons playing football or cricket, it was a joke to him, though
not one that he much enjoyed because it was also treason, all those
hours when I could have been doing something intelligent, by

which he meant being with him in the cloisters, where we could hold hands, or in the Wren Library, where we could sit together in one of the rooms off, in the armchairs, and of course we talked about his impending death – he would be lucky to live until he was twenty, he said, would certainly be dead before he was twenty-five. He said it loudly and comfortably, or matter-of-factly or dramatically, and of course I didn't believe him, although I wanted to, death being a great and romantic adventure that seemed almost an aspiration – yes, I thought it was a boast, really, and admired him for its extravagance, because death was also something that didn't actually happen, at least to anybody one knew, apart from elderly relatives, who had been alive one month and then were dead by post the next.

A LOVE STORY: PART FOUR

It was true that on some of the days when I came to the yard and found him absent he was in the infirmary, his stomach bad again, but generally he would be back the following morning, or the morning after, his large pale cheeks slightly sunken as he hadn't eaten during the attacks – his stomach was rotting, he said, so yes, there's a fragment of a sentence I remember, his stomach was rotting and killing him – the rot had started at his prep school. He had been served a meal with little shards of glass in it, one of the cooks had broken a glass in the school kitchen, some of it had got onto his plate, he had swallowed it and – peritonitis, yes, he'd had peritonitis, which had become recurrent. I don't know how feasible this is medically – nowadays I imagine that you wouldn't die of recurrent peritonitis because they wouldn't allow it to become recurrent, if you survived the initial swallowing they could probably repair the stomach lining – or is it wall? Anyway, the infected area – yes, they'd solve the peritonitis problem, and you would merely die of something you'd caught in the hospital, from a dirty instrument or a pair of unwashed hands or because of language handicaps in the surgical team – in those primitive days you died, as Robert did, of your illness, not because of the people who were treating you – so half a dozen of one, six of the other, I suppose, given that the outcome is the same.

He was at Oxford, in his second or third year, I think that's right, and I think I'd just come back from Halifax, Nova Scotia, and was on my way through to France – no, back from Vancouver, where I'd been teaching at the University of British Columbia – back from somewhere, from somewhere, perhaps from France – no, this is irrelevant, I can't remember the chronology, all I really remember is the phone call to his house, his mother's voice on the line telling me that Robert wasn't there, he was in hospital, it was his stomach – his stomach again. Oh well, I said, when do you think he'll be out? She said she wasn't sure – she wasn't really sure he would be out, he was very, very ill. Then she told me which hospital he was in and asked me to go and see him. He'd love to see you, she said, he was seeing all his friends, and he'd mentioned me, that he'd had a letter saying I would be in England and that I'd phone – and here I was, having phoned, she was so glad that I had, before it was too late, so that I could go and see him. Well, I said, well, I'd love to go, I hoped very much I'd be able to go, I'd find some way of fitting it in, if I possibly could, before I went on to wherever it was I was going on to, Halifax, Nova Scotia, Clermont-Ferrand, France, Vancouver, British Columbia, wherever the hell it was I was going on to –

A LOVE STORY: PART FIVE

The thought of Robert, in a hospital, dying – it was too complicated, dark and grown-up a thought, I couldn't allow it in properly. I talked to several friends from school who had been with Robert at Oxford and who visited him in hospital – prepare yourself for a shock, they said, he's very thin, his voice is thin, you almost won't recognize him – but there's still something about him that's Robert, the smile of course, and the way his eyes light up when he sees you, he doesn't seem to mind that he's dying, that's the most Robert part of him, so exactly Robert – he'll be so glad to see you, you and he were always so close, everybody knew that it was a special friendship, he loved getting your letters – he used to read bits of them aloud and laugh, laugh – be so glad to see you –

I set out one day, in fear and trembling. I can't remember how far I got, but it was nothing like far enough – I think I knew before I set out that I wasn't going to arrive. Nor after that did I phone the hospital, or his mother, or his friends, to find out how he was doing, whether there was any chance – a reversal of fortune, it had all been a bit exaggerated, panicky – but suppose he recovered, how would I be able to meet his eye, explain my failure to see him when he was supposed to be dying? I could imagine him telling me that really, it had been a test, and I'd failed it.

If it did, in fact, feel like a test, it was because I knew I'd failed – I was ashamed, but the shame wasn't as strong as my fear, I could live with my shame if it meant not having to see him, it was a price willingly paid. I was in that respect in complete sympathy with myself – the truth is I'd rather have died than seen Robert when he was dying, it would have been far less taxing, I could coast through my own death, which was after all an impossibility, and besides both events were unimaginable, though his came to pass whether I'd imagined it or not –

I'm at an age now when I should be able to forgive my young self – I could claim that I'd had too little experience of life to be expected to deal with death, the death of a friend – it was precisely because I'd had such a tangled and intimate relationship with him, because I'd held hands with him and longed to please him, had in my imagination saved his life on numerous occasions, had loved him more freshly and intensely than I'd loved any human being before, etc. – I wish I could say all those exonerating things, but the truth is that the shame has not only persisted but grown, I see that first failure as the most abject, because it seemed to mark my way in life – all my failures to come, including my present failures, were somehow licensed by that one – when you've been cowardly once you can be cowardly twice, indeed come to expect it of yourself, and then accept it in yourself – I am what I am, not my fault, childhood or genes to blame, and so forth –

A LOVE STORY CONCLUDED

I made it to the funeral. I remember absolutely nothing about it. Surprising, really, as it was my first.

AT HEART I AM A MERRY MAN

A playwright friend says he doesn't 'do' funerals. I point out to him that there's one he'll have to do, willy-nilly. He says that that one doesn't count, as he'll have no choice. But the other thing about him is that he loves memorial services, or 'celebrations of a life' as they're called these days, which I find baffling – I mean, how can you celebrate a life when it's no longer there? I can quite see that you can't celebrate a death, at least publicly, though there are quite a few deaths coming up during my lifetime, I hope, which I won't allow to slip by without a grateful thought – 'Yes, I admit I hated him/her,' suspects frequently say in thrillers, 'but I never wanted her/him dead!' But why not? I could reel off, right now, a list of people I want dead, and I don't think I hate them, I just don't like the thought of them, and if they were dead I'd stop thinking about them, and the point really is this – that so many people are going to die today, how much grief and suffering there's going to be, much of it anticipated, some of it not – in a film once a woman dying between putting on the kettle and the kettle coming to the boil – the shot of the kettle whistling as the steam flowed out – do kettles whistle any more? – but all those deaths bringing all that grief, why not hope that one or two from your list will be among them, bringing a little spasm of pleasure to at least your sad self?

A RESOLUTION

Enough of this. This must stop. You have to cultivate a new ambition, which is to continue writing this without again mentioning death or dying, friends dead or dying, and it really should be quite easy, as most of your closest friends are dead, none of the few left are dying, as far as you know, except in that they're living and therefore, etc., so enough of this. At your heart, you are a merry man, I am a merry man – so on to some merry thoughts, memories –

LAST DAY IN SUFFOLK

Suffolk, at two in the morning, after a warm and beautiful September day, with a large section of the moon, cold and beautiful, visible through my window when I push my chair forward and then tilt it backward – no, I've just done that and it's no longer visible, it must now be behind my study – I'll go out and look. No, not behind, at right angles to it, it's a three-quarter moon, the fourth quarter not gone but shaded down, so the eye fills it in and gives you the impression of a full moon that isn't properly round, slightly deformed, that fills the garden with light, and there is Tom. I left the door open and I can see her standing in the middle of the garden, her legs bent with age but her face lifted attentively, so there's a mouse about, or a vole – oh, I hope not, Errol did one this afternoon in front of me, a vole, held it in his paws and juggled with it before gouging it to death with his claws, he did it in a very detached manner, as if he had more important things on his mind – I don't, really don't, want Tom doing the same thing in the moonlight. Her body may be old but her eye and teeth are sharp, and she's more businesslike than Errol, no posturing and playing, a quick but ghastly dispatch, and all to show for it a speck of blood on her neat, white little chin, and a little red heap, there in the moonlight – solution, my favourite solution to a problem – shut the door, shut the door and the problem or corpse is no longer there. At least until you go out. Which you have to, in the end, even if the end doesn't come until dawn – but in the dawn there it'll be, a claim on your attention, and there I'll be, scooping it up in kitchen roll, carrying it to the fence, hurling it into the field – an elderly man at dawn, disposing of the remains, and Tom will be in the kitchen, waiting for my step and a saucerful of dry nodules, which is what we give our two cats for food these days, as dry nodules are said to be good for their health, makes them springier and more active, according to the package, which means that they're bad for the health of birds, mice, moles and voles – perhaps it would be an act of mercy to put Tom and Errol back on their previous diet, tins of compressed rabbit, chicken, etc., which they much preferred, I think, even if it made them bloated and ponderous – almost everything I eat makes me bloated and ponderous, I hope it doesn't occur to Victoria to serve me up saucers of dried nodules, if she does she might find me in the garden one night, with something between my jaws that she won't care to identify –

This is all because I am waiting for the telephone to ring. Dreading its ring. You can't shut the door on a mobile telephone, which is why I sometimes wish I could see its inventor between the paws or jaws of Errol or Tom.

PART FIVE

A BIRTHDAY CHECK-UP

Trafalgar Day – I am now officially sixty-eight, having from time to time during the year thought I was already sixty-eight. I suppose in a month or so I shall be claiming that I'm sixty-nine. But then my father used to say that I have a tendency to get ahead of myself, hence the troubles that befall me – but let us, today of all days, not get ahead of ourselves, let us look in the mirror in the cupboard in the hall outside our bedroom and study what there is here, in the present, on the first day of his sixty-ninth year. I've looked, I've studied, and what did I see but a man of my sort of age, with swollen cheeks, uneasy eyes, a lot of blackish hair sticking out in tufts, eyebrows that do much the same, plump lips, no visible teeth, general impression of paunchy slackness, of low self-esteem comfortably lived with – nothing, in fact, to surprise, all quite as expected.

We're talking of sixty-seven years ago, after all – just think of that, a man who, in 1936, was the age I am now would have been born into a world in which Dickens was alive, Tennyson, Browning, Matthew Arnold, Carlyle, Thackeray – Thackeray, not sure about Thackeray – so how the world changed between 1867 and my real birthday in the summer of 1937, when I was self-perambulating around the garden in my pram, with Mummy smoking away somewhere in the distance, Nigel in the kitchen with the Nanny, Daddy in his surgery behaving well or badly with a patient – and changed since then to now, when here I am sitting in my study, brooding on what I found in the mirror of the cupboard outside our bedroom – what will I find next year? Well, you can't look in the same mirror twice, that's for sure.

A VICTIM OF HIS APPETITES

I've just come back from an unsavoury walk. I always intend to settle for a quarter of an hour plodding away from home, and then quarter of an hour plodding back, thus giving me a full half-hour of walking – when I'm stopped by traffic lights I jog on the pavement until they change, keeping to the same pace and rhythm as when I'm actually on the move, but the sad fact is that I'm not getting past the Renaissance these days, I make it to there, and have two or sometimes three cups of espresso with hot water on the side, read whichever newspaper or a magazine I've brought with me, and then a quick bit of shopping, as if to explain to myself that that's really why I've come out, not to walk meaninglessly around and home again, but to perform certain necessary duties – today, after I'd finished my espressos and read most of the book reviews in the *Spectator* I ransacked my mind and became convinced that I had run out of chocolate – in this desk, in the first drawer to the right, level with my knee, I keep envelopes and postcards and bars of Green & Black's organic white chocolate, which I guzzle down – it really is a sort of guzzling, if I understand the word properly, in that I cram it into my mouth in lumps, sucking at it until it turns into a kind of custard, gulp it down even as I cram more lumps into my mouth, and I think I also make snorting and gulping noises – this is not a pleasurable exercise, I assume it's connected in some way to my alcoholism, some time after I stopped drinking I began to crave sweet things, all the things I used to loathe, biscuits, cakes, ice cream and so forth. Usually at dinner I'm the only one eating a pudding – in Barbados Harold and Antonia are always very keen to watch me eating my pudding, there I sit while the band plays on, usually out of tune, a girl with a raspy voice strangles a beloved ballad, elderly couples reel about in the moonlight, there I sit, under the benevolent gaze of wife and friends, with their glasses of wine in front of them or uptilting down their throats, yes, there I sit on display, a prize pig at his trough is what I feel I look like, but, trying to maintain a degree of dignity, I don't lower my snout into the bowl, I wield a spoon in a leisurely fashion, make between swallows interesting observations on this or that aspect of life and literature – but I believe I've already described my pudding behaviour in Barbados, probably described it when we were in Barbados, and anyway there it's a social matter –

GREEN & BLACK, RED-HANDED

But here, alone in my study at this sort of hour, when an awful gnawing begins in the pit of my stomach as if rats were at me there, and I begin to double up with hunger cramps, hunger-for-sugar cramps, I jerk the drawer open, scrabble a bar of Green & Black organic white onto my lap, tear off the wrapping and proceed as described above, grunting and snorting, custarding or should it be custardizing – guzzling. Yes, guzzling. So inevitably I need to be sure that there are lots of bars in the drawers, I dread running out of them as I dread running out of cigarettes, and even if I buy more when I've already got a drawer full it doesn't matter, I'll get to them in the end, I like to eat in sequence, as I like to smoke in sequence, pushing the new bars to the bottom, piling the old cartons of cigarettes on top of the new ones. In other words, it was perfectly reasonable to justify my outing, during which I happened to have consumed a couple of coffees, by bustling on up to Tesco's and emptying the shelves of Green & White's black organic chocolate, or whichever way around it is, Green & Black's white organic – I didn't actually empty the shelves, I took two handfuls and dropped them into my wire shopping basket, on top of the *Spectator*, and, trying to give the impression that I was shopping for a children's party, joined the queue in an orderly fashion. The service is very quick at Tesco's, they have a long counter with five or six cashiers, one minute there are a dozen people in front of you and you get irritable at the prospect of a long wait, the next you are at the counter, and a smiling young man is greeting you, and asking you if you have a club card or something – I don't know what a club card is, perhaps I should find out as it may entitle you to certain Tesco privileges, or reduced rates – anyway I said no, I didn't have a club card, and he said would I like one? And I said not immediately, perhaps the next time I come in – 'Ten bars,' he said, picking them up and counting them. 'Yes,' I said, 'ten bars,' and smiled an unembarrassed smile. 'And the magazine,' he said. 'No,' I said, 'no, I came in with the magazine. The *Spectator*,' and picked it up, and for some reason held it aloft, and out from between the pages slipped another bar, the eleventh bar, of Green & Black's white organic chocolate. There was no doubt about it – it had the look of something that someone had tried to hide – and probably no doubt either that I looked – the expression on my face, my eyes shifting about, the Welshness of me – as if I'd been the one who'd tried to hide it. I made no attempt to explain it, anyway, what could I say but that I didn't know, I really didn't, how it got between the pages of the *Spectator*, because in fact I didn't know, and saying it would make me sound as if I did know, know

perfectly well, as mothers and wives are in the habit of saying –
'You know perfectly well that you, how you, why you – how could
you!' etc. I lowered my head and stood with it bowed, so that I
didn't have to see his face as we completed our transaction. I gave
him a twenty-pound note that I keep in my back trouser pocket,
instead of my credit card, which I'd planned to give him – I had
some idea that tendering cash might make me seem more honest,
although it probably has the reverse effect these days, that I get by
on cash gleaned from other people's pockets, or from begging. I
took my change, and the carrier bag with the eleven bars of white
and black and green in it, and also the wire basket – this was
entirely a matter of nerves, false guilt, false shame, etc., and I have
to admit that he didn't behave as if he thought I were trying to
make off with the wire basket, in fact he was quite gentle, reached
over the counter and took it from me, and I left. Annabelle was on
the pavement in her usual spot, but facing the road, so I could pass
her without her seeing me, I didn't feel in the mood really, for
giving her cigarettes or receiving a compliment, but something
made me stop and touch her on the shoulder. She turned around,
and I took all my change out of my pocket and put it into her
hand. It was quite a lot, because there was a fiver included, at least
I hope it was a fiver, it might have been a tenner, or even a
twenty – no, couldn't have been a twenty, it was change for a
twenty, so all she got, really, was what was left of a twenty-pound
note after the price of eleven black and green whites had been
extracted from it. 'Thank you,' she said, in her usual dead-when-
receiving voice, 'much appreciated, I really appreciate it, thank you
very much.' Thus I atoned for a crime I hadn't committed, and
didn't feel any the better for it – I suppose I wanted the young
cashier to have witnessed it, to know that I wasn't the sort of man
who, at sixty-eight years old, stole bars of chocolate, in fact that

I was the sort of man who – what? The sort of man who is, I think, getting a bit absent-minded.

COMPLICATIONS AND MUDDLES

From one point of view it's perfectly reasonable for me to hate my work, lots of other people, all of them probably perfectly reasonable, also hate it. I like to think they hate it for obvious reasons, that they're bored by it because it's slow and undramatic, they find the dialogue irritating and predictable, etc., but it's possible that they dislike it for more complicated and personal reasons – they can actually hear my voice, feel my personality, running under the scenes, or possibly on top of them, and they recoil. Well, the personal and complicated is what I feel when I go to one of my own plays, although I'm not too sure about the complicated – my feelings, it's true, are a terrible muddle, dark muddle, but muddle isn't necessarily complicated, complicated suggests all kinds of subtle interconnections that you might be able to work out – as in the Shakespeare sonnet, for instance, 'Those that have power to hurt, and will do none' – whereas muddle is what you get when you buy a theatre ticket on one credit card and take along another one to collect it, or sign a bill in a restaurant where you think you have an account and don't, as I did the other evening. I signed with a flourish and left, and only wondered in the taxi going home whether I actually had an account, became increasingly convinced that I had or why would I have signed – 'Oh, by the way,' I said to Victoria when I got in, 'we do have an account there, don't we?' 'No,' she said, 'we don't.' 'Well,' I said, 'I think we may have now.' On the other hand we may not, what we may have is a criminal prosecution and/or a civil action, either of which could end in my ruination – what's the difference between ruin and ruination? But

WHY AM I HERE?

Oh yes, I've just looked back, I'm attempting to describe my feelings when I go to one of my plays, they're not complicated, as in a Shakespeare sonnet, but muddled, as in realizing you've signed for a bill at a restaurant where you haven't arranged an account – so furtive comes into it, a sense of having committed a criminal act – that's it, the public aspect, I feel like a criminal forced to sit with the jury and witness my own crime, witness myself committing it, and then showing it off. One of the things that might strike other people as odd, but doesn't strike me as odd, which is probably the oddest part of it, is that my sympathies, no, more than my sympathies, my whole digestive system and nervous track, are with the jury, at least its hostile members. I remember at the Huntington theatre in Boston last year, with Nathan Lane as Butley, a middle-aged and distinguished-looking man, almost certainly a Harvard professor, was actually slumped sideways as the play began – I was sitting on the aisle seat in the row behind him, he was about three along to my left, his spectacles dangled like mine from a cord – I couldn't keep my eyes off him, for the whole of the act I watched him, my fervent hope being that he was dead – but he started awake the moment the lights came up, turned to an equally distinguished-looking woman beside him, and spoke quite animatedly and warmly about something – and then they got up, laughing, and went off to the foyer and out, I presumed, into the muggy Boston night, mugging Boston night I hoped. They came back during the interval, sat close together as he expounded something erudite to her, down went the lights, and out he went, a few seconds into the second act, slumped in the same position, spectacles dangling, but this time he was less inert, I could see his shoulders twitching occasionally, as if something was interfering with his sleep, but – though here, in the early-morning calm of my study, I feel in retrospect a certain loathing for this man – then, as I watched him sleeping through both acts, the person I really loathed was myself. I always loathe myself when I see a member of the audience bored or made irritable by my work, it seems to me manifestly my fault that they're having a terrible evening, which they might even have paid for – sometimes, I suppose I should admit, I also blame the actors for having agreed to do the parts, the director for having chosen to do the play, the producer for making it all possible, but there is no getting away from the fact that the responsibility is mine – those hours and hours and hours spent toiling away, the long periods of worry, fret, sleeplessness, struggling to get a scene right, an exchange of dialogue telling and natural, I see myself there, at the typewriter, as a combination of fool and criminal, as if all those hours of worry, fret, sleeplessness were actually spent on planning a hopelessly unworkable robbery, for instance, or a vile sex crime which furthermore I intended to commit in public. So shame, really, is what I'm writing about, shame at seeing my work produced on the stage – or is it mortification? I think there's a difference, well, there must be inasmuch as I've sometimes felt both simultaneously – shame being a kind of hot washing down of oneself, a sort of sluicing, and mortification, a violent bitterness of the self against the self, when you're in shame you want to hide, when you're mortified you want to give yourself a hiding. Can these two states coexist? Well, that's what I meant by muddle as opposed to complicated.

FOR PURPOSES OF GRAMMAR

Let's treat shame and mortification as singular and ask – where does it come from, and why? Or is that the same question, the whence and the why? – I've not met any other playwright who experiences anything like this, in fact I know several who take an immense pride in the public performance of their plays, and not only consider that they're entitled to money from them, but get angry when it seems insufficient, talk about prosecuting the producer for fiddling the box-office returns, or suing him for not spending enough on advertising, I know of one or two who even blame the critics and the audiences when their plays fail – and there is one in particular who is fearless, one might almost say shameless, in his pride in his work – when years ago I went to see one of his plays, a well-written autobiographical piece in which he traced the roots of his present flowering back to his childhood – he'd been a misunderstood boy of quick feeling and powerful, original and, by his immediate family, discouraged talent – at one point, I glanced away from the stage and spied the author leaning so far out of a box that he was in danger of falling into the stalls, on his face an expression of sublime joy as he looked down on the boy on the stage impersonating the creative genius that was to become the figure in the box gloating down on him – I really don't think I have envied a fellow playwright as I envied him, with his proper and healthy pride in himself and his works, in contrast with my own cringing, cowardly dog of a spirit that would rather be skulking in a dark alley with a goat – goat? What do I mean? What do I imagine myself doing in a dark alley with a goat? Get to the question, which is: is *The Old Masters* a good play, or even an OK play? Now I've put it down, I gaze at it with dread, because I can see that it contains an implicit injunction: 'Go and see *The Old*

Masters, then come back and tell us in all honesty whether you think it's an OK play, let alone a good play. Go and see for yourself.'

I SEE FOR MYSELF

I didn't think I could do it, actually, get myself to the theatre. I haven't been near the play since its opening night five months ago, though I was constantly proposing plans to Victoria – 'I'll go next Thursday, if I'm up to it.' 'Why shouldn't you be up to it?' 'Well, you know, the West End at night –' 'You can take a taxi to the theatre, have one waiting when you come out, taxi straight home again.' 'I'd rather go by tube.' 'But you hate the tube.' 'Yes, that's the problem –' I refrained from ordering a taxi until the last possible minute, and didn't phone the stage management to say I was coming until I was in the taxi and past Notting Hill Gate, and even then I made it contingent – 'The traffic's very bad,' I said into my mobile as we sped along Bayswater Road, hitting a succession of green lights, 'so I may be late, and if I'm very late I won't come in, don't want to disrupt proceedings.' As I got out of the taxi, at the corner of Panton Street, I could see the hoarding for *The Old Masters*, and I thought of walking on and away, down the Haymarket, but my feet carried me to the doors, and then I was in the foyer, head down, shovelling my way through the crowd – crowd? Well, there was a definite cluster of people at the bar, almost enough to block my way to the little corridor that led to the private room. In the private room the stage manager who calls herself Pea had set out two Diet Cokes, a glass, a saucer for an ashtray, and from behind the door to the box came the peculiar hum and rustle of an invisible audience close by. I sat on the sofa, lit a cigarette and poured a Diet Coke in a kind of this-is-the-life manner, elderly and experienced playwright looking in on his successful play. Pea put her head around the door, and I told her not to tell the cast I was in, thinking that if they knew, I couldn't leave at the interval. I went into the box, which was long and narrow and could seat six, sat in the chair at the very end, adjusted it so I could get a proper view of the stage, crossed my legs, glanced down into the stalls, briefly took in the people moving along the aisle to their seats, the tops of the heads of the people already seated, got up, hurried back into the private room, and on into the lavatory, had a pee, flushed the lavatory, lowered its lid, sat on it and lit another cigarette. I was shaking. I wondered if I could get out onto the street without being noticed, wondered if I could leave a note for Pea saying I'd been taken ill, had had to go home, realized I hadn't got a pen, thought that perhaps I could go backstage and find Pea to ask her if I could borrow her pen so that I could write her a note telling her that I'd gone home because I was ill – flushed the cigarette down the lavatory, wondering if the flush could be heard in the auditorium, went back into the box and sat on the chair in the furthest corner just as the lights were going down to signal that they were about to come up. And they did, on Barbara Jefford in the garden of I Tatti, reading a letter, clutching suddenly at her stomach and moaning in pain, then forcing an appearance of ease on herself as Edward Fox and Sally Dexter – Bernard Berenson and his mistress, Nicky Mariano – entered, Edward quacking like a duck – this is not a criticism of Edward's vocal delivery or acting, he is in fact imitating a duck.

I hoped that the actors couldn't see me – or, what would be worse, couldn't just make out an unidentifiable and ominous bulge deep in the shadows of the box, and imagine perhaps an armed psychopath seeking care in the community, or a theatre critic – but they went on playing the play as if I weren't there, and almost as if the rest of the audience weren't there – they hadn't quite achieved the perfect arrogance that separates the world of the play from the world in the auditorium, there were moments when they paused slightly too long to accommodate a response they'd become used to but last night didn't come, then suggested by other pauses or a break in a line that they had become used to laughter there and there, but that didn't come either – so, assuming a slowness in the audience, they developed a thoughtful, expositional tone, to help it follow the line of the story, but the crucial thing was that even when they did their pauses for one reason or another, and fell into expositional mode, they were still listening to each other, keeping their concentration on each other's lines, and so the play moved naturally if a bit ponderously through the exchanges. Altogether, the production was as solid as it had been on the first night –

Which only leaves the play to be all right to make it an all-round all-right evening. Well, here goes. The play, *The Old Masters*, seemed to me, it seemed to me that *The Old Masters*, my play – what's on? Let's have a look –

IN DENIAL

bowls on the sports channel, bowls – well, I always think that if I forced myself to watch bowls often enough, for long stretches at a time, I could get hooked on it, but then it's not, for me, a very interesting game, so why would I want to get hooked on it? I don't think that, even if I got hooked on it, I'd find it interesting, although there's no reason to believe that I would feel guiltier watching something I'd made myself become addicted to, that wasn't interesting, than I feel watching all those other things I'm addicted to, cricket, soccer, tennis, rugby union, and now even rugby league, and sometimes even golf, that I do find interesting. The guilt has to do with what I'm not doing instead – writing – rather than with what I'm actually doing, so it doesn't matter what it is I'm doing if it isn't what I think I ought to be doing – let's change the channel. Oh, here's

CARY GRANT

in black and white – God, he's beautiful, extraordinary, I've never seen a modern face, a young face – how old is he in this film? Early forties? – I've not seen a face like that on any man in his forties in these days, not that it's an old-fashioned face, his haircut doesn't look particularly old-fashioned, although the film was probably made in – what? At a guess early 1950s, let's have a look at the title. It's a marvellous thing about Sky Plus, you press the blue-coloured crescent-shaped button on your remote control and the name of the film you're watching, *People Will Talk* in this case, comes up on the screen, but you have to be careful, if you hold the button down too long it tells you what's on the next channel, and then the next, and you get confused, not remembering which title belongs to the film you're actually watching – ah, he's a doctor, putting on a white coat, lighting up a cigarette – in a bit of an old film I saw recently there was old James Coburn, well, a very young James Coburn – I came in on it when he was lighting a young woman's cigarette, in close-up, and then he lit his own cigarette, they spoke intensely to each other as the camera moved back, and you saw that they were both wearing surgical gowns, the scene went on for a bit, they talked movingly to each other and it was about then that we discovered, no, everyone who'd been watching the picture already knew, it was I, coming in late, who discovered that this conversation between a smoking surgeon and a smoking nurse was taking place over the operating table on which the patient, full of the usual tubes etc., with the anaesthetic mask over his face, was laid out – otherwise he or she would have been smoking too, I hope – now those really were the days, and in Technicolor. So Cary Grant as Dr – she's just said his name, Preorious was it, Pythagoras, no, obviously not, well someone will say it again soon, the girl is obviously the other star of the film, I know her face well from a memory of all the films I saw when I was in my early teens, but I can't remember her name, if I ever bothered to take it in, a neat little face, pretty, I suppose, but slightly foxy and knowing, not quite right for the part, which is a mess of a part, as far as I can make it out, she's pregnant by a man she's not married to, and who is probably going to remain off-screen because here she is, falling in love with Dr Pergorious, whatever, anyway Cary Grant – and furthermore she's just tried to commit suicide by shooting herself in the hospital corridor having left Cary, who first of all told her, his face and voice full of cheer, a good-news doctor, that she was pregnant, and when she told him that being pregnant was in fact bad news, given her circumstances, he told her to look on the bright side, though I don't think Cary was quite sure what the bright side was – she leaves his office, we stay with him while he lights a cigarette, there is the sound of a shot and we go to her lying in the corridor –

(BUT WHY SHOOT HERSELF?)

It seems a bit odd, to me, to be visiting a doctor with a gun in your handbag, and using it on yourself when you find out that you're pregnant, which you didn't even realize was on the cards –

the reason she'd wanted an examination from Cary was because she'd fainted suddenly while attending a sort of post-mortem Cary was giving, no, that he took over because the old doctor who was meant to be giving it was in somebody or other's office, snooping about for information on Cary, of whose success with patients he has become jealous, leaving his first-year medical students idle – so Cary, who popped his head into the lecture room, immediately grasps that the students have been abandoned, and starts to discuss the corpse of the young woman spread out on the table in front of him, discusses it with relaxed authority, elegance, charm, wit, etc. – absolutely pure Cary, as self-possessed with a corpse as when dodging bullets from the nozzle of a crop-spraying plane. Is all this clear? Why do I want it to be clear? Why am I writing it down? Oh yes, it began with turning on the television in order to avoid doing something distasteful – oh yes, thinking about *The Old Masters* – and seeing Cary, Dr Cary, smoking a cigarette – and realizing yet again what a beautiful man he was,

CARY GRANT AGAIN

with something secret about him, all the merriness, the sparkle in the dark eyes – what colour were they when he was in Technicolor? – but in black and white they're dark – the voice with its odd, engaging accent, neither English nor American, not transatlantic either, entirely his own accent, it's merry too, a merry, intimate, crisp voice, but it also has something secret about it, it's almost the most important thing about Cary's charm, the feeling that he's withholding, will always withhold the self that is the source of all this sparkle and merriment, so he's also a bit dangerous, in a way that has nothing to do with his slightly studied unpredictability – an odd, out-of-place gesture or an over-extended vowel that is nearly a mispronunciation, those are gimmicks, actor's personality gimmicks – now what was it he said about himself? 'Everybody wants to be Cary Grant. Even I want to be Cary Grant.' And then there were all those rumours, even before his death, about him and Randolph Scott, the rock-solid hero of lots and lots of B-movie westerns, he was really an off-the-peg version of

GARY COOPER

– no, that's not fair to either of them, there could never be an off-the-peg version of Gary Cooper, he was unique, inimitable, impossible to follow the contours of his smile even if you had it in a photograph in front of you, impossible to capture the shifting shyness in the eyes, the odd, wayward furrows of his brow – the face of a poet, really, that a poet never has, the most beautiful poets' faces have never expressed the poetry of Gary Cooper's face, and very few of them could express it in their poetry, either. Now there's a question for an old-style examination paper, which poet has come closest to expressing the poetry of Gary Cooper's face? I suppose we ought to try and think of an American one, but actually I'd go for Andrew Marvell myself – but you wouldn't look to Marvell for Randolph Scott's face, which wasn't poetry anyway, it was prose, sturdy, workmanlike prose, almost inexpressive apart from the rather rugged smirk he always wore, as inexpressive as his voice, which was rugged too, of course, almost without inflection, robotic, but he had presence, no getting away from that, he looked right in cowboy clothes, deer-skin type, and usually a hat – so let's

give up the intended comparison between Randolph Scott and
Gary Cooper, and get back to the question – which was whether
Randolph Scott used to tie Cary Grant up in his gym and whip
him? And to the next question, which is why I'm asking this
question, as I'm not keen to know the answer, especially if it might
be yes, yes, Randolph did hang Cary up in his gym and whip him –
but why should I mind, there's nothing particularly wrong in
wanting to be tied up and whipped, I suppose, unless it's the
thought of Randolph Scott doing, and of Cary Grant receiving, the
whipping – it offends not as an act in itself, people who get pleasure
from whipping should whip whom their whipping pleases and so
forth, but there's something about Cary Grant –

LET SCOTT WHIP SCOTT

well, what it comes down to is that I can't bear to think of
Randolph Scott even lighting Cary's cigarette, let alone whipping
him, they shouldn't ever have been in the same room together,
Randolph Scott should be whipping Lizabeth Scott (no relation,
as far as I know), who was a regular villainess, femme fatale, etc.,
in B movies of the 1950s, she had a husky, lisping voice, and a
boldly androgynous face, and a sheaf of hair that fell down one
side of her profile, masking it almost, and she made me
uncomfortable every time I saw her on the screen, not in the way
that Virginia Mayo made me uncomfortable, aroused, quite the
opposite, she made me feel that she was – was – well, now I can
identify her, I think, as a lesbian, at least my memory transforms
her into a lesbian because it brings knowledge and experience
gleaned over a number of decades, not that I believe for an instant
that I can identify lesbians by their expressions, voices,

mannerisms, unless they're wearing earrings, nose-rings, tattoos, have spikily cropped hair, purple lips, growling, angry voices and biceps – in other words are actually presenting themselves to me and the world as bull-dykes – but Lizabeth Scott was sleek and silky and, as I say, lisping, and used to like to stand with her hand on an out-thrust hip, or her arms around a man's neck, smiling intimately into his eyes, and all the time she was letting you know, making you feel, that she wasn't feminine, not in relation to men anyway, that she was a snake, poisonous, that her kiss would be a bite and you'd sicken from it, become corrupt, die – in fact, she scared me when I was eleven or so, and I hated her being in films with men I loved, like Glenn Ford – I don't think she was classy enough ever to get into a film with Gary Cooper and certainly not Cary Grant, but she'd have been perfectly right in any frame of a Randolph Scott film, they could whip each other in scene after scene, as far as I'm concerned.

CARY GRANT: PART THREE

I still haven't got Cary's name in this film, irritating, as people keep saying it perfectly clearly but it slips straight through my consciousness – it's moved on quite a bit since I started writing about it, the rodenty girl has introduced us to her family, a grisly, pipe-smoking father who tells us that he's a failure in everything he does, which we're meant to find lovable, but as far as I'm concerned he's failed in that too, in fact I vastly prefer his completely unlovable brother, off whom he sponges, a mean-spirited, small-minded bigot of a farmer – the sponging, lovable brother, by the way, lets us know that in the heart of himself he's a bit of a poet – horrible to see Cary having to pretend to lap all this up, having to pretend to love this phoney old father, as well as be in love with his rodenty, pregnant, suicidal daughter – it's a ghastly film, really, Cary is far too good for it, and so is the dialogue. That's strange, but it's the case, the dialogue flows along, some of it smart, some of it witty, always eloquent, with long sentences that are not only grammatical but elegantly constructed and yet sound natural when spoken – now those really were the days, cigarettes and proper dialogue properly and easily spoken – everybody in the film, minor roles included, gets to speak it – in a silly, psychologically nonsensical film there is proper dialogue, while nowadays we get – oh, don't bother, don't bother to go into what we get nowadays, instead get on to

LOOK AT ME

which is the idiotic English title for the French film *Comme une image*, we saw at the Gate last week – a freak of a film, full of intelligent and civilized people behaving to each other as such people frequently behave to each other, egocentrically, thoughtlessly, narcissistically, with mainly accidental but sometimes deliberate cruelty, all of them perfectly observed in their smallest reactions, all of them intensely sympathetic even when they go against the grain of one's own good manners and kindness, which are always at their most evident to oneself when one is witness to the bad behaviour of people rather like oneself – there is a marvellously painful moment when the novelist father goes to a concert in a church at which his daughter, a fat girl with a great deal of prickliness in her, to do with her consciousness of her fatness, and the ways she is constantly slighted, or feels she is – though at moments the film catches her in an expression which makes her the most beautiful – I mean physically beautiful – creature in it, and one sees how one could fall in love even with her ill-temper and her swiftness to take offence – anyway, it is one of the most important moments in her life, her singing solo at this concert, and we watch her, and then her friends, her boyfriend, her music teacher, and then and above all her father, in the back of the church. As his daughter sings, he gropes in his pocket – for what? We don't know, but whatever it is he can't find is something he needs urgently. He turns to a faithful acolyte beside him, makes a gesture, the acolyte fumbles through his pockets, until further down the row someone produces a pen, it is passed from hand to hand to the father, who nods thanks, gets up and slips out of the church, his daughter in full, haunting flow – we see shots of him from a distance, slightly hunched, walking with a purpose, the music from the church following him as he recedes, and then we go back to the church, to the daughter unaware of his departure – such an everyday sort of treachery, which should nevertheless have robust consequences, and in fact the daughter minds, the father is embarrassed, when they sit alone and discuss it later, on the doorstep of their country house, the moon out, a few guests inside, he manages a hint of an apology, she accepts with a daughterly laugh of incredulity, and the moment is gone, an amusing moment because it's true, and a sad moment for the same reason – so here is a film, a film worth going out for, looking for, travelling across London and the Channel for too, if it's stopped showing in London, a film that makes you ask –

WHY CAN'T WE MAKE SOMETHING LIKE THAT?

And how can the French do it? How do they get the funds to do it? Of course it's elitist, one imagines the British whatever, lottery, I suppose, is what you go to when you want to make a film – they say, what's it about? And you say, it's about this rather fat girl who wants to sing professionally – not pop and crap but proper music, cantatas and so forth – and is the daughter of a talented but selfish (unusual combination) novelist who thinks his creative balls are shrivelling, and about another younger but rising novelist whose wife teaches the rather fat girl singing, about these sorts of people and how they get involved with each other, take advantage of each other, fail with each other etc. Now, can one seriously imagine anybody from the lottery, anyone from our film industry, putting up money for a film with a story like that, with people like that in it? What they put their money into, our money into, is

GUNS AND BUMS

vile gangsters films in which disgusting people mangle and shoot each other and every next word, and sometimes the word in between, is an obscenity – or into a lumpish comedy in which much the same people, using much the same language, expose their bums etc. It's true that there's an occasional classy product, once every few years or so, in which a mixture of English and American stars fall in love with Hugh Grant, who frowns and frets and stammers and tumbles his hair about in that charmingly old-fashioned way, and shows his teeth a lot – they're probably very good, the fact that I can't stand them myself is not really the point, they make money without being on the one hand violent or on the other infantilely lavatorial – but I don't want to give the impression that the vile and violent gangster films we make, or the infantilely lavatorial films we make, also make money – they lose it, as they certainly should in a just world, but in a just world they wouldn't get made, in a just world the English, British, whatever name we go by these days, director would be forced to sit through *Comme une image* – and then he would be given a gun, as from one of his vile gangster films, and then locked in a lavatory, as in one of his infantile lavatorial comedies, no, not locked in it, bricked up in it, and he there can mess about with his favourite prop in his favourite location until shame, hunger, madness and so forth compel him to raise it to his mouth.

None of the above speaks well for the civilizing influence of *Comme une image*, at least on me – in fact, thinking about it with affection and admiration seems to have driven me into a frenzy of disgust – but sometimes the contemptible awfulness of this culture of ours – but what about your own play, eh? Which is what started you off on all this. Well, at least you can claim that a) there are no guns in it, b) there are no lavatory jokes in it, c) there is no nudity in it, d) nobody swears in it, not once, and e) everybody speaks in complicated and mostly intelligent sentences, and they do it as if it were natural to them – which makes them freaks in our world, and the play a freak in London's West End. How amazing that anyone comes to see it, regardless of whether it's any good or not, which is a completely other consideration, and one that I'm trying to avoid addressing – so, so how come Cary Grant and the disgusting British film industry have between them led me

OUT OF DENIAL?

Because you can never walk in a straight line away from a thought you want to avoid, the thought is controlling your escape route, making your straight line into a circular one, back into the mouth of the thought – the thought being in this case that though the director and the actors had given the evening a rich and polished shape, and found a way of engaging the audience's attention, the playwright, the playwright, well, let's put it out there in its most unavoidable form, no, what I'll do is wait until I go in again, which will be three Saturdays hence, the last night, and I'll sit through it without flinching, no, I can't promise that, let's just commit myself to sitting through it, and concentrating on it with the intention of – well, just sitting through it. The good thing about this promise is that I can now abandon the subject for at least three weeks. So out with you, out and about with you. No, actually what is worrying me about *The Old Masters* is whether the scenes grow out of each other organically – Christ! Or Jee-zus! – 'grow out of each other organically' – the sort of horticultural vocabulary I used when I lectured on English literature at Queen Mary College, University of London, 'organically' was a particular favourite, long before it marked all those packages of everything from pork pies to yoghurt on the supermarket shelves, everything in *Hamlet*, for instance, was organically related to everything else, plot to character, character to theme, theme to structure, structure to symbol, symbol to image, image to plot, plot to character and here we go again – when of course the truth about any play – well, take *Hamlet*, as we've already taken it, take *Hamlet*, for example, particularly appropriate, as we're going to it soon – I must ask Victoria when – 'Hey!' I called out, 'when are we going to *Hamlet?*'

WHEN DO YOU THINK?

No reply from her study, so I went into the bedroom. George was on the bed, looking depressed, which suggested that she knew Victoria was going out. I could hear noises from the bathroom, the shower running and what might have been singing. 'When are we going to *Hamlet*?' I bellowed. She came out with a towel draped around her, hair damp, cheeks pink, charming to look at, obviously preparing for a night out. 'Where are you going? I didn't know you were out tonight.' 'So are you,' she said. 'What? Where? Where are we going?' which was almost a rhetorical question really, answered by the lurch in my stomach. On the other hand Toby Stephens is Hamlet, he's a friend and a terrific actor, so two excellent reasons for going, and really, when it comes down to it, the only slight thing against going is the play itself, which is bound to run well over three hours, it always does, and furthermore I can't bear – But I'd better go and get ready, ready for going out to *Hamlet*, which means popping a couple of co-praxamol against the anticipated longueurs, packing chocolate in my pocket against the inevitable hunger, and changing my shoes twice for no particular reason, that's what I do these days before going out, change my shoes twice, sometimes three times, usually ending up in the ones I started with – I expect Victoria would prefer it if I changed my shirt once, but I never promised her a rose-bush.

AND ONE JAUNDICED EYE

We had a smashing dinner, with Toby and his wife, Annie-Lou, who is very tall, with a stalk of a neck and a face like a sunflower, beautiful, in other words, and a very good actress. Toby, of course, is also beautiful, both on and off stage, has a glow about him – aura, is it? – that makes me think sometimes of Rik Mayall, who sometimes made me think of the Sun King, *Le Roi Soleil*, because of the glow or aura, as in those icons, Toby has that as Hamlet, and it's a fine thing, a royal body containing a royal mind – a quick, sarcastic, sometimes desperate royal mind, so there was that going for the production, and that, really, was all there was. The set was a circular grey wall, with sliding doors to keep the action flowing along, but the action that flowed along flowed along for far longer than registered by my watch – it was colourless, that was the thing, perversely colourless, when Claudius and Gertrude are reprimanding Hamlet for his mourning attire they themselves are kitted out in dun-coloured costumes, as was everybody in the court, so that Toby, with his starkly contrasting white and dark outfit, and his paley-pinky handsome face and luxuriously abundant golden hair, was by far the most striking figure, as of course he should be, but not in reverse, his bleakness should contrast with their opulence, he the funeral, they the wedding, etc. – but then it seemed unlikely that this couple, Gertrude and Claudius, had ever spent a moment together in bed, he was a bristly bureaucrat, meaninglessly emphatic, who'd knocked off Hamlet Senior because he thought he could do a better job as king, anyway would put in more hours at the office, and she was so agonized and bereft, so much the widow and so little a wife – what rank and enseamed bed, one kept wondering, or who's been sleeping in it, to make it rank and enseamed? Nobody in this court, not even Laertes and Ophelia – when they have the routine grope, the grope that most directors get them into these days while lecturing each other on the need for sexual discipline, pretty disgusting stuff actually, they behaved like two strap-hangers on the tube accidentally and irritatingly entwined, and they did their exchanges in much the same manner, their sentences meaninglessly but irritably entwined – now this Laertes wears funny white make-up when we first see him, and walks and postures in a manner usually described as camp, not that he has an interesting interest in Hamlet, either, or in anyone but himself and what shampoo to use – while Ophelia, who struck me as possibly a good actress unsuited, by temperament and, it has to be said, physique, to be Ophelia, comes into her own when madness descends, stalking everyone on stage with fingers pointing at their eyes or crotches, voice rasping, so that really you want her to get to the pond as quickly as possible – but on the other hand you can't imagine her sinking passively to the bottom after lying on top with flowers, you imagine her entering the pond with something of a splash, then realizing where she is, striking out for the bank with a powerful crawl. Osric, who requires plumage in dress and speech, is dun-coloured in both, Rosencrantz and Guildenstern not only indistinguishable from each other but from Osric – this court has neither life nor echoes, no distinguishing characteristics of any kind, although Polonius tries his hand at comedy, developing a self-important but lunatic laugh as the evening progresses. Bernardo, by the way, is inaudible in Welsh – you know he's Welsh, or is assuming a Welsh accent, because you half-catch a sort of lilting noise when he speaks, and his body has a lilt to it too, though it makes no more sense than his speech – he doesn't help himself or us by mainly addressing the back of the stage or the wings, which at least makes him different from most of the other actors in the production, who speak out front, to the audience, even when purportedly speaking to each other. This is the famous RSC house style, entrenched through decades – I first noticed it during the famous Henry IVs about thirty, could even be forty years ago, and what's more, no, nothing more, think positively, think – ENTER Fortinbras, thank God, surveying in stately fashion the proliferation of bodies generated by poisoned onions in the wine, mishaps, cunning, false slaughter, etc. He rolls his eye from corpse to corpse, pauses, hunches a shoulder, as if about to make an absolute corker of a joke, yes, please, then speaks in the rolling tones of an actor whose only scene is the last scene, only speech the last speech, announcing that Sheekey's is just around the corner, thank you.

AN ENDANGERED GHOST

But it strikes you, if you allow the thought to enter, that it's a narrative for an audience with lots of other things to do – drink, brawl, fornicate, eat oranges, urinate, etc. – it lollops all over the place, and to so many places, some of them unreachable even by academics and theatre critics – the two have a lot in common when it comes to Shakespeare, above all received opinion, which they send out in their turn to be received by others in their turn, so the view rolls on, through the generations, from generation unto generation, that Hamlet is one of the greatest masterworks of the human spirit etc. the completest expression of Western man's consciousness etc. – which speech by speech it possibly is – and that seeming anomalies and idiocies can be explained by intelligent (i.e. academic or theatre critics') analyses. The truth is that Shakespeare, although indisputably the greatest genius of moment-to-moment drama etc., and the greatest poetic intelligence in the history of the world etc. was in the making of plays – well, you get the feeling that his left hand is holding down the pages of his source, Plutarch, Holinshed, whatever, while his right hand is investing a character with character and translating his reported speech into iambic pentameters that pulse in the here and now of the stage. The trouble is, he follows the stories almost sentence by sentence it sometimes seems, and while it's OK to be haphazard in a chronicle, discursive, anecdotal, so forth, it's not OK with polite modern audiences, who can't skip the longueurs, unless they're lucky enough to have nodding-off tendencies. The undeviating nature of his transcriptions accounts for the oft-pondered mysteries – the ghost in *Hamlet*, the witches in *Macbeth*, etc., on which so many articles, theses, no doubt published books have been written – 'What function do they serve, these supernatural influences that Shakespeare insists on bodying forth and on which directors devote so much ingenuity? How do they connect symbolically, thematically, above all ORGANICALLY, etc., to the poetic dramatic unity, so forth?' – In the current production of *Hamlet* we have the ghost as a star turn, he has a ghastly and chalky glamour, and drags an immense sword that is both a weapon and an anchor to the underworld. He also has a slow, creaky agility – he leaves the stage by clambering up into a box, an interminable process which involves him in heart-stopping feats of balance and concentrated muscular strength, as well as nerves of steel – there was a moment when he hovered and trembled, one leg stretched forward to the rim of the box, another straining back to keep him upright, when we were in a sort of catatonic circus, the audience gripped by the intensity of the physical danger to the actor. But how can a ghost be in physical danger? – Well, that's the problem created by this production's ghost, that however spectacular a spectre, he belongs to a different order of underworld mythology from any suggested by his environment. But it doesn't really matter, because the problem created by Shakespeare is one that no production can solve, whatever sort of voice the actor gives him, booming, husky or hollow, it only works when it's issuing injunctions – 'Swear!' and so forth – it won't carry him convincingly through his bits of narrative. When he describes how he was murdered, there is too much detail – you can't go into narrative and detail in a cavernous, husky or hollow voice, you are working against yourself, losing your ghostly dignity with every sentence, turning yourself into a grievance – bore with a chest problem – the play would be vastly more interesting if Hamlet had to deal with the naturally perceivable facts, his father dead from a snake-bite while dozing in the garden, his mother remarried within a month, a little month, to his father's brother, and thrilled to be so – why not? A satyr is a satyr, after all, and knows a thing or two, while Hyperion isn't going to do the business where it counts – a sequence of thoughts along these lines might lead Hamlet to bleak speculations about what really happened in the garden, the snake crawling into his father's ear – now there's an image to jumble a son's emotions – and with the fangs striking and squirting into the dark whorl everything changes, Hyperion's court becomes the satyr's playground, funeral cold meats become a wedding feast, incest in the corridors of power, carnality and festivity throughout the kingdom, riot in Mummy's bed, Daddy's bed, Uncle's bed, whose bed? Shakespeare didn't need the ghost, but in it goes, because there it was in his source, and besides they always like a ghost or some such, and isn't old Bundlebap in town, he specializes in comic gravediggers, ghosts – so on with the story, what comes next, let's have a look, scribble, scribble, scribble, Mr Shakespeare –

Same with the witches in *Macbeth*. They're in the source, they're in the play therefore, therefore on the stage, and therefore they're a nonsense that has given rise to a steady stream of nonsense in the academies – that is, they used to, I don't know if Shakespeare is taught in schools and universities any more, though I think he must be, going by the number of teenagers in the theatre last night, why would they be there unless they were doing him in exams? If they have exams any more – anyway, exams or not, I must admit that they sounded as if they were having a good time whenever Toby was on stage, screamed with joy when he took his many curtain calls – which, by God, he deserved, because after all he'd given us Hamlet and the Prince, even though the director had left out Denmark, and there wasn't a state to rule over, or die in. Or for, therefore.

A GLUM PROSPECT

And oh Christ! there's another Shakespeare tragedy coming up in a few months, with a friend in it, so another night like this one in the offing –

WORDS OR INSECTS?

Offing? What on earth is the etymology of offing? But is etymology the right word, or does it mean the study of insects and such, and is the word I want entymology – I've just looked entymology up on Google, and the first item that caught my eye was An Entymology of the word FUCK, with FUCK in bold letters, like that, and the entry directly underneath it was (still is, I suppose) Entymology for Utah Fly Fishers, so I think I'll leave the question open for the moment, though I'd guess that my initial instinct was correct, and the word I wanted was the word I used, etymology, which brings me back to the etymology of Offing. In the offing – an extraordinary phrase, it almost ceases to mean what you know it to mean the moment you look at it, it becomes particular, as if it were a place – if it's in the offing, who put it there? Could you imagine saying, 'He left it in the offing,' and if you could, what would you imagine he'd left there? Stockings, he left his stockings in the offing. What would be the opposite of offing, onning? Yes, yes, they got tired of her perpetual offing and onning, people would know what you meant by that, especially if they spoke English – it would mean that she kept saying that she would, and also that she kept saying that she wouldn't. I must try it out on someone when they least expect it, to see if they look bewildered, or if they take it in their conversational stride – Harold would be a good person for this little experiment, as soon as the right context comes up – there's the problem of Peter Bowles, for instance, who has said several times that he'll do a tour of *The Old Masters*, but then again has said several times that he won't, so I'll raise the subject with Harold, and it'll be easy at some point to slip in, no, not slip in, I'll make it emphatic – 'I wish to God Peter Bowles would stop offing and onning' – and Harold will either say, 'Quite. I quite agree with you, we need to know one way or the other,' or he will look puzzled, he'll start up slightly, he'll say, 'What exactly do you mean by offing – and thing – what was that other word –?' 'Onning.' 'Yes, well, what exactly do you mean by that? That word onning?' To which I'll have to say, 'Well, you know – now on, now off, now off, now on, onning and offing, offing and onning,' and then he'll probably say, 'Oh. Prevaricating, in other words,' and 'Yes,' I'll say, 'prevaricating, in other words,' and the conversation will move to a different subject – though I doubt if it will be as important as finding an actor to do the tour, because the tour will bring in some money, which I will need when the London run ends next Saturday.

BUGGINS'S TURN

Judy Daish phoned this morning to say that a letter had just arrived at her office, it was from the Office of the Prime Minister, 10 Downing Street, it was marked on the envelope as urgent and private, so she had opened it, to make sure it contained nothing abusive, should she send it around, as it was in fact an enquiry as to whether I would be prepared to accept an honour in the New Year's list? Yes, I said, do send it around, let's have a look at it. It arrived half an hour later, inside a large brown envelope which was in the grip of a helmet-headed, leather-jacketed delivery man – we did a scuffly business on the doorstep, with him giving me the envelope while he sorted out his clipboard and pen, me returning the envelope to him as he gave me the clipboard and pen, and then us both fending off Toto and George, who were scampering around our feet trying to gnaw his boots and the bottom of my dressing gown, a tattered blue-towelling affair that looks more stained than it is – I signed my name twice, once as a signature and then with a scrawl to identify my signature, handed him back his clipboard and pen, ushered the dogs back into the house, climbed the stairs back to my study, climbed down them again when the doorbell rang again, opened the door to see the same man, in his helmet and leather, holding a brown envelope out to me exactly as he'd done a few minutes before. It was, of course, the same brown envelope, which he'd taken away with him, along with his clipboard and pen. We had a little laugh about it, each blaming ourselves – a pleasant alternative to the common human practice – I got the dogs in again, got up to my study, sat down at my desk, not this one, the other one, with the typewriter on it, this one has the computer, lit a cigarette, put on my spectacles, opened the brown envelope, took out the white envelope, slim, elegant, official, and, as Judy had said, with the words From the Office of the Prime Minister at the bottom left, and Urgent and Private, top left. Inside were a couple of sheets of extremely white paper, one of which, couched in courteous but impersonal language, asked if I would consider accepting a jumble of letters with a B in it, the other resembled the sort of form you have to fill out when going through Customs, with little empty boxes that had to be ticked or written in. I wondered if I oughtn't to shower, shave and get dressed, there was something a little indecent about this companion and almost colleague of Annabelle and – and her partner, what name did I give him, can't be bothered to thumb back through all the pages, think, think, James, Annabelle and James, no, that's not right. Henry? Annabelle and Henry – Henry James, yes, of course, dreary little Robinson from *The Awkward Age*, *Tragic* – no, *The Princess Casamassima*, Hyacinth, Hyacinth Robinson, Hyacinth and Annabelle! Yes, so this companion and almost colleague of Hyacinth and Annabelle is sitting half naked, belly hanging, cigarette between his fingers, spectacles halfway down his plump and shapeless nose, stubble grey and growing, studying a letter in which he is being asked if he would like to have his name submitted to Her Majesty for consideration etc.

IMAGINED DELIVERY BY ROYAL MALE

On the other hand there is a distinct possibility that I am the victim of a joke, nobody in this country who was serious about communicating with someone else would send a letter through the post, especially if it involved the Prime Minister, the Queen and so forth, they would send it by a special messenger, who would run with it through the streets on naked feet, or thonged sandals, in a tunic and carrying the message slung over his shoulder in a special satchel with an insignia on it, and in his right hand an official stick which would possess such authority that it would work like a magic wand, traffic would gather to the side of the roads down which he ran, as would pedestrians when he ran along the pavements, traffic lights would change from red to green as he approached, the citizens would lower their heads in respect as he passed them, and on the door behind which the recipient waited, he would give three knocks with the knob of his wand, and when the door opened there would be a brief exchange – 'I have an Urgent and Private message from the Office of the Prime Minister, 10 Downing Street, for the playwright and man of letters Simon Gray.' 'I am Simon Gray, the author of the play *The Old Masters*, and of many letters to newspapers and to my son.' He would fall to one knee, the message extended. I would take the message, and have the messenger escorted to the kitchen, there to be treated with the courtesy due to, etc. – this is how, it seems to me, a serious man in 10 Downing Street, the Office of the Prime Minister, would send a letter to a man who might be seriously interested in acquiring an honour from Her Majesty the Queen. Needless to say, the same process would be repeated with the response, the refreshed messenger again on his knee, the letter placed in his hand, then through the door, the streets, back to the office in 10 Downing Street. It would be difficult, of course, to send an equivocal answer in such circumstances – 'I need a few days to talk it over with my wife, Victoria –'

A HUMBLE ACCEPTANCE

I woke at midday, got up for a pee, ate two sour plums, brushed my teeth, went back to bed, thought for a while, then called out for my wife, Victoria. I'd like to report that she came running from her study, which is next to the bedroom, but she merely answered my call, and only at the third or fourth time of calling, with a brisk noise that meant 'Wait.' When she came in she had the letter and the form in her hand. She sat on the edge of the bed, and I asked her if I were honoured what form would it take. A medal, presumably, she said, what other form could it take? Well, a garter, or a belt, or a combination of both, so a garter-belt, but how would I, albeit modestly, manage to show it off – wear a kilt? I'm entitled to a kilt of some sort, being half-Scottidge, a descendant of the Macdonald-slaughtering Campbells – my wife, Victoria, is descended on her mother's side from the slaughtered Macdonalds, which perhaps explains why I feel we were destined for each other, a happy variation on the Romeo and Juliet theme, although it's taken a few centuries to work itself out –

My wife, Victoria, filled out the form – she's practised from filling out medical forms on my behalf, though this was less complicated, just date of birth and some ethnic stuff when it came down to it. She said there was no point in going into all the quarter-English, quarter-Welsh, half-Scottidge, I'll put down British and have done with it, she said, and she did, then she handed me the form to sign, and I did, then she put it in the envelope and said she'd post it when she went out later, which she did. Everyone in the Prime Minister's Office, 10 Downing Street, now knows that they have an unambiguous 'Yes' on their hands, but from them I shall only have an ambiguous silence, I won't know if I'm in fact honoured until it's announced, or not announced, in the papers on New Year's Day.

LAST NIGHT AT THE COMEDY

I saw it pretty clearly, sitting at the back of the dress circle with Victoria, only missing a few minutes at the beginning of the second act because I couldn't tear myself away from the little private room in which we spent the interval. I wanted to have a cigarette on my own and savour the moment – although I don't quite know what the moment was that I was savouring, the run was coming to its end, the characters who'd walked the stage of the Comedy would walk it no more, the actors would go back to their homes, some of them start new jobs, they might never meet again except fleetingly, at those events where actors bump into each other, and, perhaps most movingly, my cheques for the week's royalties would stop arriving at my agent's office – so I doubt if I really wanted to savour the moment, I just wanted to savour a cigarette where a cigarette is best savoured, on one's own, in a room where you're not really allowed to smoke – so I missed that much of the second act, a cigarette's length, furthermore I only missed the sight of it, Edward Fox and Peter Bowles were perfectly audible in the little room, I could even hear the silences, one of which went on for so long that I thought Edward, whose turn it was to speak, had either dried or died – but then it came, Edward's voice, floating into the little private room like a phrase from a Gregorian chant, he gets into the mode sometimes, not exactly singing but not exactly speaking either, which I suppose is why I think it sounds like Gregorian chant, perhaps plainsong would be better, or the way we used to intone psalms at school, anyway definitely ecclesiastical, starting the sentence very high, dipping down a notch or note or two, rising again, then a pause, which you assume is an invitation to the other actor to speak but is actually ended eventually by Edward, so it's rather as if he is plain-singing back and forth with himself – this is

the experience you get, or rather I got last night, listening to him
through thin walls in the little private room before I dropped my
cigarette into the lavatory bowl in the rather large private lavatory,
peed over it and then flushed it away. This time it occurred to me
that the flushing noise might be audible not only in the auditorium
but also on stage, so I slunk out, down the little corridor, through
the curtains into the dress circle, and sat at the end of the back row,
next to Victoria – there was a thin pillar in front of us, whenever
the action moved from one side of the stage to the other one had
to reincline one's body and shift one's head – that's the thing about
the theatre, it always keeps you engaged, active, even when nothing
much of interest is going on on the stage.

THE JURY RETURNS A VERDICT

Nevertheless and – I wasn't shamed/mortified by what was going
on, on the stage. The acting was very fine. Edward, as I've already
hinted, slow, but so rooted in his Berenson that he was utterly
convincing, not one of his pauses seemed phoney or willed, but an
integral part of his sense of the character, so that my eagerness for
him to hurry along there, please, went really against the other grain
in me, which relished the sheer Edwardness of what he was doing.
Peter Bowles was – everybody knows, of course, that he's
technically one of the most accomplished actors of our time, and
he brought all his accomplishment to Duveen, but there was also
a world revolving within the razzmatazz, geniality, panache that
made you feel that the more he exposed the less you knew – the
moment in the second act when he becomes befuddled, then
absent, then seems about to lapse into unconsciousness, one grasps
that it has a physical cause, something has jammed in his brain, but

one also feels that he has actually been somewhere else, seen and experienced something at the dark heart of things, and the effect of it lingers through the rest of his performance, giving a poignancy to his apparently triumphant exit. Sally Dexter as Nicky was as she had been from her first performance, sexy, graceful, loving and alive in every moment, I adore watching her just walk across stage, she flows, head held high, the line of her so delicate – and so unlike her off-stage movements, which are boisterous, not exactly clumsy, but jolly and impetuous – in her scene with Fowles, when she sits neatly, somewhat primly, in fact, on the bench, she suggests layers of humour, sensuality and reserve, not only available to Fowles, but you feel almost a mistress to the world at large, she could have conversations of this equivocating intimacy with any man she met, and possibly any woman – yet we also feel her complete faithfulness to Berenson, the love of her life – and her loyalty to her lover's wife – a good woman, she seems to me, whose little treacheries and deceits do her credit. So that's the cast, apart from Barbara Jefford, who plays Mary Berenson and Steven Pacey who plays Fowles, Duveen's intermediary. Now I'll make no bones about this, why should I? – I think Barbara Jefford is a great actress, have thought so from the first moment I saw her in rehearsals – and yet I can still only define this greatness by negatives that I've already used, the simplest of which is that she doesn't appear to act – there is not a tremble, a drained, angry look, a sudden playful smile, a stricken laugh that isn't Mary's, and it's extraordinary to me, extraordinary that – stop here. Getting overwrought. Still, I'll just add – I don't know who'll get the various awards this year for best actress, but I'll bet it won't be Barbara Jefford. Their eye will fix with their usual sightlessness on the unique real thing, move sightlessly on to the sort of acting that happens all over the place, and light blindly up when it finds it happening at one of the subsidized theatres, in a part that appeals to heterophobes, which quite a few current theatre critics are, or feel obliged to make themselves into – some, of course, have arrived there by a direct route, a consequence of genes, hormones and ill-nurture – I wonder if what I've just written is against the law, and whether my computer is tapped in to by a government agency – I must be careful when transcribing it onto the computer – although it's possibly within the reach of modern technology to tap in to the yellow pads themselves, in which case my goose is cooked, goodbye to the future, certainly goodbye to the honour – to be stripped of it before getting it, the characteristic feat, no, I mean fate, of a Libran, or a homophobe, some people would call me, I suspect. They can call me homophobe, and it's thumbs down for me and my future, but if I call them heterophobes, it's also thumbs down for me and my future – well, I've addressed elsewhere the question of whether I'm homosexual a.k.a. gay, I can't remember what my findings were, but whatever they were let's put them aside and address the question of whether I'm a homophobe –

WELL, AM I A HOMOPHOBE?

Start by examining what it means. *Phobia* is Greek for 'fear', right? And *homo* is either the Latin for 'man', or the Greek for 'the same'. Assume it's not the Latin-for-man meaning – after all, lesbians are also considered to be homosexual – so it must mean the same – a homosexual is someone who has sex with a person of the same sex, simple really, and therefore a homophobe is someone who is frightened of someone of the same sex, which in my case is male. Am I frightened of other males? Well, it depends entirely on who they are, I don't think I'm frightened of them because they're males, only if they're dangerous, angry, violent males – but on the whole I'm not as frightened of dangerous, angry, violent males as I am of dangerous, angry, violent females, so really – on the grounds of semantic logic – I can't properly be called a homophobe, can I? But I'm being disingenuous, I know perfectly well that a homophobe is someone who is frightened of homos in the demotic sense of the word, so down to the knuckles at last, am I frightened of homosexuals, of either or both sexes?

I've been sitting here, trying to think it through, with no result, just a whirl of images, memories, experiences best left forgotten – so I shall try thinking it through as I write it down, and when I've finished I'll read it back, and then I'll know where I am on the question of whether I'm frightened of homosexuals – no, no, this will never do, as somebody said of *The Lyrical Ballads*. It'll never do to go on pretending that *phobia* means 'fear', which is actually what it means, when it's come to mean – through years and years of the usual sloppiness and misuse – hatred. So the genuine question I have to think through as I write is, do I hate homosexuals of either or both sexes?

Here I go, writing blind, so to speak. The reason I'm having difficulty is that I really don't know what a homosexual is, other than that he or she prefers to have sex with someone of the same sex, and I can't really imagine what the sexual act would be like – no, what it would be, when it comes down to it. I suppose if I work on it I can visualize the acts of buggery and sodomy, though at the moment I wouldn't do it very clearly because I've forgotten what the difference between the two acts is, do men sodomize other men as well as buggering them, or are they synonyms? That's hard to grasp, because they're such different words, so let me begin by pursuing –

BUGGERY

How can I? For one thing I haven't the slightest idea where the word comes from, its root, but it has an Anglo-Saxon feel to it, dense, clotted. But no, one can say it quite lightly, so that it trips off the tongue, I've just tried it with a French accent, *la bogarie*, it sounded pleasant, rather vague – and the verb, *Je me bogue, tu te bogue, il, elle se bogue, nous nous boguons*, no, no, hang on, it can't possibly be reflexive, *so vous boguez, ils, elles boguent* – but the act itself, one assumes, isn't at all vague, though it may well be pleasant, depending on which one you are – perhaps it's pleasant for both parties – and that's as far as I can go with buggery, so on to

SODOMY

I know where the word comes from, of course, from the Old Testament, the town of Sodom, but what did the residents of Sodom call it when they did it to each other? They can hardly have been conceited enough to name the act after their town, as if no one in any other town had thought of it before – or perhaps the people in all the towns in the Old Testament named the act after the name of their own town – ah, but not Gomorrah, there is no verb derived from Gomorrah, as far as I know, merely the noun for the ailment. No, that's another word entirely, gonnoreah, not sure of the spelling – pity, really, the sentence 'She gomorrahed him' is full of interest, as long as you refuse to let the Irish aspect seduce you – I'm sure there's a joke about that, there must be, I can't have got to the age of sixty-eight without hearing some joke made out of the confusion between Gomorrah and Begorrah, if that's how it's spelt. Now, that's about as far as I can go on the sodomite aspect of homosexuality, though I still haven't worked out whether it's a different act, and the only friend to whom I could put the question – what is the difference between sodomy and buggery? – is no longer available, although I could presumably simply look it all up in a dictionary, or even on the Internet, but I feel embarrassed at the thought of doing that. Nonsense, I mean I'm too lazy, especially as I know that the moment I stop writing this down I will lose interest in the subject, and the last thing I'll want to do is to write down all the definitions of sodomy and buggery, especially as one thing is bound to lead to another, it always does in dictionaries and on the Internet – my departed friend once confided to me – he didn't confide it, he told me in an open and above-board manner – that the best sexual experience of his life came when he was twelve, he would go into town – he was a Shropshire lad – on market day and hang about the pig and sheep pens asking the farmers and shepherds there to give him a treat, which several of them invariably did, being simple and kindly country folk. What made it so perfect, he said, was that they had no teeth, just these old gums masticating away – bliss, he said, bliss, and he was a man who'd had a great variety of sexual experiences, with men and women, from early boyhood right up to his death in a windsurfing accident off Nmeth Island – I've never understood why he wanted to take up windsurfing, as he wasn't really much of a swimmer, in his soul he was a landlubber. None of this has brought me any closer to finding out whether I'm a homophobe, in the current meaning of the word. So

cf Edmund White – so much for paedophilia – .

WHAT WOULD MUMMY HAVE WANTED?

She'd have wanted me to be a homophobe, an anti-Semitic, racist homophobe, as would have befitted her idea of the complete, middle-class public-school all-rounder – actually, it probably doesn't work like that, that's what she would have wanted me to have been then, because it's what she thought was mainstream, patriotic, Churchillian, but if she were alive now she would want me to be mainstream now, which means she would have wanted me to be a homophiliac, heterophobic, anti-racist and – no, not pro-Semitic, in fact politically anti-Semitic, I assume, and pro-Palestinian, but no talk of noses and avarice, no Fagin and Shylock – my cousin Betty, who became my stepmother, once told Nigel, when I was out of the room, that she thought I had Jewish blood, 'Not you, Nigel, no, no!' she said. 'But Simon – I mean –' and she made a gesture, a hook-shaped gesture, over her nose, which was pert and neat. 'And some of his ways!' Though there she might have been muddling my seeming Jewishness with my seeming homosexuality – in her view, which Mummy half-shared, they, both 'theys', Jews and homosexuals, liked the same things – art, music, books – and natural, healthy gentiles preferred manly things, like rugby and war in Nigel's case, and bonking little Betty, along with other friends and relations of my mother's, in my father's case. If little Betty really believed I had Jewish blood, and saw my nose as a literal statement – a sort of involuntary confession – rather than a symbol, then who did she believe was my biological father? Where was the Jew who had entered mine father's spouse, and made me, and my nose? It was an attractive thought at the time, explaining why I always felt uneasy in my father's company, and why I often wished, dreamed indeed, that I would turn out to have been Jewish and adopted – being only half-parented, and through my anti-Semitic mother, was the closest I could hope to get –

POOR OLD THINGS

But facts are facts. DNA tests would doubtless resolve the conundrum, but really there is no conundrum to resolve – I know that I am my father's son, know it more with each passing year, as I find developing in myself all the attitudes and some of the mannerisms that so irritated me when I observed them in him – I am more my father's son at sixty-eight than I was at eight, eighteen, twenty-eight, fifty-eight . . . It's not that I understand him better or that I love him more – in fact, I despise myself in the way that I used to despise him, the younger creatures that I once was somehow unify into a still-present self who catches me in some elderly, inherited movement or gesture, and sneers, 'There he is, there you are, one and the same, poor old thing.' I probably have inherited characteristics from my mother, but I've never recognized them, never recognized them in either of my brothers – though I recognized him in them all right, he was strongly present in Piers's face, his features, his expressions, but they never irritated me in Piers, nothing about Piers irritated me, though at the end his drinking infuriated me until I realized, half-realized, it was terminal. On the other hand his presence in Nigel irritated me when I first consciously noticed it, when he was twelve or so, and I eleven or so, about then, until we were both in our forties, when I began to find it reassuring – grown-up, sensible and kindly – paternal, actually.

THE FAMILY TREE

We sit when we're tired with our lower jaws thrust out, shoulders hunched, our right hand clamped into our left armpit – simian. I remember writing about this once, somewhere, describing looking around the room one Christmas about forty years ago, I suppose, and seeing my father, Nigel and Piers sitting in that posture, and realizing that I was sitting watching them with my shoulders hunched, hand in armpit, jaw thrust out – my grandfather did it too, I think I remember, but I may be imposing it on him, wanting to see him as part of a procession that goes back to the crack of time, the gang of us sitting in a tree, lower jaws thrust far out, shoulders hunched up to our ears, but there'd be women too, or females, perhaps the more tactful word in these times of ours, you can't really talk of women apes, can you, without giving offence, whereas I suppose ape women could be merely descriptive, neutral therefore, but better not try it out, may not sound exactly neutral, not neutral at all to say, for instance, that there was this ape woman, apish woman, ape of a woman, in the Renaissance this afternoon, buying carrot cake – better visualize this tree from time's early light as cluttered with entirely male apes, with senior ape – Grandad, mine on the lowest branch, about to fall off, Daddy in the middle, keeping one eye on his dad below and one eye on his own son on the branch above, while at the top of the tree, his own son's one furry hand at work in his armpit, the other reaching for a banana in the sky, and more likely, in his confusion of appetites and yearnings, to topple to his doom than his great-grandad, who clings to his low bough with the intensity of senility. I wonder if apes get Alzheimer's. Are humans the only creatures to get Alzheimer's? Probably only humans are intelligent enough to prolong consciousness into imbecility, and only humans are imbecile enough to want to continue life – this comes of taking two sleeping pills. I'd like to think I took two by mistake, but I know better, I took two because I was afraid that one wasn't enough.

A WILLINGNESS TO MOURN THE DEATH, BY ANY MEANS, OF A BLACKBIRD IN LONDON

There is a bird that sings through the night, from about 11 p.m. on it warbles away until – I don't know, it's still warbling when I go to bed at 5 or 6 a.m. It seems to live in the little alley between our house and the house next door, at least that's where the warbling sounds as if it comes from, but I suspect that the bird is actually on one of the streetlamps on the pavement, and that it sings because it mistakes the artificial light for natural light, which means it lives in a perpetual day, and gives up its song without a break, from dawn to dawn, dusk to dusk, dusk to dawn and dusk. It sings and sings away – its warble is charming for the first moments, but it never changes, it's the same warble, with little fractures of silence that become as offensive to the ear as the sound it is interrupting, but have I heard it in the daytime? I think not. The traffic might cover it, though. What sort of bird is it, anyway? One or two people I have consulted say it must be a blackbird, my imitations have a blackbirdy sound, they say, and blackbirds are notoriously stupid – for instance, they build their nests in hedges at cat level – anyway, I have come to hate it, and believe it is mainly responsible for my taking two – and I'm afraid that one night it will be three or four or five – each one shortening my memory span, so that I ask after the fifth or sixth whether I've already had one of these. And I'm afraid, in short – I am afraid.

A SUNDAY MORNING IN SPRING FIFTY-SEVEN YEARS AGO

I can still remember the feeling, as I crouched in an alley off the King's Road and a man walked towards me carrying a large piece of wood which I'd seen him take out of his truck, he had gone back to fetch it, after seeing where I was hidden, and sized up what was necessary for what he wanted to do – had walked quite slowly back to his truck, and searched out the piece of wood, knowing that I couldn't possibly get out past him without his catching me, and possibly bundling me into his truck and driving off to murder me slowly, in a private place he knew about, where he'd done it before – of course it was my own fault, as these things often are, with me anyway, also the fault of a beautiful morning, which gave rise to an enormous sense of exhilaration, a devil-may-care exuberance, and a conviction of complete lovability. I had come up Manresa Road from Oakley Gardens, mid-morning on this beautiful Sunday, going nowhere in particular, out and about on my own – I have an idea that I must have had some money in my pocket, but I don't think I had any actual plans to spend it, there really wasn't very much to spend money on in London 1946, especially if you'd already used up your sweet ration and if your sexuality was a year or so away from being on the rampage, and dictating the course of most of your thinking and planning – there was nothing but the day itself, and me in it, and precious little traffic, very few pedestrians, the King's Road on a Sunday, immediately post-war, springtime, and I bouncing and jumping and darting along and forking two fingers at a trundling rubbish truck as I bounced, jumped and darted across its path, two fingers raised in defiant *joie de vivre*, something I'd never done in my life before, but it felt terrific, what did I care if he cared –

It didn't occur to me that he cared until I realized he was driving steadily behind me, when I picked up speed he picked up speed, and when I looked at his face for the first time, the face that I had insulted with my gesture was a blob of fury with a cap on top, I had never before seen such fury on a face that didn't belong to my family, from which I at least knew that it would pass, and it was a fury that also expressed an overriding purpose – to hurt me, really, to do more than that – I ran, I ran very fast in those golden, pre-pubescent days, when my energy was unspent in idle, hard-working devotions – ran very fast along the pavement of the King's Road, turning into squares that inevitably led back to the King's Road, he trundling implacably just behind me – twice I stopped in doorways, hoping that having hunted me down he'd go on his way, game over – but he stopped too, and got out, a large but squat man, I now see him as, in overalls and thick boots – the overalls and thick boots are accurate, I'm sure, but about the size, really all I saw was that he was a full-grown man, the size of my father. He got out, and off I ran again, back along the pavement of the King's Road, and when he stopped at a traffic light I ran behind him, crossed the road into Dovehouse Street, a street of small houses, for the poor, in those days, that led to another street that brought me down into the King's Road, although this was by choice, my intention of course being to get home, please get home, and there he was, parked at the kerb, engine running. I crossed the road again, ran towards Manresa Road, then, as he was making his turn, ran back, then completely outwitted myself by running down the alley, which had a wall at its end, and nothing but a doorway to crouch in – so he parked, got out, went back to fetch the piece of wood, walked steadily down the alley until he was a few yards away, and I crouched with my hands around my ears, please, please, please. It seemed like a minute that he stood there – as I didn't look at him I'd no idea what he was doing, frowning, scowling, grinning, thinking, deciding – then I heard him walk away, and when I looked up he was getting into the truck and it trundled across the top of the alley, and out of sight.

I went up the alley, saw the truck going down the King's Road towards World's End, then walked to Oakley Street, down it to Phene Street, into Oakley Gardens. I could see Mummy's face at the upstairs window, the living-room window, the cigarette in her mouth, behind her, Daddy, his hand on her shoulder, the sight that made me feel as protected and safe as I've ever felt, the immortal parents, guarantors of my immortality, though I was still trembling, the fear still hadn't left my body. She appeared at the top of the stairs, again looking down, pointing her cigarette at me.

'You bloody little fool!' she said. 'How could you be so shaming!'

I couldn't think what I'd done while I'd been out, except running for my life.

'Why?' I said. 'Mummy.'

'James, you tell him. Your father will tell you.'

'Come on up,' he said. He was wearing his troubled, stern expression, usually summoned up by his wife.

I went into the living room. They sat down, he in his usual chair in the corner, next to the table on top of which, some years later, the television set would be. He picked up his dead pipe, pulled on it, eyes over his spectacles. She sat on the sofa, coiled, seeming to chain-smoke her cigarette – in and out of her mouth, puff, puff, she was furious, furious! And humiliated, she said, humiliated! I'd humiliated her. Them. The family.

Nigel came into the room.

'Leave us alone for a few minutes, old boy,' my father said.

'Unless you've done something bloody stupid too, Nige,' she said, with extra dollops of affection.

'I've been upstairs in my room.' He spoke with mournful dignity, as he went back up there. I'd seen from his expression, though, that he knew what I'd done, he'd been listening upstairs in his room, or outside the living-room door, and what I'd done was so bad that it was outside his experience, outside his imaginative experience of bad behaviour, his expression had let me know as much –

'Sit down,' my father suggested.

'Yes, sit down.' She wouldn't look at me, just the profile, and the puffing.

'Where have you been?' asked the father.

'Just out. Up to the King's Road.'

'Running about on the King's Road.' From the mother.

'Well, and up Sidney Street – and by the church.'

'What were you doing?' He held the pipe away from his mouth, brow furrowed and wise.

'Nothing. Just – well running . . . about.'

'Hah!' Puff cough cough. The coughs were explosive, because she was trying to suppress them. 'Jenkins saw you. The younger brother.'

The Jenkins family, the milkmen, on a rota system.

What the younger Jenkins had seen me doing, my father explained with that grave kindness that was worse than a beating, was their boy Simon running up and down the King's Road, making obscene gestures at people, people like him, the younger Jenkins.

'I didn't,' I said. 'I didn't even see him.'

The point was that he'd seen me, running about, with two fingers up, and then running all over the place, not looking where I was going, bumping into people without so much as an apology – it was a wonder somebody hadn't given me a good thrashing, it was

no more than I deserved, and how could I expect to get in to
Westminster if I went running around with two fingers up, and
worst of all –

'To hear this from little Jenkins!' She'd opened the door to
him, had expected the usual respectful but insolent conversation
about the bill, which was always delivered too early, from her
point of view, or paid too late, if you were a Jenkins. 'I've never
been so mortified – mortified! That a son of mine! From a
Jenkins!'

'I'm sure he won't do it again. Will you, old boy?'

I said I wouldn't, under any circumstances.

Puff cough, went my mother, puff cough cough, and then the
coughs exploded, and revealed themselves to have been suppressed
laughs. Daddy laughed too, splutteringly, jamming his pipe into his
mouth to help stop himself.

'It's all very well,' she said, struggling to change her mood, by
aiming a blow in my direction, 'but what were you thinking of, you
fool?'

'Yes –' Daddy, no longer peering over the rims, but packing
tobacco into the bowl, in a spirit of real enquiry – 'why did you do
it?'

'What on earth's the matter with you? It's not worth snivelling
over. Really, really, Si!'

And 'Really, old boy!' too, from him. But he got up quickly, put
his hand on my forehead. 'He's very hot,' he said, 'and damp.' It
was his professional voice, James Davidson Gray, MD.

She put her hand on my forehead, probably but not necessarily
the one without the cigarette. 'Yes, hot and damp. Feverish.'

So, crying and shaking, I was put to bed, she put the
thermometer in my mouth, he took my pulse, it was agreed that I
was running a light temperature, I was given a something –

aspirin? – from her a kiss on the forehead, from him a pat on the head, they had a brief conversation about whether it would be all right to go to the Phene Arms, where they went every Sunday before lunch, for a drink with their friends the Lumsdens. They decided it would be, I seemed calm enough now – 'Aren't you, Si?' – cooling down by the second, anyway they would only be half an hour, and there was Nigel to keep an eye on me – won't you, Nige? – and off they went.

Nigel loitered briefly, with a knowing smile, he knew me better than anyone else in the world, after all. He asked me what I'd been up to, really up to? I told him. 'Well, you got away,' he said, 'so what were you crying about?' I couldn't tell him, because I didn't know – but it was probably to do with being safe, that would likely be it, safe in their anger, then safe in their laughter, then safe in their worry – and it was also a bit to do, perhaps, with the discovery that a small, impulsive gesture to celebrate the bounce in your blood could lead almost immediately to your running in terror from a man who could trap you in an alley, with a piece of wood in his hand, walk slowly towards you, and next time not change his mind about killing you – though perhaps he hadn't intended to kill me, perhaps he'd intended to do precisely what he'd done, which was to teach me a lesson – a lesson well taught, I've never since forked my fingers at an approaching vehicle, never forked my fingers at anyone unless I loved them, and felt pretty sure that they loved me –

I've just remembered a sentence I wrote, and checked on it – yes, there it is, 'I think Nigel came into the room about then, yes, the whole family present, as I started to cry –' The whole family? But where was Piers? Let me think, work this out. If I was ten when it happened, Piers was either just born or just about to be – but I don't remember Mummy pregnant then, nor his presence in the house – but one or the other was the case. Nowadays, of course, her smoking and going out for a drink would suggest that she was no longer pregnant, but back then, in 1946, a pregnant woman wasn't pregnant with moral complications – nowadays a pregnant woman can have her unborn baby killed off virtually at her convenience, but let her try smoking and drinking in a public place. 'It was a nightmare,' a very nice woman who came to interview me last month told me – she was in her early thirties, with a baby, now about six months old, that she hadn't really wanted, but now that she had it, had her, I seem to remember, now that she had her, she couldn't imagine not having wanted her – during her pregnancy, after a long day's work, she liked to go to her local wine bar, as she'd been doing for years, and people she'd never seen before, complete strangers, would come up to her and admonish her – wag their fingers and sometimes almost spit at her, for having a drink – she only ever had one drink, at the most two – and as for smoking! Smoking and drinking and pregnant! How dare she! Perhaps if she'd said it's OK, not to worry, I'm getting rid of it some time next week, so no harm done, at least none that would make a difference to its future –

I think Mummy must have been pregnant. It was a cool sunny morning, which suggests spring, so she would have been, well, at least seven months – but I don't remember it, can't see it, just the smoke, anger, laughter, worry and love – still, I'd better cross the sentence out – there it is: 'I think Nigel came into the room about then, yes, the whole family present, as I started to cry –' crossed out.

PART SIX

A PRAYER OFFERED

Christmas is over, thank God, and we're into the New Year, without anyone close to me ill, or dying, except inasmuch as we're all, etc., and with luck, God willing, DV, etc., next week – or is it the week after? – we'll be in the hotel in Barbados. The Pinters are going before us this time, so it'll be their job to nab the table, check the room – no, they won't have to check the room, we'll have the same room that we always have.

Harold phoned this evening from the hotel. 'It's pissing down!' he barked, quite cheerfully. 'Been pissing down ever since we arrived – four days of it.' 'Oh,' I said. 'How bloody awful.' 'Yes,' he said. 'I just thought you should know.' Well, yes, perhaps, perhaps I should. But then things change in Barbados, in a blink there's sunshine, and after an hour or so you can't remember the rain. It's four days before we go, four days to blink.

It's still pissing down, it hasn't stopped since he last phoned, he said, they've had a week of it, and it shows no sign of letting up. 'Be of good cheer,' I said, 'be of good heart. We will bring sunshine, and there'll be sunshine thereafter.' He didn't sound convinced. 'All shall be well, and all manner of things shall be well,' I almost crooned at him. 'Not a wink of sun!' he said, 'not a wink of it, all the time we've been here.'

The threatening-looking baby in the seats behind us remained comatose for the whole journey. It had been raining almost up to the moment we touched down, we were the first off the plane, first through Customs and Immigration, first out of the airport into the sunshine, then into the waiting car, half an hour to the hotel, and half an hour after that into the sea, which was warm and clear, unruffled. Now we're on our balcony, a balmy night, the torches are flickering around the restaurant, the band's in place, and the music sounds OK, it really does, a bit bland, but soft and jazzy – it won't last, though, because it's Thursday, and Thursday night is limbo night, the band will get boisterous and drown out the sea. If I stand up and look down into the bar, I can see Harold's profile, and beside him Antonia's face, partly obscured by one of her majestic hats. At their table are two elderly ladies, whom I can't identify – I think they're playing bridge – yes, Harold made a movement, an emphatic putting-down-a-card-take-that! kind of movement. In half an hour or so we'll join them, and then, minus the two elderly ladies, we'll go in to dinner, sit at our usual table, and all, all manner of things –